VOICES OF
THE EARTH

VOICES OF
THE EARTH

AN ANTHOLOGY
OF IDEAS
AND ARGUMENTS

J.J. CLARKE

GEORGE BRAZILLER, INC.
60 Madison Avenue,
New York, New York 10010

Dedication

To my students,
past and present,
at Kingston University

First published the United States
in 1994 by George Braziller, Inc.

Published in the UK in 1993 as *Nature in Question* by
Earthscan Publications Limited
120 Pentonville Road, London N1 9JN

For information, write to the publisher:
George Braziller, Inc.
60 Madison Ave.
New York, NY 10010

Library of Congress Catalog Number: 93-74174

ISBN 0-8076-1344-4

Printed and bound in the UK
1st U.S. edition

CONTENTS

9   The Nineteenth Century: Science and Materialism   145

10   The Twentieth Century: Positivism and its Rivals   166

PREFACE

This anthology arose out of a course I have been teaching for a number of years to first year students as part of a History of Ideas programme of studies. The course makes use of a wide range of historical writings, from philosophy to poetry, from Eastern as well as Western sources, and from the ancient to the contemporary world. The issues it raises are of a broadly philosophical kind – What is the nature of the cosmos? What is our place within it? Is nature blind or purposeful? – and so forth. These issues are treated in an historical way by tracing their development in different historical epochs and in different cultural settings. But they are also dealt with as issues which are of deep contemporary concern, issues which are not purely 'academic' in the conventional sense, but which are closely linked to urgent moral, social and political questions about the environment and ecology, indeed about our very future on this planet.

The chief aim of this anthology is to help in the clarification of these questions, and in the broadening of our understanding and our sympathies in dealing with them. It is offered in the belief that, by opening up and exploring the riches of humanity's intellectual treasure-house, we can trace the source of many prevailing notions, and we can begin to place our present concerns, our prejudices, our hopes and values, in a broader context. This is not an exercise in nostalgia, nor a romantic retreat into the past, but one of recognising the limitations of our present standpoint, and of trying to find ways of invigorating our thinking by standing beyond it. Neither is it an exercise in special pleading, for the extracts have been selected with a view to representing as wide a range of views as possible, not merely those which are in harmony with 'green' thinking.

It will be evident from this that the book does not set out to be a history of philosophy through original sources alone, nor a definitive canon of great writings on the subject of nature. Its aim is to stimulate rather than to instruct, to open up rather than to close off options, and this is expressed in the sheer variety of sources which has been selected, embracing the views of poets and theologians as well as philosophers and scientists, of the marginal as well as of the orthodox. My aim has, in fact, been to trace a path deliberately winding and circuitous, not one which follows the well-trodden highways of many studies in the history of thought, but one which veers this way and that, taking in both famous and less well-known writers, in the hope that new and surprising vistas may emerge for the reader.

After the opening chapter on non-European traditions I have adopted a conventionally chronological framework. I hope that this will enable readers to place the ideas in historical context, and I have added short notes to help in this respect. At the same time it must be remembered that such a framework is oversimplified and carries its own rigidities and pre-judices. It must be treated as a matter of convenience rather than demonstrating any definitive way of carving up the history of ideas, and should not mislead the reader into thinking that each period represents a distinct 'world-view'.

In selecting pieces for inclusion I have, as I have indicated, endeavoured to cast the net widely and to encourage thereby a pluralistic approach to the problems raised. But at the same time I have limited the scope of these selections in two ways. First, I have used only original rather than secondary sources, a limitation which virtually excludes non-literate traditions. There are plenty of secondary sources available, and a selection of these is included in the Further Reading section at the end. Secondly, I have excluded material from the past few decades. The environmental debate began in earnest in the 1960s, and since then literature on the subject has grown exponentially, requiring a different kind of anthology. The present work may be seen as a preface to that debate.

I have dedicated this book to my students, not only because of their enthusiasm for the ideas presented in this volume, and the encouragement this has given me in my teaching on this subject, but also because they are the ones who will need to carry this debate forward, and in so doing may help in creating a world in which there is, as the Indian Chief Standing Bear expresses it, 'Kinship with all creatures of the earth, sky, and water'.

My grateful thanks are due to Alison Barrington and Jill Boezalt for their research and editorial assistance, to Sally Richardson of the World Wide Fund for Nature for her enthusiastic encouragement and support for the project, and to the Faculty of Human Sciences at Kingston University for financial support.

INTRODUCTION

Nature in Question

Nature and our relation to it is one of the most urgent questions of our time. More and more people are coming to see that if we continue to abuse the planet in our present fashion, the very foundations of human life will be threatened. Questions about the ozone layer, global warming, the pollution of the seas and the air, the conservation of rain forests and other precious resources can no longer be viewed as temporary and local issues that can be solved by a quick fix or eliminated by a clean-up. Where once green concerns and arguments, and practices like vegetarianism and campaigning for endangered species, were seen as the province of a dedicated and mildly dotty minority, they are now stirring us all, slowly but inexorably, into rethinking our whole relationship with the planet Earth. They are forcing us into raising fundamental questions about our moral, political, and even our metaphysical and religious, values and beliefs. We can no longer take for granted our long-cherished convictions about such things as endless economic growth, our right to exploit living things for our purposes, the legitimacy of our dominion over nature. The very world-view which we have inherited from the Judaeo–Christian tradition, from the Greek philosophers, and from the revolutionary Age of Enlightenment is beginning to be questioned at the most fundamental levels. Even science and technology, those sacred symbols of Western pride and civilization, are no longer beyond criticism. The severity of our situation, and that of our planetary home, is indeed forcing us to go back to basics. As Peter Marshall puts it in an important new book:

> Ecological thinking is rising in human minds like sap in spring. What is taking place is not merely a concern with cleaning up our environment but a fundamental shift in consciousness – as momentous as the Renaissance . . . What is wrong is nothing less than the way we see and act in the world. (*Nature's Web*, p5*)

---

* Books referred to in the Introduction are listed in Further Reading section at the end of this volume.

The chief aim of this anthology is to serve as a catalyst in our thinking and our discussions concerning these questions. Its primary purpose is to help us to conduct our debates on these broad environmental and ecological issues in a wider intellectual and historical context. To borrow a metaphor from genetics: it aims to enhance the *gene-pool of ideas* from which we can draw in considering the contentious issue of our contemporary under-standing of the natural world; just as genetic variety is necessary to the ongoing health of ecosystems, so too the health of our intellectual life depends on our capacity to retain variety and to avoid limiting ourselves by dogmatic narrowness and conventional blinkers. The issues we face now are in many ways new and unique in the history of the human race, but this makes it all the more urgent that in addressing them we open our minds to the collective wisdom of humankind, and in the light of this have the courage to re-examine long-held convictions and practices. Many of our attitudes to the natural world are embedded in ways of thinking which run deep, which seem immutable like the laws of nature themselves, and whose foundations are therefore rarely examined. One way of opening up and exploring them is by taking seriously a number of radically different ways of thinking about nature which other societies in different times have found useful. This process, moreover, will not only help to place our current debates in wider context, but will also enable us to observe and reflect on the historical sources of our current world-views, and to identify the philosophical roots of many of our current prejudices and assumptions.

This is the reason why we need to go back into the *past* in order to address questions which are patently about the *future*. Until recently the task of gathering together remnants of apparently outdated attitudes to the natural world would have seemed little more than an antiquarian exercise. The positivistic and Marxist mentalities which dominated the intellectual life of the middle decades of this century might well have dismissed a large proportion of this anthology as either meaningless or as the faded propaganda of defunct ruling classes. But our present age has become less self-assured and may once more be prepared to listen to and open its mind to the voices of the past. The urgency of our present situation has forced us to rethink our beliefs at a fundamental level. The philosophical assumptions on which our civilization is based seem to be failing us, and we are now more ready to appeal to the past for fresh inspiration. The passion for progress, and the converse contempt for the past, appears to be giving way to a more modest, less arrogant attitude which regards history, not as endless progress, but as endless recycling, of bad ideas and good, of mistakes as well as successes, and hence a resource on which we must continually draw.

This anthology, then, is offered in the belief that we can learn from the past, indeed that we *must* learn from the past. This is not because history literally repeats itself, or because we can derive general laws from its study; such notions can no longer be seriously entertained. The sort of learning that is advocated can be summed up in the idea of *dialogue*. It implies a willingness to learn, a capacity to listen and to change one's views, an openness to beliefs and systems of thought which at first sight seem alien, and which challenge one's own self-assurance. It implies especially an absence of dogmatism, and an awareness of the relativity of one's own point of view. The idea of dialogue has become especially fashionable in recent years in the field of theology where old confrontations between religious groupings are giving way to a spirit of openness and mutual exchange. Nowadays dialogue between differing religious traditions is replacing polemics, debate, and the monologue preaching of the past. In the field of environmental debate it means the capacity to re-examine our own current beliefs concerning the natural world by measuring them against a range of alternatives, from non-Western as well as Western sources, alternatives which can at least place our current views into relief and into wider perspective.

The dialogue we need to engage in is not just one for specialists, for nature is now everybody's business. Since the nineteenth century there has been a tendency to allocate to the sciences the leading role in under-standing and interpreting nature, leaving the philosopher, the poet, and the layperson toiling in the rear. The Australian philosopher John Pass-more is typical of many when he writes that 'ecological problems . . . can be solved only by the joint efforts of scientists, technologists, economists, statesmen, administrators' (*Man's Responsibility for Nature*, p173). This anthology is offered in the belief that the present situation demands that we *all* look again at the fundamental, and often hidden, attitudes that underlie our treatment of the natural world. Scientists and technologists no doubt have a special role to play in this, as do philosophers and theologians, but the issues to be faced require that we all get involved in the debate, for it is the common assumptions of humankind that are in question, not just the opinions of specialists and intellectuals.

To assist the debate we need to go back to basics, and to recognize the role that our belief systems play in all this. For many people 'nature' simply refers to all that stuff out there. The natural world represents the domain which is essentially external to human beings, and on which we rely from time to time for sustenance and recreation. If we want to know more about it, or need to manipulate it more effectively, then we turn to science or to technology. This anthology offers a different perspective. It suggests that in a very important sense we do not *discover* the natural world but rather *construct* it. So diverse are the images of nature contained in this volume that we are inevitably led to the conclusion that what we are dealing with is not so much nature itself as so many different pictures or models which, like other human products, have a history. In a sense we do not experience reality direct, but rather in a form which is filtered through the lenses of our conceptual and symbolic creations – through our mythologies, sciences, philosophies, theologies, through language itself. Let us see how this idea works in the various different fields of thought.

Nature in Myth and Mythology

All the endeavours to understand nature, whether scientific, philosophical, theological, or occultist, have inherited an approach which can be traced back to mythology, and to pre-literate traditions whose ideas have been handed down orally. The notion of 'myth' and of 'mythology' has in the past, partly under the influence of Christian attitudes, partly impelled by scientific ones, often been associated with childish confusion and the more bizarre reaches of the human imagination, and the term has frequently been taken as synonymous with 'error'. Under the impact of Romantic thinkers such as J G von Herder myth came to be viewed in a more favourable light, but the domination of the scientific mentality from the late nineteenth century onwards has meant a continuation of negative attitudes in this regard. A more sympathetic approach now prevails and, as a result of the work of twentieth century thinkers such as the anthropologist Claude Levi-Strauss, or the psychologist C G Jung, it is now possible to view myth as a serious and highly intelligent endeavour to make sense of the world and to construct a coherent understanding of it. Indeed it might be possible to view *all* the world-views outlined or hinted at in the selections that follow as so many myths, for they all in a sense tell us stories which enable us to grasp the meaning of things and so to find our way about in the world.

Let us begin with one of the seminal myths of the Western world, 'the Fall', which rests on the idea of a primitive paradisal state from which humanity has been catastrophically expelled. In the Book of Genesis we are told of a happy original condition in which the founding members of the human race enjoyed a harmonious relationship, not only with God and each other, but also with the natural world. This state of innocent and blissful integration has, according to the myth, unhappily been broken through humankind's own wilfulness. Through some primordial act of defiance and self-assertion humankind became excluded from this garden of delight, and has been exiled to an altogether harsher world, one which is riven with disharmony and suffering. Indeed, on one reading of the Book of Genesis it is in that very act of defiance that we can discern the moment at which humanity took a step back from nature and confronted it as an independent, alien reality. As a consequence our relationship with nature has become problematic, often beset with toil and pain, a domain, not of easy communing but of anxiety, struggle, and conflict.

Theologically this anxiety has sometimes been expressed in the idea that nature, as well as the human race, is implicated in the Fall of Adam and Eve, and that our struggle to survive in the face of a hostile external world is sanctioned by divine ordinance. Philosophically this anxiety can be seen in the writings of twentieth-century Existentialist philosophers who conclude that, in the absence of God, we are simply 'thrown' into the world (Heidegger's word), or that the world we find ourselves in is simply 'absurd' (a term used by Camus and Sartre), however much we may try to disguise this fact from ourselves. On this view, there is no reason why the world along with its inhabitants should be the way it is, or indeed why it should exist at all. From a more political or sociological perspective, human alienation from nature, for example in the writings of Karl Marx, has been seen as the consequence of particular economic and social systems, and that humanity's 'fall' is an inevitable consequence of modern revolutions in the means of producing goods and ordering society.

At the present time this inharmonious character of our relationship with nature has become a matter of much wider, indeed of universal, concern. The issue is no longer – if it ever was – a purely theological or philosophical one, but is to do with our very survival as a species, some would even say the survival of nature itself. The symbolic act of defiance contained in the myth of our first parents may at one time have appeared as a sin against God, perhaps even as an act of heroic rebellion. Now it reads like an episode in a tragic drama, whose plot begins with humanity's ever-growing sense of its ability to manipulate and control nature, continues with its acquisition of almost god-like powers, and ends with its self-destruction. Where the Bible began with the injunction to subdue and master all living creatures, science and technology provide people with the tools to achieve this end to perfection. Indeed, Francis Bacon, who in many ways set the agenda for the modern world, saw in the new post-Aristotelian science the means to reverse the tragic effects of the Fall, and to give to humankind complete domination over the natural world. The ancient Greek myth of the hero Prometheus, who stole fire from heaven to give to humankind, is perhaps an even more appropriate myth for our age, and one which may tell us something about the role of science in shaping our attitudes towards the natural world.

Nature in Science, Philosophy and Religion

The myths of science have indeed to a considerable extent replaced those of religion in the modern world. Our compulsion to stand back from and to reflect upon nature has led to the production of some of our most magnificent intellectual and cultural achievements, works that can be admired and studied alongside all the other creative works of humanity. In the extracts which follow you will find references to a rich variety of such works. There are some modern writers who, like Peter Medawar, believe that the greatest of these works is to be found in natural science which has succeeded in creating a remarkably coherent and systematic account of the natural world. Though it has become highly specialised, and in many ways closed off to the layperson, its theories are not merely technical instruments in the hands of the initiated, but project a picture of nature which has become deeply embedded in our common consciousness. Even if we are poorly educated in natural science, or feel some hostility towards it, we cannot avoid the fact that its world-picture permeates all our thinking, as much as the myths of old, and also puts into our hands a tool of unprecedented power, a huge potential for both creation and destruction.

One of the most powerful myths to emerge from science in modern times is that of the *world machine*, a model which clearly raises fundamental problems about our relationship with the natural world, and is a focal point for much recent ecological debate. The machine model is essentially the idea that nature, despite all its overflowing complexities and sensual excesses, is really nothing but a machine driven by quite simple and mathematically elegant principles. Where in earlier times the natural world, even the cosmos as a whole, was seen in organic terms, as a kind of living being articulated like an animal or plant, and valued as such, from about 1600 onwards in Europe the world was viewed increasingly as a gigantic clockwork made of inert matter. This conception, originally conceived by Descartes, has proved to be a remarkably successful model out of which has proliferated the scientific exploration of the whole of the natural world, and the means of exploiting it for human purposes. These successes, however, are now increasingly looked upon as double-edged. While the removal of old animistic 'superstitions' about hidden purposes and driving spirits within nature has enabled us to subject nature to rational understanding and control, it has also meant the loss of a sense of the sacredness of nature and has encouraged us to treat it as a dead object which can be used for our purposes with impunity. It has also helped to engender a materialist and determinist philosophical climate which has contributed to our sense of alienation from the world of nature.

Science as we now know it was created in the seventeenth century by Galileo, Newton and others who, following Descartes' inspiration, forged this view of nature as a great machine. Philosophy in general, and natural philosophy in particular, is older than science, and can be traced back as far as Thales at the end of the seventh century BCE* who is usually acknowledged as the first Western philosopher. His chief concern was not so much with the human world of values and morals, but with the natural world and with the cosmological stage on which humans act out their lives. Even prior to Thales, the Egyptians and Babylonians had demonstrated a deep interest in the shape of the heavens and the relationship betweeen the heavens and the human world. The search for an understanding of the cosmos at large could indeed be seen as humanity's oldest philosophical concern. Cosmological speculation flourished during the great era of Greek philosophy which followed Thales in the period from the sixth to the fourth centuries BCE, from Pythagoras and Heraclitus to Plato and Aristotle. Though such speculations largely died out in Europe in the centuries following the fall of the Roman Empire in 470 CE, they were revived again by Christian philosophers such as Thomas Aquinas in the Middle Ages. Aquinas himself was deeply indebted to Arab philosophers such as Averroes who absorbed and developed many of the ideas of Greek thinkers concerning the natural world.

There has been growing interest of late in the philosophies of East Asia such as Buddhism and Taoism, and increasingly they have been drawn into modern debates about ecology and the environment. As with traditional philosophies of the West, they have also shown a tendency to place human issues within the broad framework of nature. Even where the main focus has been on specifically human concerns – good government in the case of Confucianism, and the overcoming of suffering in the case of Buddhism – these concerns have been expressed within a cosmic setting and have been intimately connected with cosmological speculations. This is especially true in the case of Chinese Taoism. Here the idea of nature takes on a central role, and out of it is created a distinctive picture of the intimate relationship between the human and the natural worlds. It is frequently pointed out that Eastern thinking is essentially *holistic* in outlook, refusing to draw any absolute distinction between the human and the natural worlds, or between mind and matter, but seeing all such elements as inextricably entwined within an organic whole. In traditional India, for example, culture and nature are closely linked together, and all life is seen as sacred. Some of the attempts of recent thinkers to reconstruct a holistic model of nature, one which is claimed to heal some of the harmful rifts and divisions thought to be endemic in the mechanical model of nature, have drawn inspiration from the East, and have even claimed to see a convergence between modern quantum physics and ancient Taoism.

---

* Throughout this anthology I will be using the abbreviations BCE 'Before the Common Era', and CE 'Common Era', as these are less Eurocentric than the more common BC and AD.

The great religious system which has dominated the West, namely Christianity, has also shown an inclination towards cosmological speculation. It is true that at one level it has sought to elevate the human mind beyond the natural world into the realm of the transcendent. It is also true that this has frequently led to a somewhat negative assessment of the worth of the things and processes of nature, and has led some to argue that Christianity is largely responsible for our present ecological crisis. But there is also a level at which Christian philosophers, along with religious thinkers of the Jewish and Islamic faiths, have felt the necessity to construct a philosophy of nature, and thereby to place what they may deem to be matters of spiritual concern into the framework of the natural world. Even where nature is not seen as a legitimate object of disinterested study, it may be viewed as a vehicle by means of which the mind can be raised to God, a set of signs in which can be discerned God's providential purposes. From the time of the ancient Greek philosophers up to Darwin's day in the nineteenth century, philosophers and theologians have toyed with the alluring idea that the natural world displays a degree of order which cannot be explained purely by chance. Indeed recent books by the physicist Paul Davies suggest that this 'argument from design' is not dead yet. This way of thinking about nature, as a set of signs that point to the beyond, may suggest a downgrading of the value of the natural world, yet at the same time it played an important role during the eighteenth and nineteenth centuries in encouraging a close and intimate examination of nature's workings and in engendering a sense of awe at its seemingly miraculous ways. Even if nature was not intrinsically holy, it appeared to have wondrous and sublime qualities which pointed to a spiritual world beyond.

The occult arts of magic, astrology and alchemy, though primarily practical in intention, have also succeeded in formulating remarkably coherent views of the cosmos. They also continue to enjoy an appeal in our 'postmodern' age. Such arts, and their related philosophies, are to be found in all societies. In Europe they were drawn from a variety of ancient philosophical and mythological sources, especially those arising from Egypt, and attained towards the end of the Mediaeval period and in the Renaissance period a considerable degree of sophistication. The core theme of these beliefs lay in the linked notions of the macrocosm and the microcosm, the greater world of the heavens above and the lesser world of humanity, animals, and plants below. These two levels of being were seen to mirror one another and to be engaged in mutual influence so that the magical practitioner was deemed able to draw on powers within the natural world that originated in, and were a reflection of, the heavens above. This was linked to the idea, universally accepted in the East as well as the West, that the cosmos was arranged in accordance with a grand hierarchy – a Great Chain of Being, as it became known – with the human world placed at a mid-way point between the realms of pure spirit and pure matter. This is a seductive image, one which appeals to our deeply felt need to see human existence and human aspirations woven into the whole cosmic fabric, and it may therefore help to explain the growing fascination with the occult in our own day and its evident link with some of the more metaphysical strands of environmental thinking. Thus astrology, in its more sophisticated forms, tells us that our lives are not just, in Shakespeare's words, 'a tale told by an idiot, full of sound and fury, signifying nothing', but are an integral part of a meaningful whole.

The great literatures of the world, aside from those obviously associated with religious and philosophical teachings, also give ample evidence of our propensity to construct images of nature. Indeed human art in general, whether literary or pictorial, or even musical, has often demonstrated the same concern as philosophy with the wider arena within which human life is conducted. Poets have frequently been able to express insights into nature which dramatically highlight, or sometimes even anticipate, the more cumbersomely expressed ideas of philosophers. This is most obviously true of the Romantic poets and artists whose insights still play an important role in shaping our attitudes towards the natural world, and which manage to capture more deftly than the philosophers the very feel and sensation of nature. The outlook of poets and painters such as Wordsworth and Turner was constructed, not in the quiet of libraries or studios, but in the hard toil of endless journeys and wanderings in which nature was experienced, not as an abstract theory, but as an elemental force, a vital principle that flows through all things. This outlook has at one level certainly educated the minds and senses of many travellers and tourists since their time, but at another it has provided a powerful myth for modern minds in search of an alternative to mechanistic and materialistic models.

Questions of Values

One implication to be drawn from all this is that questions about nature involve questions concerning *values*. How we think about nature has implications for what value we place on it and its various components, and hence on how we treat it. As John Stuart Mill pointed out in the last century, the terms 'nature' and 'natural' carry all kinds of evaluative assumptions which shape the way we think and behave, and for this reason alone we need to develop a critical awarness of how we employ these terms. For example: some people hold that certain kinds of sexual acts are 'unnatural', and hence wrong; for some people certain kinds of medical treatment are deemed to be 'natural', and hence good; certain kinds of human institution, such as slavery and the family, have at various times in history been thought to be 'natural'. Furthermore, if we think of nature as dead matter then we may be inclined to value it differently from the way we would if we believe nature to be invested with spiritual beings and forces. Someone who believes that animals have a close kinship with humanbeings is likely to value animals differently from someone who holds that animals, unlike us, are automata.

The question of humanity's relation to animals does indeed help to focus attention on the broad issues concerning our relationship with nature, and in the extracts which follow there are several which are directly concerned with this question. In Western society it has long been assumed that our natural place lies above that of the animals. Authority for this view is sometimes traced to the Book of Genesis where Adam is given command over the animals, an authority seen to be confirmed by the fact that God allowed Adam to name the various species. It can also be traced to the Aristotelian idea of a ladder of nature, or chain of being, in which all things are ranked in terms of relative excellence from matter below to the heavens above, with plants, animals and humanity ranged in the centre. In this hierarchy, humanity is placed above other living beings and is thereby endowed with greater nobility, and hence with authority over them. In Descartes' philosophy this hierarchical model is completely rejected, but his view that animals are automata, unlike human beings who possess rational souls, has a similar consequence in confirming humanity's sense of its own superiority, and of its inherent rights with respect to other living beings. It can be seen from this that the issue of animal rights broadens out to encompass wider considerations about nature: how we regard and treat animals is a clue to our general attitude towards nature, and is a consequence of prevailing philosophies concerning the natural world. And we can see that from this point our treatment of animals broadens out to the whole question of our treatment of the natural world – of plants, forests, oceans, habitats.

A similar widening out of perspectives can be seen in relation to the question of women's rights. It is of course possible to treat this as a specifically sociological, political, or even theological issue, and it is in these sorts of ways that it has typically been dealt with in this century. Of late, though, attention has increasingly been paid to the wider ecological dimension. Writers such as Carolyn Merchant, in her book *The Death of Nature*, have argued that the philosophy of nature which has prevailed in the modern world since the time of Galileo, Descartes, and Bacon in the early seventeenth century has carried with it an implicitly – sometimes even explicitly – anti-feminine bias. Where in an earlier period nature was seen as something living, even sacred, and hence worthy of respect, the mechanistic world-view which emerged at that time encouraged an exploitative attitude towards nature, one which encouraged masculine attitudes of dominance and exploitation, and which correspondingly demoted the supposedly more feminine qualities of co-operation and mutual support. Some modern writers such as C G Jung have even suggested that the whole underlying psychological attitude of modern Western civilization has an essentially anti-feminine bias which expresses itself in part in our attitude towards the natural world.

It is evident from this that any re-examination of our values and attitudes with regard to nature is bound to have *political* implications. A cursory glance at the extracts contained in this book might lead the unwary reader to suppose that our ideas of nature have nothing directly to do with the conduct of society's affairs, and are matters of pure philosophical contemplation and of individual belief. Nothing could be further from the case. Careful study of these extracts will reveal that they can carry hidden, if consciously unintended, messages concerning how society should be ordered. For example, the idea that nature is arranged in a grand hierarchy could be seen as furnishing a powerful justification for a particular social order. If nature is ordered in accordance with a scheme of 'higher' and 'lower', with the former controlling the latter, then human society should follow suit, and hence certain forms of human authority may acquire cosmic justification. Such implications were explicitly drawn in the case of Mediaeval societies both in Europe and in China where the natural order was seen to embrace and to validate the political order.

It is sometimes pointed out, too, that the mechanistic model of nature gives expression to a particular form of political absolutism, an idea that became explicit in the philosophy of Thomas Hobbes. The idea that society is a sort of machine which works in accordance with laws analogous to those which govern the natural world has continued to play a part in social and political theory, and to shape popular attitudes, right up to the present time. Atomistic theories, likewise, which depict nature in all its complexity as being reducible to independent elementary particles, may also be seen as providing a model for political attitudes. This particular conception of the natural world is clearly mirrored, for example, in the liberal doctrine of individualism where complex social structures are viewed as the product of the activity of free and independently acting persons. Similarly the principles of the free market economy, adumbrated by the French Physiocrats and the Scottish philosopher Adam Smith in the eighteenth century, were quite deliberately modelled on the prevailing ideas of natural philosophy, and in the following century Darwin drew an explicit parallel between his own conception of natural selection and the intrinsically competitive nature of the prevailing economic system.

Contemporary debates concerning green issues are also linked to fundamental political questions. It is obvious that at one level environmental questions, such as atmospheric pollution, resource depletion, or the conservation of the rain forests, are political in nature, for they concern the public interest and the well-being of peoples, and hence have implications for government and social action. Even the belief that such matters should be left to the dictates of market forces is itself a political decision which might require legislation. But some have argued that these matters demand a deeper probing of basic assumptions, and perhaps even a fundamental revision of our whole attitude towards nature and society. According to this view we cannot possibly solve our present environmental problems within the framework of the central philosophical traditions which underpin the modern world, for it is precisely these traditions which have given rise to those very problems.

Old Philosophies, New Paradigms

This deeper probing of environmental questions has led to the distinction between *deep ecology* and *shallow ecology*. Shallow ecology means the treatment of environmental problems without tackling the underlying causes, and without confronting the philosophical assumptions that underlie our current political and economic thinking, especially the assumption which views these issues from a purely anthropocentric perspective. The argument for deep ecology could be expressed in the following way: the dominant world-view of modern times regards nature as a machine and human beings as isolated and fundamentally separate from nature, superior to and in some sense in charge of the rest of the natural world, and in competition with each other, values arising solely from the needs and rights of human beings. In this world-view the mental and the material, the spiritual and the physical, are sharply divided from one another, with the mental and the spiritual realm completely excluded from the realm of nature, a view usually known as *dualism*. This view has led to the belief that we have a right to dominate and exploit nature, for nature in itself has no intrinsic spiritual or moral qualities, and is simply there for us to use and enjoy. Hence, while we might be concerned about environmental questions, this concern is wholly anthropocentric and in no way challenges the prevailing world-view. Deep ecologists, such as the Norwegian philosopher Arne Naess, argue that we need to return to a conception of nature which rejects the dualism and the narrow materialism of the modern world-view, and which re-integrates humankind within nature, nature perceived not as a collection of separate material entities, but as a living whole, one which recognizes the interdependence of all natural phenomena, and which fuses together again the spiritual and the material aspects of reality. We need, in brief, to locate our moral priorities, not in the narrow world of the human species, but in the world of nature as a whole. Such a conception of nature, which Naess characterizes as *biocentric*, is wholly at odds with the modern materialist, consumerist outlook, but is, nevertheless, to be found in various forms, prior to the modern world, in for example Taoist writings, and in the sayings of North American Indian sages, and it is from these, it is argued, that we must learn in our attempts to reconstruct an ecologically sound philosophy of nature.

It is not difficult to see that deep ecology carries with it highly controversial and revolutionary political implications. In the first place it implies that today's political and social arrangements are inadequate to deal with the population–resource–environmental crisis, for they tend to involve short-term and narrowly sectarian solutions which may only serve to aggravate the problems that we face. In the second place it points to a radical rethinking of our social and economic institutions, implying such policies as the drastic decentralizing of power, the realignment of the relationship between town and country, and between industry and agriculture, and a rethinking of the principle of perpetual economic growth. A sustainable society, it is argued, can only be achieved by a sustainable relationship with the natural world, and hence only if the political, economic, and even philosphical assumptions on which Western society has been based for the past few centuries are revised.

Some believe that such a fundamental philosophical shift of attitudes is already under way, even if the full political and economic implications of deep ecology have yet to be grasped. The American scientist Fritjof Capra, for example, has argued in his book *The Turning Point* that we are already undergoing a *paradigm shift*, namely a reappraisal of the fundamental assumptions underlying our attitudes, not only to the natural world, but also to our understanding of human nature and human consciousness. This transformation, he argues, has largely been precipitated by revolutions within science itself, especially those associated with the so-called 'new physics' of relativity and quantum theory. These new ideas call into question some of the basic principles underlying Newtonian physics, and hence the whole mechanistic world-view. They force us to think again about the traditional notions of space, time, and causality. They reject the determinism, reductionism, and dualism of the old model, and postulate instead a holistic model in which nature is seen as a constant flux and flow of energy transformations, a network of interactions which cannot be reduced to the activity of discrete particles, in which rigid determinism no longer applies, and where human consciousness can no longer be separated out into a distinct compartment of reality.

Capra sees this new paradigm as being essentially ecological. Where the old mechanistic model encouraged us to see nature as a collection of dead and valueless entities existing independently of human consciousness, the new paradigm offers us a picture in which all things are interconnected, and which resembles far more closely a living organism than a machine. This model has important implications, he believes, in the fields of human sciences and medicine, for not only does it enable us to see human life as integral to the whole life of nature, but it also enables us once again to view human beings as mental–physical wholes. Where the old paradigm had encouraged us see the world and its inhabitants as distinct entities, the new paradigm sees the world as a living community of beings who are inseparably linked, and in which therefore the sense of our responsibility for the planet is heightened. It is a view, furthermore, that goes beyond the bounds of the empirical sciences, for, as Capra admits, its image of the oneness of life, in which the human spirit is understood as the mode of consciousness in which the individual feels connected with the cosmos as a whole, is a truly spiritual one.

This quest for a new philosophy is one which links contemporary ecological concerns with some of the great metaphysical and mystical traditions of the past, traditions which have sometimes been summed up as *the perennial philosophy*. This conception was first mooted by fifteenth-century Renaissance humanists such as Marsilio Ficino and Pico della Mirandola who pursued the synchretistic ideal of reconciling the seemingly opposed world-views of Christianity, Judaism, Platonism, and Hermetic and Cabalistic magic. The term itself was probably first coined in the eighteenth century by the philosopher Leibniz who conceived it as the distillation of the essence of diverse philosphical and theological traditions. His aim was not simply theoretical but was part of a wider scheme to reconcile the warring religious factions that were tearing Europe apart at that time, and even beyond that to seek a way of bringing the nations of the earth, East as well as West, into some sort of political harmony. He even conceived the idea of an international forum – a United Nations, in effect – in which differences between nations could be conciliated and resolved. Aldous Huxley, who is responsible for popularizing the term 'perennial philosophy' in recent times, characterized it as 'the metaphysic that recognises a divine Reality substantial to the world of things and lives and minds; the psychology that finds in the soul something similar to, or even identical with, divine Reality; the ethic that places man's final end in the immanent and transcendent Ground of all being' (*The Perennial Philosophy*, p9). This description of the perennial philosophy, with its strong mystical overtones, finds echoes among the more religiously inclined wing of the green movement, and there are many who would go a long way down the road towards the metaphysical approach advocated by Huxley, viewing the new ecological movement in essentially religious terms. Many on the other hand would find this whole approach too esoteric, too far removed from pressing social and economic reality, even politically dangerous. Murray Bookchin, an exemplar of the latter view, is sceptical of those 'mythical' and 'supernatural' ecological beliefs, whose roots lie in Romantic and mystical traditions, which in his view easily become 'means of social control and political manipulation'. The philosophy of interconnectedness he says can, if unregulated by critical reason and a passion for truth, lead to brutal movements like National Socialism which, 'fed on a popular anti-rationalism, anti-intellectualism, and a personal sense of alienation', and have led to an 'antisocial form of perverted "ecologism"' (*The Philosophy of Social Ecology*, p10).

Whatever the political inclination or outcome of these current debates, it is clear that standing behind them, and the whole ecological and new-paradigm discourse, are the philosophies and debates of past ages. On all sides we see a renewed willingness, reminiscent of the Renaissance spirit of Ficino, Pico, and Leibniz, to bring into play, and to give serious consideration to, philosophies which were long ago relegated to the childhood of humankind, fragments of past wisdoms which could thankfully be dismissed as 'primitive', and viewed as little more than historical curiosities. This new eclecticism, however, does not mean that we are simply engaged in recycling old philosophies, in reviving outworn creeds. Nor is it merely the product of a resigned and uncritical nostalgia for a past dream-world into which we can escape from our present predicament. I spoke earlier in terms of a *dialogue* with the past, and we are hopefully now in a better position to understand what this implies in the present context: it means that, starting from a perception of our present situation, we engage with an 'other' in order to clarify and put into wider perspective our current ideas and concerns. It is based on the belief that only by standing outside our usual circle of belief and understanding, and by trying out alternative perspectives, can we enter into a critical relationship with our present situation.

It is in the spirit of such an open-ended dialogue that the following selections are offered.

1

NATURE AS A LIVING BEING: NON-EUROPEAN TRADITIONS

It is no longer possible for Westerners to ignore non-European philosophies of nature, or to consign them to histories of superstitions and pre-scientific errors. It seems more evident to us as the century draws to a close that peoples from the traditional cultures of the East, of Africa, of North America, and of Australasia have developed and preserved attitudes towards the natural world from which we have much to learn. What is common to them is a feeling for the affinity between the human and the natural worlds, and a sense that all things belong together and work together like the organs of a living thing. Animism, the belief that nature is activated by spiritual forces, is ancient and widespread, and can be seen in the sacred writings of the Hindus as well as in the oral traditions of the North American Indians. In both, too, there is a strong sense of the earth as a maternal being to whom due reverence and respect must be given. The sense of respect, even reverence, for all living things, non-human as well as human, is a characteristic feature of the philosophies that have emerged from India. Perhaps best known in the West is the central Buddhist doctrine of compassion which is based on a rejection of any absolute distinction between self and others, between mind and non-mind. In the Buddhist, as well as in the Hindu, view, all things flow endlessly into each other, and the distinctions we make between things, or between categories of things such as minds and bodies, are in the final analysis illusory. One of the most refined philosophies of nature from the non-European traditions is that of Chinese Taoism. It is a philosophy which has many faces, from the popular and the medical to the metaphysical and the mystical. Unlike the Judaeo–Christian–Islamic religions, it has no concept of an almighty creator god who stands above and rules nature, but rather understands the processes of the natural and the human world in terms of the *Tao* (or *Dao*), a term usually translated as 'the way'. The operation of Tao comes about through the spontaneous and creative interaction of the opposite principles of *yin* and *yang*, and the natural way for humankind is to live in accordance with the flow of nature, to work with nature, not struggling to dominate or to control it. In this philosophy, as in so many other pre-modern traditions, the emphasis is on the need to co-operate with nature, to respect its inherent wisdom, and to live in accordance with its ways.

The Vedas *are the oldest Hindu scriptures, dating back to about 1500* BCE, *which express in poetic form an extraordinary religious sensitivity to the beauties of nature. The ineffable mysteriousness of creation is expressed in the first passage, which should be compared with the opening of the Book of Genesis. The second passage gives a strong sense of nature as animated, and hence as an object of reverence.*

There was neither non-existence nor existence then; there was neither the realm of space nor the sky which is beyond. What stirred? Where? In whose protection? Was there water, bottomlessly deep?

There was neither death nor immortality then. There was no distinguishing sign of night nor of day. That one breathed, windless, by its own impulse. Other than that there was nothing beyond.

Darkness was hidden by darkness in the beginning; with no distinguishing sign, all this was water. The life force that was covered with emptiness, that one arose through the power of heat.

Desire came upon that one in the beginning; that was the first seed of mind. Poets seeking in their heart with wisdom found the bond of existence in non-existence.

Their cord was extended across. Was there below? Was there above? There were seed-placers; there were powers. There was impulse beneath; there was giving-forth above.

Who really knows? Who will here proclaim it? Whence was it produced? Whence is this creation? The gods came afterwards, with the creation of this universe. Who then knows whence it has arisen?

Whence this creation has arisen – perhaps it formed itself, or perhaps it did not – the one who looks down on it, in the highest heaven, only he knows – or perhaps he does not know.

The Rig Veda, 'The Creation Hymn'

Homage to the Breath of Life, for this whole universe obeys it,
Which has become the Lord of all, on which all things are based.

Homage to thee, O Breath of Life, [homage] to thy crashing;
Homage to thee, the thunder; homage to thee, the lightning;
Homage to thee, O Breath of Life, when thou pourest rain.

When upon the plants the Breath of Life in thunder roars, they [then] conceive and form the embryo;
Then manifold are they born.

When upon the plants the Breath of Life, the season come, roars loud,
All things soever upon [this] earth rejoice with great rejoicing.

When the Breath of Life [this] mighty earth with rain bedews,
Then do the cattle [too] rejoice: 'Great [strength] will be our portion'.

Rained upon by the Breath of Life, when thou comest, when thou goest:
Homage to thee when standing still; homage to thee when sitting!

Homage to thee, O Breath of Life, when breathing in,
Homage when breathing out:
Homage to thee when thou turnest aside, homage to thee when thou facest [us].
To all of thee, [yea, all,] is this [our] homage [due].

O Breath of Life, that form of thine so dear [to us],
O Breath of Life, that [form] which is yet dearer,
And then that healing which [too] is thine,
Place it in us that we may live.

The Breath of Life takes living creatures as its garment,
As father [takes] his beloved son.
The Breath of Life is the Lord of all,
Of whatever breathes and what does not.

The Breath of Life is death, is fever;
The Breath of Life the gods revere.
In the highest world hath the Breath of Life
Set the man who speaks the truth.

The Atharva Veda, 'To the Breath of Life [prana]'

Where the Vedas *are polytheistic and emphasize ritual, the* Upanishads, *dating from about 500 to 200* BCE, *move towards a monotheistic outlook and emphasize knowledge and meditation, leading ultimately to a sense of the unity of all things.*

This is the truth: As from a fire aflame thousands of sparks come forth, even so from the Creator an infinity of beings have life and to him return again.

But the spirit of light from above, never-born, within all, outside all, is in radiance above life and mind, and beyond this creation's Creator.

From him comes all life and mind, and the senses of all life. From him comes space and light, air and fire and water, and this earth that holds us all.

The head of his body is fire, and his eyes the sun and the moon; his ears, the regions of heaven, and the sacred *Vedas* his word. His breath is the wind that blows, and this whole universe is his heart. This earth is his footstool. He is the Spirit that is in all things.

From him comes the sun, and the source of all fire is the sun.

From him comes the moon, and from this comes the rain and all herbs that grow upon earth. And man comes from him, and man unto woman gives seed; and thus an infinity of beings come from the Spirit supreme ...

From him the oceans and mountains; and all rivers come from him. And all herbs and the essence of all whereby the Inner Spirit dwells with the elements: all come from him.

The Mundaka Upanishad

Believe me, my son, an invisible and subtle essence is the Spirit of the whole universe. That is Reality. That is Atman [Soul]. THOU ART THAT.

The Chandogya Upanishad

Buddhism, an offshoot of Hinduism that became a world religion, is not primarily concerned with nature but rather with the release from suffering, but to achieve this release it is necessary to recognize the power of the mind to project illusory beliefs about oneself and the world. The principle of compassion for all sentient beings belongs not only to Buddhism but to all the Hindu traditions, and is connected with the doctrine of samsara (rebirth), a teaching which embraces the animal as well as the human worlds.

All phenomena originate in the mind, and when the mind is fully known all phenomena are fully known. For by the mind the world is led ... and through the mind Karma is piled up, whether good or evil. The mind swings like a fire-brand, the mind rears up like a wave, the mind burns like a forest fire, like a great flood, the mind bears all things away. The bodhisattva, thoroughly examining the nature of things, dwells in ever-present mindfulness of the activity of the mind, and so does not fall into the mind's power, but the mind comes under his control. And with the mind under his control, all phenomena are under his control.

Mahayana Buddhist Sutra

This is what should be done by the man who is wise, who seeks the good, and who knows the meaning of the place of peace.

Let him be strenuous, upright, and truly straight, without conceit of self, easily contented and joyous, free of cares; let him not be submerged by the things of the world; let him not take upon himself the burden of worldly goods; let his senses be controlled; let him be wise but not puffed up, and let him not desire great possessions even for his family; let him do nothing that is mean or that the wise would reprove.

May all beings be happy and at their ease! May they be joyous and live in safety!

All beings, whether weak or strong – omitting none – in high, middle, or low realms of existence, small or great, visible or invisible, near or far away, born or to be born – may all beings be happy and at their ease!

Let none deceive another, or despise any being in any state! Let none by anger or ill-will wish harm to another!

Even as a mother watches over and protects her child, her only child, so with a boundless mind should one cherish all living beings, radiating friendliness over the entire world, above, below, and all around without limit. So let him cultivate a boundless good will towards the entire world, uncramped, free from ill-will or enmity.

Standing or walking, sitting or lying down, during all his waking hours, let him establish this mindfulness of good will, which men call the highest state!

Mahayana Buddhist Sutra

———————————

Philosophical Taoism, which is traditionally traced back to the Chinese sage Lao-Tzu (sixth century BCE) and to Chuang-Tzu (fourth century BCE), is characterized by a sense of the essential unity of humanity with nature and the fundamental harmonizing of all things through the balancing of yin and yang. It is usually thought of as a mystical teaching since it avoids rational explanations and expresses its insights in terms of poetic, and often paradoxical, utterances. Virtue consists in following the way – the Tao. Affinities have recently been suggested between the holistic concept of nature propounded by Taoists and aspects of modern quantum physics.

The way that can be told
Is not the constant way;
The name that can be named
Is not the constant name.

The nameless was the beginning of heaven and earth;
The named was the mother of the myriad creatures.

The whole world recognizes the beautiful as the beautiful, yet
this is only the ugly; the whole world recognizes the good
as the good, yet this is only the bad.

Thus Something and Nothing produce each other;
The difficult and the easy complement each other;
The long and the short off-set each other;
The high and the low incline towards each other;
Note and sound harmonize with each other;
Before and after follow each other.

The spirit of the valley never dies.
This is called the mysterious female.
The gateway of the mysterious female
Is called the root of heaven and earth.
Dimly visible, it seems as if it were there,
Yet use will never drain it.

There is a thing confusedly formed,
Born before heaven and earth.
Silent and void
It stands alone and does not change,
Goes round and does not weary.
It is capable of being the mother of the world.
I know not its name
So I style it 'the way'.

The way is broad, reaching left as well as right.
The myriad creatures depend on it for life yet it claims no
    authority.
It accomplishes its task yet lays claim to no merit.
It clothes and feeds the myriad creatures yet lays no claim to
    being their master.

One who knows does not speak; one who speaks does not
    know.

Lao-Tzu: *Tao Te Ching*

In the great beginning there was non-being. It has neither
being nor name. The One originates from it; it has oneness but
not yet physical form. When things obtain it and come into
existence, that is called virtue. That which is formless is divided
into *yin* and *yang*, and from the very beginning going on
without interruption, is called destiny. Through movement and
rest it produces all things. When things are produced in
accordance with the principle of life, there is physical form.
When the physical form embodies and preserves the spirit so
that all activities follow their specific principles, that is nature.
By cultivating one's own nature one will return to virtue. When
virtue is perfect, all will be one with the beginning. Being one
with the beginning, one becomes receptive to all, and [so] one
becomes great. One will then be united with the sound and
breath of things. When one is united with the sound and breath

of things, one is then united with the universe ... this is complete harmony.

Chuang-Tzu

I venture to ask whether the creator is or is not. If he is not, how can he create things? If he is, then (being one of these things) he is incapable of creating the mass of bodily forms. Hence only after we realise that the mass of bodily forms are things of themselves, can we begin to talk about the creation of things ... The creating of things has no Lord; everything creates itself. Everything produces itself and does not depend on anything else. This is the normal way of the universe.

Kuo-Hsiang

Nature [*T'ien*] operates with constant regularity. It does not exist for the sake of [sage-emperor] Yao, nor does it cease to exist because of [wicked king] Chieh. Respond to it with peace and order, and good fortune will result. Respond to it with disorder and disaster will follow. If the foundations of living [ie agriculture] are strengthened and are economically used, then Nature cannot bring impoverishment ... if the Way is cultivated without deviation, then Nature cannot cause misfortune.

Hsun-Tzu

Therefore the *yin* and the *yang* are the great principles of Heaven and Earth. The four seasons are the great path of the *yin* and the *yang*. Punishment and reward are the harmonizers of the four seasons. When punishment and reward are in harmony with the seasons, happiness is produced; when they disregard them, there comes calamity. But what will [the sovereign] do in spring, summer, autumn and winter?

The [correlates of the] east are the stars. Its season is spring. Its influence is the wind. Wind produces wood and bone. Its characteristics are those of a time of joyousness, plenty and regular growth. The duties to be performed are to put in order and cleanse the places of the spirits, and respectfully to use presents in their worship; to make the *yang* supreme; to repair the dikes; to cultivate and plant the fields; adjust properly the bridges and dams; repair canals; repair rooms and gutters; make compromises of resentments; pardon those who have sinned; and open communication between the four quarters. Thereupon the soft wind and sweet rains will come; the common people will live to a great age; and the various animals will flourish. This is the virtue of the stars ...

The [correlate of the] south is the sun. Its season is summer. Its influence is *yang*. *Yang* produces fire and vapors. Its characteristics are those of giving and pleasure ... This is the virtue of the sun.

The [correlate of the] central quarter is the earth. The virtue of earth acts back and forth throughout the four seasons as an assistant [to the other four stable elements], and wind and rain give it additional strength. It produces skin and flesh. Its characteristics are those of harmony and equability. It is central, correct and impartial. It assists the four seasons. Thus through it spring produces and engenders; summer nourishes and matures; autumn collects and receives; and winter closes up and stores away ... This is the virtue for the year ...

The [correlate of the] west are the stars of the zodiac. Its season is autumn. Its influence is *yin*. *Yin* produces metal, horns and nails. Its characteristics are those of sadness, quietude, uprightness, severity and compliance. Occupying it, one dares not be dissolute ... This is the virtue of the stars of the zodiac ...

The [correlate of the] north is the moon. Its season is winter. Its influence is that of cold. Cold produces water and blood. Its characteristics are those of purity, scattering, mild anger and secret storing up ... This is the virtue of the moon.

Therefore withering in spring, flourishing in autumn, thunder in winter and frost in summer, are all perversions of these forces. When punishments and rewards become mixed up and lose their orderliness, perversions of the forces come ever more frequently. And when this happens, the country suffers many calamities. Therefore a Sage-king establishes government in accordance with the seasons; accompanies education with the art of war; and performs sacrifices to display virtue. It is through these three that the Sage-king can put himself into union with the movements of Heaven and Earth.

Kuan-Tzu

Although the universe is vast, its transformation is uniform. Although the myriad of things are many, their order is one.....When all things in general are seen through *Tao*, the response of things to each other is complete. Therefore it is virtue [*li*] that penetrates heaven and earth, and it is *Tao* that operates in all things...To be in accordance with *Tao* is completeness.

Chuang Tzu

For North American Indians human life is deeply interwoven into the meaning of the cosmos, and all their activities are viewed as being connected with the life of nature – with the sun, the seasons, the animals, the plants, all of which are infused with a divine quality.

The Lakota was a true naturist – lover of Nature. He loved the earth and all things of the earth, the attachment growing with age. The old people came literally to love the soil and they sat or reclined on the ground with a feeling of being close to a mothering power. It was good for the skin to touch the earth and the old people liked to remove their moccasins and walk with bare feet on the sacred earth. Their tipis were built upon the earth and their altars were made of earth. The birds that flew in the air came to rest upon the earth and it was the final abiding place of all things that lived and grew. The soil was soothing, strengthening, cleansing, and healing...

Wherever the Lakota went, he was with Mother Earth. No matter where he roamed by day or slept by night, he was safe with her. This thought comforted and sustained the Lakota and he was eternally filled with gratitude.

From Wakan Tanka there came a great unifying life force that flowered in and through all things – the flowers of the plains, blowing winds, rocks, trees, birds, animals – and was the same force that had been breathed into the first man. Thus all things were kindred and brought together by the same Great Mystery.

Kinship with all creatures of the earth, sky, and water was a real and active principle. For the animal and bird world there existed a brotherly feeling that kept the Lakota safe among them. And so close did some of the Lakotas come to their feathered and furred friends that in true brotherhood they spoke a common tongue.

The animal had rights – the right of man's protection, the right to live, the right to multiply, the right to freedom, and the right to man's indebtedness – and in recognition of these rights the Lakota never enslaved the animal, and spared all life that was not needed for food and clothing.

This concept of life was humanizing and gave to the Lakota an abiding love. It filled his being with the joy and mystery of living; it gave him reverence for all life; it made a place for all things in the scheme of existence with equal importance to all. The Lakota could despise no creature, for all were of one blood, made by the same hand, and filled with the essence of the Great Mystery . . .

The old people told us to heed *wa maka skan*, which were the, 'moving things of the earth.' This meant, of course, the animals that lived and moved about, and the stories they told us of *wa maka skan* increased our interest and delight. The wolf, duck, eagle, hawk, spider, bear, and other creatures, had marvelous powers, and each one was useful and helpful to us. Then there were the warriors who lived in the sky and dashed about on spirited horses during a thunder storm, their lances clashing with the thunder and glittering with the lightning. There was *wiwila*, the living spirit of the spring, and the stones that flew like a bird and talked like a man. Everything was possessed of a personality, only differing with us in form. Knowledge was inherent in all things. The world was a library and its books were the stones, leaves, grass, brooks, and the birds and animals that shared, alike with us, the storms and blessings of earth. We learned to do what only the student of nature ever learns, and that was to feel beauty . . . Bright days and dark days were both expressions of the Great Mystery, and the Indian reveled in being close to the Big Holy.

Standing Bear: *Land of the Spotted Eagle*

2

FROM MYTH TO PHILOSOPHY:
THE CLASSICAL WORLD

It is sometimes claimed that philosophy began in Greece with Thales, and that philosophy is a peculiarly European phenomenon. This may be disputable as an expression of Eurocentric chauvinism, but what cannot be denied is that from the sixth century BCE onwards in the Greek world – a world embracing modern Turkey, the Aegean islands, Egypt and Southern Italy as well as Athens and mainland Greece – there emerged an extraordinarily creative tradition of speculation and argument concerning all aspects of human experience from morality and politics to religion and cosmology. Some of this speculation clung on to and refined older ideas about the divine order of things and the pervasive presence of soul in nature, while others sought to demolish completely the ancient myths and to establish a completely rationalistic view of nature. At one extreme we find Plato arguing that the cosmos is a single living, ensouled being, created by a god in accordance with an eternal rational plan, in which human beings, the possessors of rational souls, have a special place. For Stoic philosophers like Cicero a contemplation of the cosmos must necessarily lead to belief in a divine intelligence. Such views were to have a powerful influence on the later development of European thought, and at the same time bear comparison with ideas from the previous chapter; indeed the remarkable affinity between aspects of Greek and Indian philosophy suggests the possibility of mutual influence. At the other extreme we find atomists such as Lucretius putting forward a model of the universe which dispenses with the supernatural and sees the order of things as arising out of the random motion of particles.

Among the Pre-Socratic philosophers, Pythagoras (sixth century BCE) and Heraclitus (540–480 BCE) are especially interesting to us today, for both anticipate in different ways models of nature with which we have become familiar through modern science. Thus Pythagoras, though deeply religious and committed to the central place of the soul in the

*universe, propounded the view that all is made of number, and held
that beneath the flux of nature as it appears to us there is a hidden order
or harmony. This idea of cosmic harmony was to exercise a powerful
influence on the imagination of the later Mediaeval and Renaissance
periods. Heraclitus, a more elusive figure given to delphic utterances,
might have been at home in the discussions of modern quantum phy-
sicists for, like these, he viewed nature as comprising, not substances but
rather energy which, like fire, is constantly being transformed and
which, though it retains its outward form, is never the same from one
moment to the next.*

[The] Pythagoreans, as they are called, devoted themselves to
mathematics; they were the first to advance this study, and
having been brought up in it they thought its principles were
the principles of all things. Since of these principles numbers are
by nature the first, and in numbers they seemed to see many
resemblances to the things that exist and come into being –
more than in fire and earth and water (such and such a modification of numbers being justice, another being soul and
reason, another being opportunity – and similarly almost all
other things being numerically expressible); since, again, they
saw that the attributes and ratios of the musical scales were
expressible in numbers; since, then all other things seemed in
their whole nature to be modelled after numbers, and numbers
seem to be the first things in the whole of nature, they supposed
the elements of numbers to be the elements of all things, and
the whole heaven to be a musical scale and a number. And all
the properties of numbers and scales which they could show to
agree with the attributes and parts and the whole arrangement
of the heavens, they collected and fitted into their scheme; and
if there was a gap anywhere, they readily made additions so as to
make their whole theory coherent. Eg as the number ten is
thought to be perfect and to comprise the whole nature of
numbers, they say that the bodies that move through the
heavens are ten, but as the visible bodies are only nine, to meet
this they invent a tenth – the 'counter-earth' ... Evidently,
then, these thinkers also consider that number is the principle
both as matter for things and as forming their modifications and
their permanent states, and hold that the elements of number
are the even and the odd, and of these the former is unlimited,
and the latter limited; and the one proceeds from both of these

(for it is both even and odd), and number from the one; and the whole heaven, as has been said, is numbers.

Aristotle: *Metaphysics*

This world, which is the same for all, no one of gods or men has made; but it was ever, is now, and ever shall be an ever-living Fire, with measures of it kindling, and measures of it going out.

The transformations of Fire are, first of all, sea; and half of the sea is earth, half whirlwind.

All things are an exchange for Fire, and Fire for all things, even as wares for gold and gold for wares.

It becomes liquid sea, and is measured by the same tale as before it became earth.

Fire is want and surfeit.

Fire lives the death of air, and air lives the death of fire; water lives the death of earth, earth that of water.

Fire in its advance will judge and convict all things.

How can one hide from that which never sets?

It is the thunderbolt that steers the course of all things.

The sun will not overstep his measures; if he does, the Erinyes, the handmaids of Justice, will find him out.

The limit of dawn and of evening is the bear; and opposite the Bear is the boundary of bright Zeus.

If there were no sun it would be night, for all the other stars could do.

The sun is new every day.

You cannot step twice into the same rivers; for fresh waters are ever flowing upon you.

Homer was wrong in saying: 'Would that strife might perish from among gods and men!' He did not see that he was praying for the destruction of the universe; for, if his prayer was heard, all things would pass away.

War is the father of all and the king of all.

Heraclitus: *Fragments*

The main concern of Plato (427–348 BCE) was with political and moral questions, but in his later years, under the influence of Pythagoras, he elaborated a cosmological picture which was to have a powerful influence on European thought for two thousand years. It assumes that the human being is an integral part of the cosmic organism – a microcosm that reflects the macrocosm – and that just as humans have rational souls which guide them towards the ideal of the Good, so too the cosmos has a soul whose rational operations are visible in the structure of the world and the heavens. Nature is therefore seen as an intelligible and purposeful whole.

We must in my opinion begin by distinguishing between that which always is and never becomes from that which is always becoming but never is. The one is apprehensible by intelligence with the aid of reasoning, being eternally the same, the other is the object of opinion and irrational sensation, coming to be and ceasing to be, but never fully real. In addition, everything that becomes or changes must do so owing to some cause; for nothing can come to be without a cause. Whenever, therefore, the maker of anything keeps his eye on the eternally unchanging and uses it as his pattern for the form and function of his product the result must be good; whenever he looks to something that has come to be and uses a model that has come to be, the result is not good.

As for the world – call it that or cosmos or any other name acceptable to it – we must ask about it the question one is bound to ask to begin with about anything: whether it has always existed and had no beginning, or whether it has come into existence and started from some beginning. The answer is that it has come into being; for it is visible, tangible, and corporeal, and therefore perceptible by the senses, and, as we saw, sensible things are objects of opinion and sensation and therefore change and come into being. And what comes into being or changes must do so, we said, owing to some cause. To discover the maker and father of this universe is indeed a hard task, and having found him, it would be impossible to tell everyone about him. Let us return to our question, and ask to which pattern did its constructor work, that which remains the same and unchanging or that which has come to be? If the world is beautiful and its maker is good, clearly he had his eye on the eternal; if the alternative (which it is blasphemy even to mention) is true, on that which is subject to change. Clearly, of course, he had his eye on the eternal; for the world is the fairest of all things that have come into being and he is the best of causes. That being so, it must have been constructed on the pattern of what is apprehensible by reason and understanding and eternally unchanging; from which again it follows that the world is a likeness of something else. Now it is always most important to begin at the proper place; and therefore we must lay it down that the words in which likeness and pattern are described will be of the same order as that which they describe. Thus a description of what is changeless, fixed and clearly intelligible will be changeless and fixed – will be, that is, as irrefutable and uncontrovertible as a description in words can be; but analogously a description of a likeness of the changeless, being a description of a mere likeness will be merely likely; for being has to becoming the same relation as truth to belief. Don't therefore be surprised, Socrates, if on many matters concerning the gods and the whole world of change we are unable in every respect and on every occasion to render consistent and accurate account. You must be satisfied if our account is as likely as any, remembering that both I and you who are sitting in judgement on it are merely human, and should not look for anything more than a likely story in such matters...

Let us therefore state the reason why the framer of this universe of change framed it at all. He was good, and what is good has no particle of envy in it; being therefore without envy he wished all things to be as like himself as possible. This is as valid a principle for the origin of the world of change as we shall discover from the wisdom of men, and we should accept it. God, therefore, wishing that all things should be good, and so far as possible nothing be imperfect, and finding the visible universe in a state not of rest but of inharmonious and disorderly motion, reduced it to order from disorder, as he judged that order was in every way better. It is impossible for the best to produce anything but the highest. When he considered, therefore, that in all the realm of visible nature, taking each thing as a whole, nothing without intelligence is to be found that is superior to anything with it, and that intelligence is impossible without soul, in fashioning the universe he planted reason in soul; and soul in body, and so ensured that his work should be by nature highest and best. And so the most likely account must say that this world came to be in very truth, through god's providence, a living being with soul and intelligence.

On this basis we must proceed to the next question: What was the living being in the likeness of which the creator constructed it? We cannot suppose that it was any creature that is part of a larger whole, for nothing can be good that is modelled on something incomplete. So let us assume that it resembles as nearly as possible that of which all other beings individually and generically are parts, and which comprises in itself all intelligible beings, just as this world contains ourselves and all visible creatures. For god's purpose was to use as his model the highest and most completely perfect of intelligible things, and so he created a single visible living being, containing within itself all living beings of the same natural order. Are we then right to speak of one universe, or would it be more correct to speak of a plurality or infinity? ONE is right, if it was manufactured according to its pattern; for that which comprises all intelligible beings cannot have a double. There would have to be another being comprising them both, of which both were parts, and it would be correct to call our world a copy not of them but of the being which comprised them. In order therefore that our universe should resemble the perfect living creature in being unique, the maker did not make two universes or an infinite number, but our universe was and is and will continue to be his only creation.

Now anything that has come to be must be corporeal, visible and tangible: but nothing can be visible without fire, nor tangible without solidity, and nothing can be solid without earth. So god, when he began to put together the body of the universe, made it of fire and earth, but it is not possible to combine two things properly without a third to act as a bond to hold them together. And the best bond is one that effects the closest unity between itself and the terms it is combining; and this is best done by a continued geometrical proportion. For whenever you have three cube or square numbers with a middle term such that the first term is to it as it is to the third term, and conversely what the third term is to the mean the mean is to the first term, then since the middle becomes first and last and similarly the first and last become middle, it will follow necessarily that all can stand in the same relation to each other, and in so doing achieve unity together. If then the body of the universe were required to be a plane surface with no depth, one middle term would have been enough to connect it with the other terms, but in fact it needs to be solid, and solids always need two connecting middle terms. So god placed water and air between fire and earth and made them so far as possible proportional to one another, so that air is to water as water is to earth; and in this way he bound the world into a visible and tangible whole. So by these means and from these four constituents the body of the universe was created to be at unity owing to proportion; in consequence it acquired concord, so that having once come together in unity with itself it is indissoluble by any but its compounder.

The construction of the world used up the whole of each of these four elements. For the creator constructed it of all the fire and water and air and earth available, leaving over no part or property of any of them, his purpose being, firstly, that it should be as complete a living being as possible, a whole of complete parts, and further, that it should be single and there should be nothing left over out of which another such whole could come into being, and finally that it should be ageless and free from disease. For he knew that heat and cold and other things that have powerful effects attack a composite body from without, so causing untimely dissolution, and make it decay by bringing disease and old age upon it. On this account and for this reason he made this world a single complete whole, consisting of parts that are wholes, and subject neither to age nor to disease. The shape he gave it was suitable to its nature. A suitable shape for a living being that was to contain within itself all living beings would be a figure that contains all possible figures within itself. Therefore he turned it into a rounded spherical shape, with the extremes equidistant in all directions from the centre, a figure that has the greatest degree of completeness and uniformity, as he judged uniformity to be incalculably superior to its opposite. And he gave it a perfectly smooth external finish all round, for many reasons. For it had no need of eyes, as there remained nothing visible outside it, nor of hearing, as there remained nothing audible; there was no surrounding air which it needed to breathe in, nor was it in need of any organ by which to take food into itself and discharge it later after digestion. Nothing was taken from it or added to it, for there was nothing that could be; for it was designed to supply its own nourishment from its own decay and to comprise and cause all processes, as its creator thought that it was better for it to be self-sufficient than dependent on anything else. He did not think there was any purpose in providing it with hands as it had no need to grasp anything or defend itself, nor with feet or any other means of support. For the seven physical motions he allotted to it the one which most properly belongs to intelligence and reason, and made it move with a uniform circular motion on the same spot; any deviation into movement of the other six kinds he entirely precluded. And because for its revolution it needed no feet he created it without feet or legs.

This was the plan of the eternal god when he gave to the god about to come into existence a smooth and unbroken surface, equidistant in every direction from the centre, and made it a physical body whole and complete, whose components were also complete physical bodies. And he put soul in the centre and diffused it through the whole and enclosed the body in it. So he established a single spherical universe in circular motion, alone but because of its excellence needing no company other than itself, and satisfied to be its own acquaintance and friend. His creation, then, for all these reason, was a blessed god.

Plato: *Timaeus*

In Plato's pupil, Aristotle (384–322 BCE), we see a middle position between the materialists such as Democritus and the idealists such as Plato. Like Plato he sees nature in organic rather than purely materialistic terms, and views the natural order as a kind of hierarchy or 'ladder of being' where, as in an organism, everything has its appropriate place and purpose, an idea which was to become a foundation stone for Mediaeval Christian cosmology. And unlike the materialists, he saw living things as having souls, and hence being guided, not by chance, but by some teleological principle, so that every living being has its 'entelechy', or purposive principle. But at the same time he avoided the 'other-worldly' tendencies of Plato, and anticipated the methods of modern science in his close observation of the natural world.

[We] must proceed to consider causes, their character and number. Knowledge is the object of our inquiry, and men do not think they know a thing till they have grasped the 'why' of it (which is to grasp its primary cause). So clearly we too must do this as regards both coming to be and passing away and every kind of physical change, in order that, knowing their principles, we might try to refer to these principles each of our problems.

In one sense, then, (1) that out of which a thing comes to be and persists, is called 'cause', e.g. the bronze of the statue, the silver of the bowl . . .

On another sense (2) the form or the archetype, ie the statement of the essence, and its genera, are called 'causes' (eg of the octave the relation of 2:1, and generally number) . . .

Again (3) the primary source of the change or coming to rest; eg the man who gave advice is a cause, the father is cause of the child, and generally what makes what is made and what causes change of what is changed.

Again (4) in the sense of end or 'that for the sake of which' a thing is done, eg health is the cause of walking about . . . This then exhausts the number of ways in which the term 'cause' is used.

Aristotle: *Physics*

[We] come to see clearly that in plants too that is produced which is conducive to the end – leaves, eg grow to provide shade for the fruit. If then it is both by nature and for an end that the swallow makes its nest and the spider its web, and plants grow leaves for the sake of the fruit and send their roots down (not up) for the sake of nourishment, it is plain that this kind of cause is operative in things which come to be and are by nature. And since 'nature' means two things, the matter and the form, of which the latter is the end, and since all the rest is for the sake of the end, the form must be the cause in the sense of 'that for the sake of which' . . . It is plain then that nature is a cause, a cause that operates for a purpose.

Aristotle: *Physics*

Nature proceeds little by little from things lifeless to animal life in such a way that it is impossible to determine the exact line of demarcation, nor on which side thereof an intermediate form should lie. Thus, next after lifeless things in the upward scale comes the plant, and of plants one will differ from another as to its amount of apparent vitality; and, in a word, the whole genus of plants, whilst it is devoid of life as compared with an animal, is endowed with life as compared with other corporeal entities. Indeed, as we just remarked, there is observed in plants a continuous scale of ascent towards the animal. So, in the sea, there are certain objects concerning which one would be at a loss to determine whether they be animal or vegetable. For instance, certain of these objects are fairly rooted, and in several cases perish if detached; thus the pinna is rooted to a particular spot, and the solen (or razor-shell) cannot survive withdrawal from its burrow. Indeed, broadly speaking, the entire genus of testaceans have a resemblance to vegetables, if they be contrasted with such animals as are capable of progression.

In regard to sensibility, some animals give no indication whatsoever of it, whilst others indicate it but indistinctly. Further, the substance of some of these intermediate creatures is fleshlike, as is the case with the so-called tethya (or ascidians) and the acalephae (or sea-anemones); but the sponge is in every respect like a vegetable. And so throughout the entire animal scale there is a graduated differentiation in amount of vitality and in capacity for motion.

Aristotle: *Study of Animals*

From all this it is clear that the theory that the movement of stars produces a harmony, ie, that the sounds they make are concordant, in spite of the grace and originality with which it has been stated, is nevertheless untrue. Some thinkers suppose that the motion of bodies of that size must produce a noise, since on our earth the motion of bodies far inferior in size and in speed of movement has that effect. Also, when the sun and the moon, they say, and all the stars, so great in number and in size, are moving with so rapid a motion, how should they not produce a sound immensely great? Starting from this argument and from the observation that their speeds, as measured by their distances, are in the same ratios as musical concordances, they assert that the sound given forth by the circular movement of the stars is a harmony. Since, however, it appears unaccountable that we should not hear this music, they explain this by saying that the sound is in our ears from the very moment of birth and is thus indistinguishable from its contrary silence, since sound and silence are discriminated by mutual contrast. What happens to men, then, is just what happens to coppersmiths, who are so accustomed to the noise of the smithy that it makes no difference to them.

Aristotle: *On the Heavens*

The Roman world did not produce any original philosophers, but in the Stoic orator Cicero (106–43 BCE) we find an early expression of an argument for the existence of God based on the order in nature, which was to become widely used in a later era. The Stoics stressed the ideal of accepting the inevitable order of nature which was deemed to be fundamentally rational.

As to [the gods'] nature there are various opinions, but their existence nobody denies. Indeed our master Cleanthes gave four reasons to account for the formation in men's minds of their ideas of the gods. He put first the argument of which I spoke just now, the one arising from our foreknowledge of future events; second, the one drawn from the magnitude of the benefits which we derive from our temperate climate, from the earth's fertility, and from a vast abundance of other blessings; third, the awe inspired by lightning, storms, rain, snow, hail, floods, pestilences, earthquakes and occasionally subterranean rumblings, showers of stones and raindrops the colour of blood, also landslips and chasms suddenly opening in the ground, also unnatural monstrosities human and animal, and also the appearance of meteoric lights and what are called by the Greeks 'comets', and in our language 'long-haired stars', such as recently during the Octavian War appeared as harbingers of dire disasters, and the doubling of the sun, which my father told me had happened in the consulship of Tuditanus and Aquilius, the year in which the light was quenched of Publius Africanus, that second sun of Rome: all of which alarming portents have suggested to mankind the idea of the existence of some celestial and divine power. And the fourth and most potent cause of the belief he said was the uniform motion and revolution of the heavens, and the varied groupings and ordered beauty of the sun, moon and stars, the very sight of which was in itself enough to prove that these things are not the mere effect of chance. When a man goes into a house, a wrestling-school or a public assembly and observes in all that goes on arrangement, regularity and system, he cannot possibly suppose that these things come about without a cause: he realizes that there is someone who presides and controls. Far more therefore with the vast movements and phases or the heavenly bodies, and these ordered processes of a multitude of enormous masses of matter, which throughout the countless ages of the infinite past have never in the smallest degree played false, is he compelled to infer that these mighty world-motions are regulated by some Mind.

Cicero: *On the Nature of the Gods*

The approach of the Stoics to the natural world, as well as that of Aristotle and Plato, is in marked contrast to that of the materialists such as Lucretius (99–55 BCE). This Roman philosopher, taking up the ideas of the Greek philosopher Democritus, attempted to show that nature, and even mind, could be explained without resorting to spiritual factors, and argued that all the phenomena of nature were due to the motion of atoms acting in the void without guidance or purpose. His ideas, for long unacceptable to orthodox Christianity, came back into fashion during the scientific revolution of the seventeenth century.

Mortals are gripped by fear, and attribute unexplainable happenings to the will of some god. This dread can be dispelled if we accept that *nothing can ever be created out of nothing* even by divine power.

If things were made out of nothing, then any species could spring from any source and nothing would require seed. Man could arise from the sea and scaly fish from the earth, and birds could be hatched out of the sky. Cattle and other domestic animals and every kind of wild beast, multiplying indiscriminately, would occupy cultivated and waste lands alike. The same fruits would not grow constantly on the same trees, but they would keep changing: any tree might bear any fruit. If each species were not composed of its own generative bodies, why should each be born always of the same kind of mother? Actually, since each is formed out of specific seeds, it is born and emerges into the sunlit world only from a place where there exists the right material, the right kind of atoms. This is why everything cannot be born of everything, but a specific power of generation inheres in specific objects.

Here is a further point. Without seasonable showers the earth cannot send up gladdening growths. Lacking food, animals cannot reproduce their kind or sustain life. This points to the conclusion that many elements are common to many things, as letters are to words, rather than to the theory that anything can come into existence without atoms.

Or again, why has not nature been able to produce men on such a scale that they could ford the ocean on foot or demolish high mountains with their hands or prolong their lives over many generations? Surely, because each thing requires for its birth a particular material which determines what can be produced. It must therefore be admitted that nothing can be made out of nothing, because everything must be generated from a seed before it can emerge into the unresisting air.

The second great principle is this: nature resolves everything in its component atoms and never reduces anything to nothing. If anything were perishable in all its parts anything might perish all of a sudden and vanish from sight. There would be no need of any force to separate its parts and loosen their links. In actual fact, since everything is composed of indestructible seeds, nature obviously does not allow any thing to perish till it has encountered a force that shatters it with a blow or creeps into chinks and unknits it.

[All] nature as it is in itself consists of two things – bodies and the vacant space in which the bodies are situated and through which they move in different directions. The existence of bodies is vouched for by the agreement of the senses. Nothing exists that is distinct from body and vacuity ... Material objects are of two kinds, atoms and compounds of atoms.

My next task will be to demonstrate to you what sort of matter it is of which this mind is composed and how it was formed. First, I affirm that it is of very fine texture and composed of exceptionally minute particles ... On every ground, therefore, it may be inferred that mind and spirit are composed of exceptionally diminutive atoms.

Lucretius: *On the Nature of the Universe*

In the following quotations from the great Greek tragedian Sophocles (496–406 BCE) and the Roman Stoic Epictetus (55–c135 CE), as well as the brief final quotation from Aristotle, we can see expressions of a widely held view in the ancient Mediterranean world concerning the excellence of human nature and its precedence over other species.

Wonders are many on earth, and the greatest of these
Is man, who rides the ocean and takes his way

Through the deeps, through wind-swept valleys of perilous seas
    That surge and sway.

He is master of ageless Earth, to his own will bending
The immortal mother of gods by the sweat of his brow,
As year succeeds to year, with toil unending
Of mule and plough.

He is lord of all things living; birds of the air,
Beasts of the field, all creatures of sea and land
He taketh, cunning to capture and ensnare
With sleight of hand;

Hunting the savage beast from the upland rocks,
Taming the mountain monarch in his lair,
Teaching the wild horse and the roaming ox
His yoke to bear.

Sophocles: *Antigone*

Be not surprised, if other animals have all things necessary to the body ready provided for them, not only meat and drink but lodging: that they want neither shoes, nor bedding, nor clothes, while we stand in need of all these. For they not being made for themselves, but for service, it was not fit that they should be formed so as to need the help of others. For, consider what it would be for us to take care, not only for ourselves, but for sheep and asses too, how they should be clothed, how shod, and how they should eat and drink. But as soldiers are ready for their commander, shod, clothed, and armed (for it would be a grievous thing for a colonel to be obliged to go through his regiment to put on their shoes and clothes), so nature likewise has formed the animals made for service, ready provided, and standing in need of no further care. Thus one little boy, with only a crook, drives a flock.

Epictetus: *Discourses*

[We] may infer that, after the birth of animals, plants exist for their sake, and that the other animals exist for the sake of man, the tame for use and food, the wild, if not all, at least the greater part of them, for food, and for the provision of clothing and various instruments. Now if nature makes nothing incomplete, and nothing in vain, the inference must be that she has made all animals for the sake of man.

Aristotle: *The Politics*

3

NATURE IN THE HANDS OF GOD: THE JUDAEO–CHRISTIAN–ISLAMIC TRADITIONS

You could be forgiven for supposing that Judaism, Christianity and Islam (which all acknowledge the authority of Moses and Abraham) had little interest in the natural world. Certainly all three have often postulated a sharp division between the natural and the supernatural, seeing the latter as immensely superior to and of infinitely greater worth than the former. Sometimes this has led to an attidude of indifference towards nature, even to the point of seeing it as intrinsically evil. In the Book of Genesis, although God finds his creation 'good', He also appears to be placing humankind in a position of rightful dominance over the natural world, and the impression is given that it is there for our use and pleasure, even though the effects of the Fall are such that nature becomes a place of struggle and pain. Furthermore the Jews by and large took no great interest in natural philosophy, and Christians in the early centuries were convinced that the world was shortly coming to an end, and hence there was little point in devoting much attention to it.

Nevertheless as time went on, and as Greek philosophical ideas were absorbed into the thinking of Jews, Christians, and the followers of Mohammed in the early mediaeval period, increasingly attempts were made to construct a natural philosophy in which the natural world was given an integral place within a total theistic cosmology. The Aristotelian idea of the 'ladder of nature', with its hierarchical order stretching from the world of matter below to the more spiritual orders above, proved especially fruitful, and generations of scholars and philosophers sought to build it into a theological world-view. According to this model, which later became known as the 'Great Chain of Being', mankind occupies a special median place within the chain which ranges from matter, plants and animals below, to heavenly bodies, angels, and God above, a conception which gave everything its proper and natural place as part of an integrated and purposeful whole. This model overcame, to some extent, the rather sharp division between the natural and the spiritual orders, since both were viewed as elements within a continuum rather than as confronting opposites, and one consequence of this was that it gradually became possible to study the order of nature as a manifestation of divine providence. This is not quite science in the modern sense, but it does represent a new willingness to investigate the rich variety of nature, if not for its own sake, at least as a bearer of God's signature and as a witness to His presence in the universe. As illustration of this, on the one hand we see St Thomas Aquinas arguing that the existence of God can be demonstrated from the examination of certain features of the natural order, and on the other we see the more mystical figure of St Francis giving expression to a new sense of delight in nature.

———————

The view of nature contained in the following extracts from the Bible is clearly God-centred, flowing as it does from the belief that God designed and created the universe out of nothing. As with Plato's view of nature, which it predates by several hundred years, and which it resembles in certain respects, the Bible sees the role of mankind as integral to God's overall design, and while nature is an object of praise for its goodness and beauty, as can be seen from the two psalms quoted, it is also a stage on which humankind plays a leading role. Nature is not a playground, though, for the result of the Fall is that our relationship with nature is one of struggle and toil, and so our 'command' of the earth's creatures is a qualified one.

God, at the beginning of time, created heaven and earth. Earth was still an empty waste, and darkness hung over the deep; but already, over its waters, stirred the breath of God. Then God said, Let there be light; and the light began. God saw the light, and found it good, and he divided the spheres of light and darkness; the light he called Day, and the darkness Night. So evening came, and morning, and one day passed. God said, too, Let a solid vault arise amid the waters, to keep these waters apart from those; a vault by which God would separate the waters which were beneath it from the waters above it; and so it was done. This vault God called the Sky. So evening came, and morning, and a second day passed.

And now God said, Let the waters below the vault collect in one place to make dry land appear. And so it was done; the dry land God called Earth, and the water, where it had collected, he called the Sea. All this God saw, and found it good. Let the earth, he said, yield grasses that grow and seed; fruit-trees too, each giving fruit of its own kind, and so propagating itself on earth. And so it was done; the earth yielded grasses that grew and seeded, each according to its kind, and trees that bore fruit, each with the power to propagate its own kind. And God saw it, and found it good. So evening came, and morning, and a third day passed.

Next, God said, Let there be luminaries in the vault of the sky, to divide the spheres of day and night; let them give portents, and be the measures of time, to mark out the day and the year; let them shine in the sky's vault and shed light on the earth. And so it was done.

God made the two great luminaries, the greater of them to command the day, and the lesser to command the night; then he made the stars. All these he put in the vault of the sky, to shed light on the earth, to control day and night, and divide the spheres of light and darkness. And God saw it, and found it good. So evening came, and morning, and a fourth day passed.

After this, God said, Let the waters produce moving things that have life in them, and winged things that fly above the earth under the sky's vault. Thus God created the huge sea-beasts, and all the different kinds of life and movement that spring from the waters, and all the different kinds of flying things; and God saw it and found it good. He pronounced his blessing on them, Increase and multiply, and fill the waters of the sea; and let there be abundance of flying things on earth. So evening came, and morning, and a fifth day passed. God said, too, Let the land yield all different kinds of living things, cattle and creeping things and wild beasts of every sort; and so it was done. God made every sort of wild beast, and all the different kinds of cattle and of creeping things; and God saw it and found it good.

And God said, Let us make man, wearing our own image and likeness; let us put him in command of the fishes in the sea, and all that flies through the air, and the cattle, and the whole earth, and all the creeping things that move on earth. So God made man in his own image, made him in the image of God. Man and woman both, he created them. And God pronounced his blessing on them, Increase and multiply and fill the earth, and make it yours; take command of the fishes in the sea, and all that flies through the air, and all the living things that move on the earth. Here are all the herbs, God told them, that seed on earth, and all the trees, that carry in them the seed of their own life, to be your food; food for all the beasts on the earth, all that flies in the air, all that creeps along the ground; here all that lives shall find its nourishment. And so it was done. And God saw all that he had made, and found it very good. So evening came, and morning, and a sixth day passed.

Thus heaven and earth and all the furniture of them were completed. By the seventh day, God had come to an end of making, and rested, on the seventh day, with his whole task accomplished. That is why God gave the seventh day his blessing, and hallowed it, because it was the day on which his divine activity of creation finished.

Such origin heaven and earth had in the day of their fashioning. When heaven and earth God made, no woodland shrub had yet grown, no plant had yet sprung up, the Lord God had not yet sent rain upon the ground, that still had no human toil to cultivate it; there was only spring-water which came up from the earth, and watered its whole surface. And now, from the clay of the ground, the Lord God formed man, breathed into his nostrils the breath of life, and made of man a living person. God had planted a garden of delight, in which he now placed the man he had formed. Here, at the bidding of the Lord God, the soil produced all such trees as charm the eye and satisfy the taste; and here in the middle of the garden, grew the tree of life,and the tree which brings knowledge of good and evil . . . So the Lord God took the man and put him in his garden of delight, to cultivate and tend it. And this was the command which the Lord God gave the man, Thou mayest eat thy fill of all the trees in the garden except the tree which brings knowledge of good and evil; if ever thou eatest of this, thy doom is death.

But the Lord God said, It is not well that man should be without companionship. I will give him a mate of his own kind. And now, from the clay of the ground, all the beasts that roam the earth and all that flies through the air were ready fashioned, and the Lord God brought them to Adam, to see what he would call them; the name Adam gave to each living creature is its name still. Thus Adam gave names to all the cattle, and all that flies in the air, and all the wild beasts; and still Adam had no mate of his own kind. So the Lord God made Adam fall into a deep sleep, and, while he slept, took away one of his ribs, and filled its place with flesh. This rib, which he had taken out of Adam, The Lord God formed into a woman; and when he brought her to Adam, Adam said, Here, at last, is bone that comes from mine, flesh that comes from mine; it shall be called Woman, this thing that was taken out of Man. That is why a man is destined to leave father and mother, and cling to his wife instead, so that the two become one flesh. Both went naked, Adam and his wife, and thought it no shame.

Of all the beasts which the Lord God had made, there was none that could match the serpent in cunning. It was he who said to the woman, What is this command God has given you, not to eat the fruit of any tree in the garden? To which the woman answered, We can eat the fruit of any tree in the garden except the tree in the middle of it; it is this God has forbidden us to eat or even to touch, on pain of death. And the serpent said to her, What is this talk of death. God knows well that as soon as you eat this fruit your eyes will be opened, and you yourselves will be like gods, knowing good and evil. And with that the woman, who saw that the fruit was good to eat, saw too, how it was pleasant to look at and charmed the eye, took some fruit from the tree and ate it; and she gave some to her husband, and he ate with her. Then the eyes of both were opened,and they became aware of their nakedness; so they sewed fig-leaves together, and made themselves girdles.

And now they heard the voice of the Lord God, as he walked in the garden in the cool of the evening; whereupon Adam and his wife hid themselves in the garden, among the trees. And the Lord God called to Adam, Where art thou? he asked. I heard thy voice, Adam said, in the garden, and I was afraid, because of my nakedness, so I hid myself. And the answer came, Why, who told thee of thy nakedness? Or hadst thou eaten of the tree, whose fruit I forbade thee to eat? The woman, said Adam, whom thou gavest me to be my companion, she it was who offered me fruit from the tree, and so I came to eat it. Then the Lord God said to the woman, What made thee do this? The serpent, she said, beguiled me, and so I came to eat.

And the Lord God said to the serpent, For this work of thine, thou, alone among all the cattle and all the wild beasts, shalt bear a curse; thou shalt crawl on thy belly and eat dust all thy life long. And I will establish a feud between thee and the woman, between thy offspring and hers; she is to crush thy head, while thou dost lie in ambush at her heels. To the woman he said, Many are the pangs, many are the throes I will give thee to endure; with pangs thou shalt give birth to children, and thou shalt be subject to thy husband; he shall be thy lord. And to Adam he said, Thou hast listened to thy wife's counsel, and hast eaten the fruit I forbade thee to eat; and now, through thy act, the ground is under a curse. All the days of thy life thou shalt win food from it with toil; thorns and thistles it shall yield thee, this ground from which thou dost win thy food. Still thou shalt earn thy bread with the sweat of thy brow, until thou goest back into the ground from which thou wast taken; dust thou art, and unto dust shalt thou return.

The name which Adam gave his wife was Eve, Life, because she was the mother of all living men.

And now the Lord provided garments for Adam and his wife, made out of skins, to clothe them. He said, too, Here is Adam become like one of ourselves, with knowledge of good and evil; now he has only to lift his hand and gather fruit to eat from the tree of life as well, and he will live endlessly. So the Lord God drove him out from that garden of delight, to cultivate the ground from which he came; banished Adam, and posted his Cherubim before the garden of delight, with a sword of fire that turned this way and that, so that he could reach the tree of life no longer . . .

And God pronounced his blessing on Noe and his sons; Increase, he said, and multiply, and fill the earth. All the beasts of earth, and the winged things of the sky, and the creeping things of earth, are to go in fear and dread of you, and I give you dominion over all the fishes of the sea. This creation that lives and moves is to provide food for you; I make it all over to you, by the same title as the herbs that have growth. Only, you must not eat the flesh with the blood still in it. The shedder of your own life-blood shall be held to account for it, whether man or beast; whoever takes the life of his brother-man shall answer for it to me. Man was made in God's image, and whoever sheds a man's blood must shed his own blood in return. And now, increase and multiply; occupy and fill the earth.

This, too, God said to Noe, and to Noe's sons: Here is a covenant I will observe with you and with your children after you, and with all living creatures, your companions, the birds and the beasts of burden and the cattle that came out of the Ark with you, and the wild beasts besides. Never more will the living creation be destroyed by the waters of a flood; never again a flood to devastate the world. This, God said, shall be the pledge of the promise I am making to you, and to all living creatures, your companions, eternally; I will set my bow in the clouds, to be a pledge of my covenant with creation. When I veil the sky with clouds, in those clouds my bow shall appear, to remind me of my promise to you, and to all the life that quickens mortal things; never shall the waters rise in flood again, and destroy all living creatures. There, in the clouds, my bow shall stand, and as I look upon it, I will remember this eternal covenant; God's covenant with all the life that beats in mortal creatures upon earth. Such was the pledge God gave to Noe of his promise to all living things.

The Book of Genesis

O LORD, our Master, how the majesty of thy name fills all the earth! Thy greatness is high above heaven itself. Thou hast made the lips of children, of infants at the breast, vocal with praise, to confound thy enemies; to silence malicious and revengeful tongues. I look up to those heavens of thine, the works of thy hands, at the moon and at the stars, which thou has set in their places; what is man that thou shouldst remember him? What is Adam's breed that it should claim care? Thou hast placed him a little below the angels, crowning him with glory and honour, and bidding him rule over the works of thy hands. Thou has put them all under his dominion, the sheep and the cattle, and the wild beasts besides; the birds in the sky, and the fish in the sea, that travel by the sea's paths. O Lord, our Master, how the majesty of thy name fills all the earth!

Psalm 8

Give praise to the Lord in heaven; praise him all that dwells on high. Praise him, all you angels of his, praise him, all his armies. Praise him, sun, and moon; praise him, every star that shines. Praise him, you highest heavens, you waters beyond the heavens. Let all these praise the Lord; it was his command that created them. He has set them there unageing for ever, given them a law which cannot be altered. Give praise to the Lord on earth, monsters of the sea and all its depths; fire and hail, snow and mist, and the storm-wind that executes his decree; all you mountains and hills, all you fruit trees and cedars; all you wild beasts and cattle, creeping things and birds that fly in air; all you kings and peoples of the world, all you that are princes and judges on earth; young men and maids, old men and boys together; let them all give praise to the Lord's name.

Psalm 148

Faced with the prospect of the Second Coming, the early Christian churches largely ignored natural philosophy as irrelevant to the scheme of salvation, but from the time of the conversion of the Emperor Constantine in the early fourth century CE, its growing confidence allowed it to confront the pagan philosophies of ancient Greece and even to some extent to integrate their ideas into Christian theology. St Augustine (354–430 CE) was one of the most important seminal figues in shaping Christian theology, and though he was wary of pagan philosophy as a distraction from humanity's supreme destiny, we find him also making use of a traditional philosophical argument based on the order and beauty of nature.

When, then, the question is asked what we are to believe in regard to religion, it is not necessary to probe into the nature of things, as was done by those whom the Greeks called *physici*; nor need we be in alarm lest the Christian should be ignorant of the force and number of the elements – the motion, and order, and eclipses of the heavenly bodies; the form of the heavens; the species and the natures of animals and plants, stones, fountains, rivers, mountains; about chronology and distances; the signs of coming storms; and a thousand other things which those philosophers either have found out, or think they have found out . . . It is enough for the Christian to believe that the only cause of all created things, whether heavenly or earthly, whether visible or invisible, is the goodness of the Creator, the one true God; and that nothing exists but Himself that does not derive its existence from Him.

St Augustine: *Enchiridion*

Thanks be to you, O Lord, for all that we see! We see heaven and earth, which may be either the upper and lower parts of the material world or the spiritual and material creations. For their adornment, whether they constitute the whole of the material world or the entire creation, spiritual and material alike, we see the light that was created and separated from the darkness. We see the firmament of heaven . . . We see the waters gathered together, so that the surface of the sea is like a great plain, and the dry land, first rising bare from the waters and then with form added so that it might become visible and order might be given to it and it should become the mother of plants and trees. We see the lights shining from above, the sun furnishing its light to the day and the moon and the stars giving comfort to the night, and all of them marking the passage of time. All about us we see how the sea and the rivers and the lakes teem with fish and the great creatures that live in the water, and with birds as well, for it is the evaporation of moisture which makes the air dense enough to support them in flight. We see the face of the earth graced by the animals that live upon it. And finally we see man, made in your own image and likeness, ruling over all the irrational animals for the very reason that he was made in your image and resembles you, that is, because he has the power of reason and understanding. And just as in man's soul there are two forces, one which is dominant because it deliberates and one which obeys because it is subject to such guidance, in the same way, in the physical sense, woman has been made for man. In her mind and her rational intelligence she has a nature the equal of man's, but in sex she is physically subject to him in the same way as our natural impulses need to be subjected to the reasoning power of the mind, in order that the actions to which they lead may be inspired by the principles of good conduct.

All this we see. Taken singly, each thing is good; but collectively they are very good.

Your works proclaim your glory, and because of this we love you; and it is in our love for you that they proclaim your glory. You created [the world] from nothing, not from your own substance or from some matter not created by yourself or already in existence, but from matter which you created at one and the same time as the things that you made from it, since there was no interval of time before you gave form to this formless matter...

I have also considered what spiritual truths you intended to be expressed by the order in which the world was created and the order in which the creation is described. I have seen that while each single one of your works is good, collectively they are very good, and that heaven and earth, which represent the Head and the body of the Church, were predestined in your Word, that is, in your only-begotten Son, before all time began, when there was no morning and no evening.

St Augustine: *Confessions*

The Roman philosopher Plotinus (205–262 CE), though not a Christian, was to have an important influence on a particular mystical strand of Christian thinking which took its inspiration from Plato and from the idea that all things emanate from the One and are infused with soul as a unifying principle. There are intimations here of Indian mysticism, too, and indeed Plotinus, who lived for a time in Alexandria and travelled to Persia, was fascinated by the philosophies of the East.

It is by the One that all beings are beings. This is equally true of those that are primarily beings and those that in some way are simply classed among beings, for what could exist were it not one? Not a one, a thing is not. No army, no choir, no flock exists except it be one. No house, even, or ship exists except as the unit, house, or the unit, ship; their unity gone, the house is no longer a house, the ship no longer a ship. Similarly quantitative continua would not exist had they not an inner unity; divided, they forfeit existence along with unity. It is the same with plant and animal bodies; each of them is a unit; with disintegration, they lose their previous nature and are no longer what they were; they become new, different beings that in turn exist only as long as each of them is a unit. Health is contingent upon the body's being co-ordinated in unity; beauty, upon the mastery of parts by The One; the soul's virtue, upon unification into one sole coherence.

The Soul imports unity to all things in producing, fashioning, forming, and disposing them. Ought we then to say that the Soul not only gives unity but is unity itself, The One? No. It bestows other qualities upon bodies without being what it bestows ... so also this unity; The Soul makes each being one by looking upon the One, just as it makes man by contemplating the Idea, Man, effecting in the man the unity that belongs to Man ...

All these entities emanate from The One without any lessening for it is not a material mass. If it were, the emanents would be perishable. But they are eternal because their originating principle always stays the same; not fragmenting itself in producing them, it remains entire. So they persist as well, just as light persists as long as the sun shines.

We are not separated from The One, not distant from it, even though bodily nature has closed about us and draw us to itself.

It is because of The One that we breathe and have our being: it does not bestow its gifts at one moment only to leave us again; its giving is without cessation so long as it remains what it is. As we turn towards The One, we exist to a higher degree, while to withdraw from it is to fall. Our soul is delivered from evil by rising to that place which is free of all evils. There it knows. There it is immune. There it truly lives. Life not united with the divinity is shadow and mimicry of authentic life. Life there is the native act of The Intelligence, which, motionless in its conract with The One, gives birth to gods, beauty, justice, and virtue.

With all of these The Soul, filled with divinity, is pregnant; this is its starting point and its goal. It is its starting point because it is from the world above that it proceeds. It is its goal because in the world above is the Good to which it aspires and by returning to it there its proper nature is regained. Life here below in the midst of sense objects is for the soul a degradation, an exile, a loss of wings.

Plotinus: *The Enneads*

Interest in natural philosophy revived in the Middle Ages with the influx from Moorish Spain in the twelfth century of the works of Aristotle, works which had been preserved and studied by generations of Arab philosophers, and the argument of the Jewish philosopher Maimonides (1135–1204) set out below was clearly influenced by the Greek philosopher's teleological view of the natural world. Of great importance was the attempt by the theologian Thomas Aquinas (1225–1274) to integrate Aristotelian philosophy with Christian theology, and his arguments for the existence of God are based on a general philosophical conception of the natural world that owes much to ancient philosophy. The view that nature displays design and purpose is used by Aquinas in his 'fifth way' (see p57), and is evident too in the extract from the theologian Peter Abelard (1079–1142).

Another method with regard to the belief in unity. It has already been established as true by means of a demonstration that all that exists is like one individual whose parts are bound up with each other, and that the forces of the sphere pervade this lowly matter and fashion it. At the same time it is impossible – and this has already been established as true – that one deity should be exclusively concerned with one part of what exists, and the other deity with another part; for one part is bound up with the other. According to the division of possibilities, the only hypotheses that remain open are that one deity acts during a certain time and the other during another time, or that both of them always act together so that no act is perfect unless it has been carried out by both of them together. Now the supposition that one of them acts during a certain time and the other during another time is absurd from several points of view. For if it were possible that during the time in which one of them acts the other should act also, what could be the cause necessitating that one of them acts during that time whereas the other remains inactive? If, however, it were impossible for one of them to act during the time in which the other acts, there consequently must be another cause that necessitates that at a given time it is possible for one of them to act whereas for the other it is impossible. For there is no differentiation in time as a whole; and the substratum for the action is one, and its parts are bound up with one another, as we have made clear. Furthermore, according to this supposition, each one of them would fall under time inasmuch as his work would be tied up with time. Furthermore, each one of them, at the time of his action, would have to pass from potentiality to actuality, and, in consequence, each one of them would need something that would cause him to pass from potentiality to actuality. Furthermore, possibility would subsist in the essence of each of them. If, however, they were supposed always to make together everything that is in existence, so that one of them would not act without the other, that also would be absurd, as I shall set forth. For in the case of any complex composed of parts, which cannot cause a certain act to become perfect except through the cooperation of each one of its parts, none of these parts is an agent in respect to its own essence or the first cause of the act; that first cause is the coming-together of the parts of the complex. Now it has been demonstrated that it is a necessary conclusion that what is necessary of existence can have no cause. Moreover the coming-together of the parts of the complex represents a certain act, which requires another agent, namely, one who causes the parts of the complex to come together. Now if the agent who causes the parts of the complex to come together – without which the act cannot become perfect – is one, he is indubitably the deity. If, however, this agent who causes the parts of this complex to come together is another complex, the same conclusions follow necessarily with regard to this second complex as with regard to the first. Thus there can be no doubt about ultimately reaching One who is the cause of the existence of this existent, which is one, whatever the manner of this may have been: whether through creating it in time after it had been nonexistent, or because it proceeds necessarily from this One. It has thus become clear, also according to this method, that the fact that all that exists is one, indicates to us that He who caused it to exist is one.

Maimonides: *The Guide of the Perplexed*

It is not to be doubted that all things, both good and bad, proceed from a most perfectly ordered plan, that they occur and are fitted to one another in such a way that they could not possibly occur more fittingly. Thus Augustine: since God is good, evils would not be, unless it were a good that there should be evils. For by the same reason for which he wills that good things shall exist, namely, because their existence is befitting (*conveniens*), he also wills that evil things should exist... all of which as a whole tends to his greater glory. For as a picture is often more beautiful and worthy of commendation if some colours in themselves ugly are included in it, than it would be if it were uniform and of a single colour, so from an admixture of evils the universe is rendered more beautiful and worthy of commendation.

Abelard: *The Essence of Christian Theology*

God's existence can be proved in five ways. First and most obvious is the way that begins with 'change'. It is obvious that some things in the world are undoubtedly in the process of changing. But anything undergoing change is being changed by something else. This is the case with anything in the process of changing, because it does not yet possess the perfection toward which it is changing, although it is capable of it; whereas anything causing change must already have the perfection it is causing, for to cause a change is to bring into existence that which previously was capable of existing, and only something that already exists can do this... Now, the same thing cannot be simultaneously both actually and potentially x; but it can be actually x and potentially y... Therefore, whatever is in the process of changing cannot cause its own changing; it cannot change itself. Anything in the process of changing is therefore being changed by something else. Moreover, if this something else is in the process of changing, it itself is being changed by another thing, and this by another. Now, the changing has to stop somewhere, or else there will be no first cause of the changing and, consequently, no subsequent causes; for only when acted upon by the first cause do intermediate causes produce any change...And so we have come to some first cause of changing that is not itself changed by anything else, and this is what everyone understands by God.

The second way is derived from the nature of causation. In the sensible world we find causes in an order of succession; we never see, nor could we, anything causing itself, for then it would have to pre-exist itself, and this is impossible. Any such succession of causes must begin somewhere, for in it a primary cause influences an intermediate, and the intermediate a last (whether the intermediate be one or many). Now, if you eliminate a cause, you also eliminate its effects, so that you cannot have a last cause or an intermediate one without having a first cause. Without an origin to the series of causes, and hence no primary cause, no intermediate causes would function and therefore no last effect, but the facts seem to contradict this [for the effects are present]. We must therefore suppose a First Cause, which all call 'God'.

The third way is drawn from the existence of the unnecessary and the necessary, and proceeds as follows. Our experience includes things certainly capable of existing but apparently unnecessary, since they come and go, coming to birth or dying. But if it is unnecessary for a thing to exist, it did not exist once upon a time, and yet everything cannot be like this, for if everything is unnecessary, there was once nothing. But if such were the case, there would now be nothing, because a non-existent can only be brought into existence by something already existing. So that if ever there was nothing, not a thing could be brought into existence, and there would be nothing now, which contradicts the facts. And so not everything can be an unnecessary kind of being; there must exist some being that necessarily exists. But a thing that necessarily exists may or may not have this necessity from something else. But just as we must begin somewhere in a succession of causes, the case is the same with any succession of things that necessarily exist and receive this necessity from others. Hence we are compelled to suppose something that exists necessarily, having this necessity only from itself; in fact, it itself is the cause why other things exist.

The fourth way is supported by the gradation noticed in things. There are some things that are more good, more true, more noble, and so forth, and other things less so. But such comparisons denote different degrees of approach to a superlative; for instance, things are hotter and hotter the closer they approach what is hottest. There is therefore a truest and best and most noble thing, and so most fully existing. Now when many things share some property, whatever possesses it most fully causes it in others: 'Fire', to use Aristotle's example, the hottest of all things, causes all other things to be hot. There is, therefore, something that causes in all other things their being, their goodness, and any other perfection they possess. And this we call 'God'.

The fifth way is taken from the ordered tendencies of nature. A direction of actions to an end is detected in all bodies following natural laws even when they are without awareness, for their action scarcely ever varies and nearly always succeeds; this indicates that they do tend towards a goal, not merely succeeding by accident. Anything, however, without awareness, tends to a goal only under the guidance of someone who is aware and knows; the arrow, for instance, needs an archer. Everything in nature, consequently, is guided to its goal by someone with knowledge, and this one we call 'God' . . .

Some people, such as Democritus and the Epicureans, completely denied that there is any providence, and they held that the world came about by chance. Others taught that only incorruptible things were subject to providence and that corruptible beings were subject to it only in their species and not in their individualities; for in their species they are incorruptible. They are supposed to have said (Job 22:14): 'The clouds are his covert'; and 'he does not consider our things; and he walketh about the poles of heaven'. Nevertheless, Rabbi Moses, while agreeing with this opinion concerning those things enduring corruption, excluded men from the generally corruptible things on account of the excellence of their intellect.

It is necessary to state, however, that everything is subject to divine providence, not only in a general way but even as individuals. What follows will clarify this. Because every agent acts for an end, the directing of effects towards that end goes as far as does the causing of the first agent. And so because an effect at times comes from a cause other than and beyond the intention of an agent, among the effects of an agent something occurs that is unrelated to the end. But the causing by God, who as the first agent, is concerned with all being, not only with the principles constituting species but also with the individualizing principles, not only with the incorruptible but also with corruptible beings. And so anything in any way existent is necessarily directed by God towards some end...And since his knowledge is related to things in themselves as art to the works of art, all beings must be subject to his ordering as all things made through art are subject to the ordering of that art.

St Thomas Aquinas: *Summa Theologiae*

Following the injunctions of the Book of Genesis concerning the right of human beings to command nature, and the belief that human beings, being made in God's image, are, unlike animals, rational creatures and possess immortal souls, Mediaeval theologians generally took the view that cruelty to animals did not constitute a sin except in so far as it tended to encourage sinful behaviour towards other human beings. A more unorthodox attitude to animals is evident in the famous 'Canticle of the Sun', or 'The Song of Brother Sun and of All Creatures' of St Francis of Assisi (1181–1226).

In the first place, then, the very condition of the rational creature, in that it has dominion over its actions, requires that the care of providence should be bestowed on it for its own sake: whereas the condition of other things that have not dominion over their actions shows that they are cared for, not for their own sake, but as directed by other things. Because that which acts only when moved by another, is like an instrument; whereas that which acts by itself, is like a principal agent. Now an instrument is required, not for its own sake, but that the principal agent may use it. Hence whatever is done for the care of the instruments must be referred to the principal agent as its end: whereas any such action directed to the principal agent as such, either by the agent itself or by another, is for the sake of the same principal agent. Accordingly intellectual creatures are ruled by God, as though He cared for them for their own sake, while other creatures are ruled as being directed by rational creatures . . .

Hereby is refuted the error of those who say it is sinful for a man to kill dumb animals: for by divine providence they are intended for man's use in the natural order. Hence it is no wrong for man to make use of them, either by killing or in any other way whatever. For this reason the Lord said to Noe (*Gen.*ix.3): *As the green herbs, I have delivered all flesh to you.*

And if any passage of Holy Writ seem to forbid us to be cruel to dumb animals, for instance to kill a bird with its young: this is either to remove man's thought from being cruel to other men, and lest through being cruel to animals one become cruel to human beings: or because injury to an animal leads to the temporal hurt of man, either of the doer of the deed, or of another: or on account of some signification: thus the Apostle expounds the prohibition against *muzzling the ox that treadeth the corn.*

St Thomas Aquinas: *Summa Contra Gentiles*

Most High, Almighty, good Lord,
Thine be the praise, the glory, the honour,
And all blessing.

To Thee alone, Most High, are they due,
And no man is worthy To speak Thy Name.

Praise to Thee, my Lord, for all Thy creatures,
Above all Brother Sun
Who brings us the day and lends us his light.

Lovely is he, radiant with great splendour,
And speaks to us of Thee, O Most High.

Praise to Thee, my Lord, for Sister Moon and the stars
Which Thou has set in the heavens,
Clear, precious, and fair.

Praise to Thee, my Lord, for Brother Wind,
For air and cloud, for calm and all weather,
By which Thou supportest life in all Thy creatures.

Praise to Thee, my Lord, for Sister Water,
Who is so useful and humble,
Precious and pure.

Praise to Thee, my Lord, for Brother Fire,
By whom Thou lightest the night;
He is lovely and pleasant, mighty and strong.

Praise to Thee, my Lord, for our sister Mother Earth
Who sustains and directs us,
And brings forth varied fruits, and coloured flowers, and plants.

St Francis of Assisi: 'The Song of Brother Sun and of All Creatures'

Much effort was expended in the Middle Ages and the Renaissance in elaborating a cosmological idea, first mooted by Aristotle, in which all beings are located in order of precedence and 'nobility' along a hierarchical Chain of Being. Humanity is placed in a middle position, above the animals and plants, and below the heavenly bodies and the angels. It is a scheme of things which placed the human world within a precisely articulated and meaningful cosmic order, and at the same time one which corresponded closely to the socio-political order of the feudal system. Dante (1265–1321) structured his poem, The Divine Comedy, *around this cosmological picture.*

Since it has been demonstrated in the preceding chapter what this . . . heaven is, and how it is ordered within itself, it remains to show who they are who move it. Therefore be it known, in the first place, that these are Substances separate from matter, that is Intelligences, whom the common people call Angels . . . The numbers, the orders, the hierarchies [of these angelic beings], are recounted by the moveable heavens, which are nine; and the tenth announces the unity and stability of God. And therefore the psalmist says, 'The heavens recount the glory of God, and the firmament announceth the work of His hands.'

Wherefore it is reasonable to believe that the motive powers [that is the beings who move the spheres] of the Heaven of the Moon are of the order of Angels; and those of Mercury, Archangels; and those of Venus are the Thrones . . . And these Thrones, which area allotted to the government of this heaven [of Venus], are not many in number, and the astrologers [or astronomers] differ about the revolutions [of this heaven], although all are agreed in this, that their number is equal to that of these revolutions; which, according to the *Book of the Aggregation of the Stars*... are three: one by which the star revolves within its epicycle, the second by which the epicycle, and the whole heaven revolves equally with that of the Sun, and the third by which all that heaven revolves, following the [precessional] motion of the stellar sphere from west to east, one degree in a hundred years. So that for these three motions are three motive powers [which are three members of the angelic order of Thrones].

Dante: *The Banquet*

The Islamic peoples inherited from the Greeks their love of the order and beauty of nature and helped to preserve and enhance the philosophical and scientific ideas which were lost to the West after the fall of the Roman empire in the fifth century CE. Like the Bible, the Koran displays a sensitivity towards the natural world which is seen as both glorifying and manifesting God (Allah), and as being an instrument for human use and welfare.

The judgement of Allah will surely come to pass: do not seek to hurry it on. Glory to Him! Exalted be He above their idols!

By His will He sends down the angels with the Spirit to those of His servants whom he chooses, bidding them proclaim: 'There is no god but Me: therefore fear Me.'

He created the heavens and the earth to manifest the truth. Exalted be He above their idols!

He created man from a little germ: yet man openly disputes His judgement.

He created the beasts which provide you with warm clothing, food, and other benefits. How pleasant they look when you bring them home and when you lead them out to pasture!

They carry your burdens to far-off lands, which you could not otherwise reach except with painful toil. Compassionate is your Lord, and merciful.

He has given you horses, mules, and donkeys, which you may ride or use as ornaments; and He has created other things beyond your knowledge.

Allah alone can show the right path. Some turn aside from it, but had He pleased He would have guided you all aright.

It is He who sends down water from the sky, which provides drink for you and brings forth the crops on which your cattle feed. And thereby He brings up corn and olives, dates and grapes and other fruit. Surely in this there is a sign for thinking men.

He has forced the night and the day, and the sun and the moon, into your service: the stars also serve you by His leave. Surely in this there are signs for men of understanding.

On the earth He has fashioned for you objects of various hues: surely in this there is a sign for prudent men.

It is He who has subjected to you the ocean, so that you may eat of its fresh fish and bring up from it ornaments with which to adorn your persons. Behold the ships ploughing their course through it. All this He has created, that you may seek His bounty and render thanks to Him.

He set firm mountains upon the earth lest it should move away with you; and rivers, roads, and landmarks, so that you may be rightly guided. By the stars, too, are men directed.

Is He, then, who has wrought the creation, like him who has created nothing? Will you not take heed?

If you reckoned up Allah's blessings you could not count them. He is forgiving and merciful.

The Koran

4

MAGIC, MYSTICISM, AND HARMONY IN THE RENAISSANCE

It is sometimes a surprise to discover that the Renaissance, that extra-ordinary period of creativity in the arts, literature, and culture that centred on and spilled out of the Italy of the fifteenth century, and which gave rise to an 'enlightened' humanism, was steeped in religious and mystical ideas, even the occult. It was, of course, a period in which we find many anticipations of the scientific revolution which was to emerge in the six-teenth and seventeenth centuries. Here one only has to think of the amazing close observation of the details of the natural world apparent in the work of the artists of the period; Leonardo da Vinci inevitably springs to mind in this context as someone whose careful studies of nature, ranging from landscape drawings to anatomical dissections, seem entirely free from philosophical or religious concerns. Yet at the same time this was an epoch still firmly rooted in Christian theological teachings, and as far as natural philosophy is concerned it represented the drawing together of many ancient traditions. Although Aristotle, as interpreted by the Med-iaeval philosophers such as Aquinas, fell out of favour, the idea of the Great Chain of Being, now underpinned by the more mystical teachings of Plato and the Neoplatonists, was more than ever the favoured model on which were built all kinds of intellectual and artistic constructs. Following mediaeval developments of ancient teachings, the Renaissance thinkers tended to see the natural world, not as a collection of material objects, but rather as a kind of text comprising a whole interlocking set of signs and symbols which, like a book, could be read, and in which could be dis-cerned the mind and intentions of the Creator. Under the influence of Plato's theory of Forms, woven into Christian theology, the world was seen as a manifestation of Spirit whose meaning was encoded in the beauty and harmony of nature. It was in effect a kind of magical universe, for its signs could not only be read but, in so far as they manifested hidden powers and influences in nature, could be exploited for human purposes.

Such was, in brief, the underlying assumption of the occult philosophy that flourished in the Renaissance, a philosophy which had its origins in the ancient world and which was beginning to filter back into the

European mind through the rediscovery of ancient manuscripts. Astrology, magic, and alchemy all represented a new – or renewed – concept of nature which, though often deemed by the Church to be heretical, still viewed the universe as an essentially spiritual being, and nature as the embodiment of Spirit. Thus astrology, widely practised in the period, and even patronized by Popes, was based on the belief that earthly and human events – the microcosm – reflect and are influenced by the motions and dispositions of the heavenly bodies – the macrocosm – and hence that nature is part of a meaningful whole whose activities can be read and, with the appropriate knowledge, used for human purposes.

Although Petrarch (1304–1374) is often seen as a forebear of Renaissance humanism, he can also be seen in the following letter as a man who still carried within him much of the Mediaeval uncertainty about the value of admiring nature for its own sake rather than as a sign of God's providence.

Today I ascended the highest mountain of this region [Mont Ventoux]...I admired every detail, now relishing earthly enjoyment, now lifting my mind to higher spheres after the example of my body, and I thought it fit to look into the volume of Augustine's *Confessions* ... keeping it always in my hands, in remembrance of the author as well as the donor. It is a little book of smallest size but full of infinite sweetness. I opened it with the intention of reading whatever might occur to me first...Where I fixed my eyes first it was written: 'And men go to admire high mountains, the vast floods of the sea, the huge streams of the rivers, the circumference of the ocean, and the revolutions of the stars – and desert themselves'.

Petrarch: 'The Ascent of Mont Ventoux'

Interest in magic and witchcraft, both of which were tied to a pagan, pre-Christian natural philosophy, flourished in the late Middle Ages in spite of the hostility of the Church, and in 1486 two Dominican priests, Heinrich Kraemer and Johannes Sprenger, published a treatise which argued that magic and witchcraft were realities manifesting the work of the devil, not mere superstitions and illusions. The Witches' Ham-

mer became the encyclopaedia of demonology throughout Christendom for the following two centuries.

Certain writers, pretending to base their opinion upon the words of St Thomas when he treats of impediments brought about by magic charms, have tried to maintain that there is not such a thing as magic, that it only exists in the imagination of those men who ascribe natural effects, the causes whereof are not known, to witchcraft and spells. There are others who acknowledge indeed that witches exist, but they declare that the influence of magic and the effects of charms are purely imaginary and phantasmical. A third class of writers maintain that the effects said to be wrought by magic spells are altogether illusory and fanciful, although it may be that the devil does really lend his aid to some witch.

The errors held by each one of these persons may thus be set forth and thus confuted. For in the very first place they are shown to be plainly heretical by many orthodox writers, and especially by St Thomas, who lays down that such an opinion is altogether contrary to the authority of the saints and is founded upon absolute infidelity. Because the authority of the Holy Scriptures says that devils have power over the bodies and over the minds of men, when God allows them to exercise this power, as is plain from very many passages in the Holy Scriptures. Therefore those err who say that there is no such thing as witchcraft, but that it is purely imaginary, even although they do not believe that devils exist except in the imagination of the ignorant and vulgar, and the natural accidents which happen to a man he wrongly attributes to some supposed devil. For the imagination of some men is so vivid that they think they see actual figures and appearances which are but the reflection of their thoughts, and then these are believed to be the apparitions of evil spirits or even the spectres of witches. But this is contrary to the true faith, which teaches us that certain angels fell from heaven and are now devils, and we are bound to acknowledge that by their very nature they can do many wonderful things which we cannot do. And those who try to induce others to perform such evil wonders are called witches. And because infidelity in a person who has been baptized is technically called heresy, therefore such persons are plainly heretics.

As regards those who hold the other two errors, those, that is to say, who do not deny that there are demons and that demons possess a natural power, but who differ among themselves concerning the possible effects of magic and the possible operations of witches: the one school holding that a witch can truly bring about certain effects, yet these effects are not real but phantastical, the other school allowing that some real harm does befall the person or persons injured, but that when a witch imagines this damage is the effect of her arts she is grossly deceived. This error seems to be based upon two passages from the Canons where certain women are condemned who falsely imagine that during the night they ride abroad with Diana or Herodias. This may be read in the Canon. Yet because such things often happen by illusion and merely in the imagination, those who suppose that all the effects of witchcraft are mere illusion and imagination are very greatly deceived. Secondly, with regard to a man who believes or maintains that a creature can be made, or changed for better or for worse, or transformed into some other kind or likeness by anyone save by God, the Creator of all things, alone, is an infidel and worse than a heathen. Wherefore on account of these words such an effect if wrought by witchcraft cannot be real but must be purely phantastical.

Kraemer and Sprenger: *The Witches' Hammer*

The rediscovery of the Hermetica, *or* Corpus Hermeticum *(also known as* The Hermetic Philosophy*), an ancient Egyptian text allegedly dating from the time of Moses, though in fact written in about the second century* CE, *was one of the most important events of the Renaissance, for, with its mystical philosophy that the cosmos is a unity in which all things express and are bound together by the divine Spirit, it provided the basis for the revived interest in the occult sciences – magic, astrology, and alchemy. The important status allotted to the sun was to have important consequences in the revolutionary ideas of Copernicus.*

If you want to see god, consider the sun, consider the circuit of the moon, consider the order of the stars. Who keeps this order? (For every order is bounded in number and in place.) The sun, the greatest god of those in heaven, to whom all heavenly gods submit as to a king and its ruler, this sun so very great, larger than the earth and sea, allows stars smaller than him to circle above him. To whom does he defer, my child? Whom does he fear? Does not each of these stars in heaven make the same circuit or a similar one? Who determined the direction and the size of the circuit for each of them?

Who owns this instrument, this bear, the one that turns around itself and carries the whole cosmos with it? Who sets limits to the sea? Who settled the earth in its place? There is someone who is maker and master of all this. Without someone to make them, neither place, nor number, nor measure could have been maintained. Everything that is an order has been made; only something placeless and measureless can be not made. But even this does not lack a master. Even if the unadorned is deficient it is still subject to a master who has not yet imposed order on it.

Would that you could grow wings and fly up in the air, lifted between earth and heaven to see the solid earth, the fluid sea, the streaming rivers, the pliant air, the piercing fire, the coursing stars, and heaven speeding on its axis about the same points. Oh, this is a most happy sight to see, my child, to have a vision of all these in a single instant, to see the motionless set in motion and the invisible made visible through the things it makes! This is the order of the cosmos, and this is the cosmos of order.

If you wish to see the vision through mortal things on earth and in the deep, my child, consider how the human being is crafted in the womb, examine the skill of the craftwork carefully, and learn who it is that crafts this beautiful, godlike image of mankind. Who traced the line round the eyes? Who pierced the holes for nostrils and ears? Who opened up the mouth? Who stretched out the sinews and tied them down? Who made channels for the veins? Who hardened the bones? Who drew skin over the flesh? Who parted the fingers? Who flattened the bottoms of the feet? Who cut passages for the pores? Who stretched out the spleen? Who made the heart in the form of a pyramid? Who joined the [ribs] together? Who flattened the liver? Who hollowed out the lungs? Who made the belly spacious? Who set the most honoured parts in relief to make them visible but hid the shameful parts away? . . .

If you force me to say something still more daring, it is [god's] essence to be pregnant with all things and to make them. As it is impossible for anything to be produced without a maker, so it is impossible for this maker [not] to exist always unless he is always making everything in heaven, in the air, on earth, in the deep, in every part of the cosmos, in every part of the universe, in what is and in what is not, for there is nothing in all the cosmos that he is not. Those that are he has made visible; those that are not he holds within him. This is the god who is greater than any name; this is the god invisible and entirely visible. This god who is evident to the eyes may be seen in the mind. He is bodiless and many-bodied; or, rather, he is all-bodied. There is nothing that he is not, for he also is all that is, and this is why he has all names, because they are of one father, and this is why he has no name, because he is father of them all . . .

You are everything, and there is nothing else; what is not, you are as well. You are all that has come to be; you are what has not come to be; you are the mind that understands, the father who makes his craftworld, the god who acts, and the god who makes all things.

The Hermetic Philosophy

Johann Kepler (1571–1630) is usually remembered as having made an important contribution to the study of planetary motion, but, like most of the natural philosophers (ie scientists) of the period his outlook was steeped in occult ideas, and in the first of the following passages we find him worrying over a question integral to astrology and much debated in his time, namely whether and how far the heavenly constellations at the time of birth predetermine human destiny and so contradict free will. In the second passage he offers a theological rationale for his natural philosophy.

Here is another question: how does the conformation of the heavens influence the character of a man at the moment of his birth? It influences a human being as long as he lives in no other way than that in which the peasant haphazardly ties slings around pumpkins; these do not make the pumpkin grow, but they determine its shape. So do the heavens; they do not give a man morals, experiences, happiness, children, wealth, a wife, but they shape everything with which a man has to do. And yet from the constellation of the birth of a man, the heavens take an infinite number of forms during the course of his life. They never remain the same; so the constellation at birth is a passing one.

Kepler: Letter to Herwart von Hohenberg

If you desire venerability – nothing is more precious, nothing more beautiful than our magnificent temple of God. If you wish to know the mysteries – nothing in Nature is, or ever has been, more recondite. *It is but for one reason that my object will not satisfy everybody, for its usefulness will not be apparent to the thoughtless.* I am speaking of the Book of Nature, which is so highly esteemed in the Holy Scriptures, St Paul admonished the Heathens to reflect on God within themselves as they would on the Sun in the water or in a mirror. Why then should we Christians delight the less in this reflection, seeing that it is our proper task to honour, to revere and to admire God in the true way? Our piety in this is the deeper the greater is our awareness of creation and of its grandeur. Truly, how many hymns of praise did not David, His faithful servant, sing to the Creator, who is none but God alone! In this his mind dwelled reverently on the contemplation of the Heavens. The Heavens, he sings, declare the glory of God. I will consider Thy heavens, the work of Thy hands, the moon and the stars which Thou has ordained. God is our Lord, and great is His might; He counteth the multitude of the stars, and knoweth them by their names. Elsewhere, inspired by the Holy Ghost and full of joyousness, he exclaims to the Universe: Praise ye the Lord, praise Him, Sun and Moon, etc. Now, do the heavens or the stars have a voice? Can they praise God as men do? Nay, when we say that they themselves give praise to God, it is only because they offer men thoughts of praise to God. Thus, in what follows, let us free the very tongues of the heavens and of nature so that their voices may resound all the louder; and when we do so let no one accuse us of vain and useless efforts.

Kepler: *Mysterium Cosmographicum*

The following three passages from Marsilio Ficino (1433–1499), who translated the Corpus Hermeticum *into Latin, Baldasar Castiglione (1478–1529), whose book* The Courtier *was one of the most widely read books of the period, and William Shakespeare (1564–1616), who is often seen as the final flowering of the Renaissance, all give voice to the idea of the cosmos as a universal and divinely constructed order. The musical/mathematical metaphor of cosmic harmony, which as we saw above can be traced back to Pythagoras, was especially attractive to the Renaissance mind.*

The motion of each of all the natural species proceeds according to a certain principle. Different species are moved in different ways, and each species always preserves the same course in its motion so that it always proceeds from this place to that place and, in turn, recedes from the latter to the former, in a certain most harmonious manner . . . If individual motions are brought to completion according to such a wonderful order, then certainly the universal motion of the cosmos itself cannot be lacking in perfect order. Indeed, just as the individual motions are derived from and contribute to universal motion, so from the order of universal motion they receive order and to the order of universal motion they contribute order. In this common order of the whole, all things, no matter how diverse, are brought back to unity according to a single determined harmony and rational plan. Therefore, we conclude that all things are led by one certain orderer who is most full of reason . . .

Reason is certainly peculiar to us. God has not bestowed it upon the beasts, otherwise he would have given them discourse which is, as it were, the messenger of reason . . . Where intellect is present, intellect which is, as it were, a kind of eye turned towards the intelligible light, there also the intelligible light which is God shines and is honoured and loved and worshipped.

As intellect is more perfect than sense, man is more perfect than the brutes. Because of this very thing, he is more perfect: he has a characteristic not shared by the beasts. Thus on account of his intelligence alone man is judged to be more perfect, especially since, by means of the function of intelligence, he approaches the infinite perfection which is God.

Ficino: *Letters*

Consider the structure of this great fabric of the universe, which was created by God for the health and preservation of all His creatures. The bowl of heaven, adorned with so many celestial lamps, and the earth in the centre, surrounded by the elements and sustained by its own weight; the sun, illuminating all things as it revolves, in winter approaching the lowest sign, and then by degrees ascending to the other side; the moon, which derives its light from the sun, in accord with whether the sun is approaching or drawing away; and the five other stars which separately travel the same course: these all influence each other so profoundly through the coherence of the natural order that if they changed in the slightest they could no longer exist together and the universe would crumble. Moreover, they have such beauty and loveliness that the human mind cannot conceive anything more graceful. Consider next the structure of man, who may be called a little universe in himself. We see that every part of his body is in the natural order of things made by design and not by chance and that his form as a whole is so beautiful that it is difficult to decide whether it is utility or grace that is given more to the human face and body by its various parts, such as the eyes, nose, mouth, ears, arms and breast. The same can be said of all the animals. Consider the feathers of birds and the leaves and branches of trees, which are given by Nature to preserve their being, and yet which are also of the greatest loveliness.

Castiglione: *The Book of the Courtier*

How sweet the moonlight sleeps upon this bank
Here will we sit, and let the sounds of music
Creep in our ears; soft stillness and the night
Become the touches of sweet harmony.
Sit, Jessica. Look how the floor of heaven
Is thick inlaid with patens of bright gold.
There's not the smallest orb which thou behold'st
But in his motion like an angel sings,
Still quiring to the young-eyed cherubims.
Such harmony is in immortal souls,
But whilst this muddy vesture of decay
Doth grossly close it in, we cannot hear it.

Shakespeare: *The Merchant of Venice*

The idea of cosmic harmony was associated with the twin concepts of the macrocosm and the microcosm: the world of the heavens above and the human world below each reflected the other and were bound together by bonds of sympathy – 'As above, so below', as the saying went. This idea was central to the theory of astrology as expressed in the philosophical writings of Cornelius Agrippa (1486–1535), and taken for granted as common knowledge by Leonardo da Vinci (1452–1519).

Man is the most finished and beautiful work and image of God, and a smaller version of the world. Therefore in his more perfect form and sweeter harmony, and in his more sublime dignity he has all the numbers, measures, weights, motions and elements. All component things stand within and are sustained in him, all things are in him as in the supreme artificer, and he has a supreme destiny beyond the common range of other creatures. As a result all ancient peoples first counted their fingers and then established numbers from them. And all the articulations of the human body itself, and all numbers, measures, proportions and harmonies that they found were measured against it. Whence, from this commensuration, temples, shrines, houses, theatres, and beyond them boats and machines and all sorts of technical devices and craft objects, and buildings in all their parts and members eg columns, friezes, etc, were brought forth from the human body ... And there is no member of the human body that does not respond to some point or sign, some star, some being, some divine name, within the archetype of it all, God.

Agrippa: *On the Occult Philosophy*

Man has been called by the ancients a lesser world and indeed the term is well applied. Seeing that if a man is composed of earth, water, air, and fire, this body of earth is similar. While man has within himself bones as a stay and framework for the flesh, the world has stones which are the supports of earth. While man has within himself a pool of blood wherein the lungs as he breathes expand and contract, so the body of the earth has its ocean, which also rises and falls every six hours with the breathing of the world; as from the said pool of blood proceed the veins which spread their branches through the human body, so the ocean fills the body of the earth with an infinite number of veins of water ...

In this body of the earth is lacking, however, the nerves, and these are absent because nerves are made for the purpose of movement; and as the world is perpetually stable, and no movement takes place here, nerves are not necessary. But in all other things man and the earth are very much alike.

Leonardo da Vinci: *The Notebooks*

In spite of the overriding sense that all beings are integrated into the cosmic harmony, many Renaissance thinkers viewed humanity as having a special, almost divine, status in the order of things, and even went so far beyond Christian orthodoxy as to claim that 'Man can do anything that he wills' (Alberti). The theologian Pico della Mirandola (1463–1494) places this somewhat anthropocentric view within the framework of a myth of creation, while the playwright Christopher Marlowe (1564–1593) expresses it more boldly through the then-popular story of Doctor Faustus who bought power at the cost of his immortal soul.

God the Father, the supreme Architect, had already built this cosmic home we behold, the most sacred temple of His God-head, by the laws of His mysterious wisdom. The region above the heavens He adorned with Intelligences, the heavenly spheres He had quickened with eternal souls, and the excrementary and filthy parts of the lower world He filled with a multitude of animals of every kind. But, when the work was finished, the Craftsman kept wishing that there were someone to ponder the plan of so great a work, to love its beauty, and to wonder at its vastness. Therefore, when everything was done (as Moses and Timaeus bear witness), He finally took thought concerning the creation of man. But there was not among his archetypes that from which He could fashion a new offspring, nor was there in His treasurehouses anything He might bestow on His new son as an inheritance, nor was there in the seats of all the world a place where the latter might sit to contemplate the universe. All was now complete; all things had been assigned to the highest, the middle, and the lowest orders ...

At last the best of artisans ordained that that creature to whom He had been able to give nothing proper to himself should have joint possession of whatever had been peculiar to each of the different kinds of being. He therefore took man as a creature of indeterminate nature and, assigning him a place in the middle of the world, addressed him thus: 'Neither a fixed abode nor a form that is thine alone nor any function peculiar to thyself have we given thee, Adam, to the end that according to thy longing and according to thy judgement thou mayest have and possess what abode, what form, and what functions thou thyself shalt desire. The nature of all is limited and constrained within the bounds of laws prescribed by Us. Thou, constrained by no limits, in accordance with thine own free will, in whose hand We have placed thee, shalt ordain for thyself the limits of thy nature. We have set thee at the world's center that thou mayest from thence more easily observe whatever is in the world. We have made thee neither of heaven nor of earth, neither mortal nor immortal, so that with freedom of choice and honor, as though the maker and moulder of thyself, thou mayest fashion thyself in whatever shape thou shalt prefer.'

Pico della Mirandola: *Oration on the Dignity of Man*

Bad Angel: Go forward, Faustus, in that famous art
Wherein all nature's treasury is contain'd:
Be thou on earth as Jove is in the sky,
Lord and commander of these elements.

Faustus: How am I glutted with conceit of this!
Shall I make spirits fetch me what I please,
Resolve me of all ambiguities,
Perform what desperate enterprise I will?
I'll have them fly to India for gold,
Ransack the ocean for orient pearl,
And search all corners of the new-found world
For pleasant fruits and princely delicates;
I'll have them read me strange philosophy
And tell the secrets of all foreign kings;
I'll have them wall all Germany with brass
And make swift Rhine circle fair Wittenberg;
I'll have them fill the public schools with silk
Wherewith the students shall be bravely clad;
I'll levy soldiers with the coin they bring
And chase the Prince of Parma from our land
And reign sole king of all our provinces;
Yea, stranger engines for the brunt of war
Than was the fiery keel at Antwerp's bridge
I'll make my servile spirits to invent.

Marlowe: *Doctor Faustus*

The spirit of human superiority and domination of nature clearly emerged in the Renaissance period with the crumbling of the old Mediaeval Catholic order, the growth of capitalism, and the opening up of the globe to European exploration and conqest. Nevertheless there were to be heard voices of warning such as those of Michel de Montaigne (1533–1592), one of the first modern writers to inveigh against cruelty to animals and to protest against our self-appointed sovereignty over them, and Blaise Pascal (1623–1662) who underlines in theological terms the humble place of man and of man's much-vaunted intellect in relation to the vastness of the universe.

As for me, I have not been able to witness without displeasure an innocent defenceless beast which has done us no harm being hunted to the kill. And when as commonly happens the stag, realizing that it has exhausted its breath and its strength, can find no other remedy but to surrender to us who are hunting it, throwing itself on our mercy which it implores with its tears ... that has always seemed to me the most disagreeable of sights.

I hardly ever catch a beast alive without restoring it to its fields. Pythagoras used to do much the same, buying their catches from anglers and fowlers ...

In Rome, once they had broken themselves in by murdering animals they went on to men and to gladiators. I fear that Nature herself has attached to Man something which goads him on towards inhumanity. Watching animals playing together and cuddling each other is nobody's sport: everyone's sport is to watch them tearing each other apart and wrenching off their limbs.

And lest anyone should laugh at this sympathy which I feel for animals, Theology herself ordains that we should show some favour towards them; and when we consider that the same Master has lodged us in this palatial world for his service, and that they like us are members of his family, Theology is right to enjoin upon us some respect and affection for them.

Montaigne: 'On Cruelty'

Returning to himself, let man consider what he is compared with all existence; let him think of himself as lost in this remote corner of nature; and from this little dungeon in which he finds himself lodged – I mean the Universe – let him learn to set a true value on the earth, its kingdoms, and cities, and upon himself. What is a man in the infinite?

But to behold another miracle no less astonishing, let him examine the most delicate things he knows. Let him take a mite, with its tiny body and its incomparably more tiny limbs: legs with their joints, veins in those legs, blood in those veins, humours in the blood, drops in those humours, vapours in the drops. Subdividing yet again, let him exhaust his powers of thought, and let the ultimate point he can reach be now the subject of our discourse. Perhaps he will think that here is nature's extreme diminutive. But in it I mean to show him a new abyss. I will paint for him not only the visible universe but all the imaginable vastness of nature in the womb of this diminutive atom. There let him see an infinity of universes, each with its firmament, its planets, its earth in the same proportions as the visible world; – living creatures on that earth, and finally mites, in which he will find again all the features that he found in the first; and in these too he will find the same, repeated ceaselessly without pause and without end. Let him stand in amazement before these wonders, as astonishing in their minuteness as the others in their immensity. For who can fail to marvel that our body, which, before, was imperceptible in a universe itself imperceptible in the vastness of the whole, should now be a colossus, a world, or rather an absolute, compared with the nothingness that is beyond our reach?

A man who considers himself in this light will be frightened for himself; seeing himself suspended in the material body that nature has given him between the two abysses of infinity and nothingness, he will tremble at the sight of these marvels. And I believe that as his curiosity changes into awe, he will be more inclined to contemplate them in silence than presumptuously to examine them.

For, after all, what is man in nature? A nothing in comparison with the infinite, an absolute in comparison with nothing, a central point between nothing and all. Infinitely far from understanding these extremes, the end of things and their beginning are hopelessly hidden from him in an impenetrable secret. He is equally incapable of seeing the nothingness from which he came, and the infinite in which he is engulfed...

Those infinite spaces fill me with terror.

Pascal: *The Pensées*

By about 1600 the old order was beginning to break apart, many traditional views were being challenged, man's place in the universe no longer seemed so secure, and the fear of chaos, religious, political, and even cosmic, was widely felt, as is evident in the following passages from Shakespeare and John Donne (1572–1631). The 'new philosophy' which 'calls all in doubt' is that of Copernicus who, as we shall see in the next chapter, upset traditional views of the cosmos, but his ideas were fore-shadowed early on in the Renaissance period by the philosopher–mystic Nicholas of Cusa (1401–1464).

The heavens themselves, the planets, and this centre
Observe degree, priority, and place,
Insisture, course, proportion, season, form,
Office, and custom, in all line of order;
And therefore is the glorious planet Sol
In noble eminence enthron'd and spher'd
Amidst the other whose med'cinable eye
Corrects the ill aspects of planets evil,
And posts, like the commandment of a king.
Sans check, to good and bad: but when the planets
In evil mixture to disorder wander,
What plagues and what portents, what mutiny,
What raging of the sea, shaking of earth,
Commotion in the winds, frights, changes, horrors,
Divert and crack, rend and deracinate
The unity and married calm of states
Quite from their fixture; Oh! when degree is shak'd
Which is the ladder to all high designs,
The enterprise is sick. How could communities,
Degrees in schools and brotherhoods in cities,
Peaceful commerce from dividable shores,
The primogeniture and due of birth,
Prerogative of age, crowns, sceptres, laurels,
But by degree stand in authéntic place?
Take but degree away, untune that string,
And hark! what discord follows; each thing meets
In mere oppugnancy: the bounded waters
Should lift their bosoms higher than the shores
And make a sop of all this solid globe.
Strength should be lord to imbecility,

And the rude son should strike his father dead.
This chaos, when degree is suffocate,
Follows the choking.

Shakespeare: *Troilus and Cressida*

Then, as mankind, so is the world's whole frame
Quite out of joint, almost created lame:
For, before God had made up all the rest,
Corruption entered, and depraved the best:
It seized the Angels, and then first of all
The world did in her cradle take a fall,
And turned her brains, and took a general maim
Wronging each joint of th'universal frame.
The noblest part, man, felt it first; and then
Both beasts and plants, cursed in the curse of man.
So did the world from the first hour decay,
That evening was beginning of the day,
And now the springs and summers which we see,
Like sons of women after fifty be.
And new philosophy calls all in doubt,
The element of fire is quite put out;
The sun is lost, and th'earth, and no man's wit
Can well direct him where to look for it.
And freely men confess that this world's spent,
When in the planets, and the firmament
They seek so many new; they see that this
Is crumbled out again to his atomies.
'Tis all in pieces, all coherence gone;
All just supply, and all relation:
Prince, subject, father, son, are things forgot,
For every man alone thinks he hath got
To be a phoenix, and that then can be
None of that kind, of which he is, but he.
This is the world's condition now, and now
She that should all parts to reunion bow,
She that had all magnetic force alone,
To draw, and fasten sundered parts in one;
She whom wise nature had invented then
When she observed that every sort of men
Did in their voyage in this world's sea stray,
And needed a new compass for their way;

She that was best, and first original
Of all fair copies; and the general
Steward to Fate; she whose rich eyes, and breast,
Guilt the West Indies, and perfumed the East;
Whose having breathed in this world, did bestow
Spice on those isles, and bad them still smell so,
And that rich Indy which doth gold inter,
Is but as single money, coined from her:
She to whom this world must itself refer,
As suburbs, or the microcosm of her,
She, she is dead; she's dead: when thou know'st this,
Thou know'st how lame a cripple this world is,
And learn'st thus much by our anatomy,
That this world's general sickness doth not lie
In any humour, or one certain part;
But as thou sawest it rotten at the heart,
Thou seest a hectic fever hath got hold
Of the whole substance, not to be controlled,
And that thou hast but one way, not to admit
The world's infection, to be none of it.

Donne: 'An Anatomie of the World'

The universe, then, has no circumference, for, if it had a centre
and a circumference, it would thus have in itself its beginning
and its end, and the universe itself would be terminated by
relation to something else; there would be outside the universe
another thing and a place – but all this contains no truth. Thus,
since it is not possible that the universe is enclosed between a
material centre and a circumference, the world is unintelligible;
the world whose centre and circumference are God ... Just as
the earth is not the centre of the universe, neither is the
circumference of the universe the sphere of the fixed stars.

What we have said above the ancients did not consider
because they were lacking in learned ignorance. It is already
clear to us that this earth actually moves although it does not
seem to, for we only apprehend movement by means of comparison with a fixed point.

Nicholas of Cusa: *On Learned Ignorance*

5

'THE MAGNIFICENT CLOCKWORK':
NATURE AS MACHINE

The idea that nature is not a great organism but rather a great machine is the central inspiration of the scientific revolution, and as a potent metaphor runs through the whole of modern thought and culture. The image of nature as an organism, ensouled and purposeful, created by God and replete with signs of His creative and loving providence, reached its culmination in the West in the Renaissance period, but in the course of the sixteenth century a new and dramatically different model of the universe began to emerge. Copernicus, who was no revolutionary but a loyal priest of the Catholic Church, replaced the old Ptolemaic geocentric universe with a heliocentric model, thereby destroying the image of a cosmos which, since Plato, had come to symbolize the central place of humanity within the Great Chain of Being. But the main task of building a new model fell to Kepler, Galileo and Newton who reordered the conception of the solar system so that it no longer resembled an organism but rather a magnificent piece of clockwork. Between them, over a period of about a century, they showed that the processes of the natural world, whether in the heavens or on earth, could be understood without reference to soul, or to purpose, but could simply be understood in terms of material particles moving in infinite space in accordance with strict, mathematically precise, universal laws. The culminating synthesis was laid out in Isaac Newton's *Principia Mathematica*, first published in 1687, a work which became a model for all future scientific endeavour. It was left to two other thinkers to uncover some of the wider implications of this new natural philosophy.

The French philosopher René Descartes was the first to give clear articulation to the idea that all the workings of nature could be understood by analogy with the workings of a clockwork machine, and hence could dispense with the mysterious occult influences and entelechies of the old model. Two momentous conclusions were drawn from this: the first was that mind and body represent two completely distinct kinds of substance, and that mind (defined as thought or consciousness) is therefore completely excluded from the natural world; the second was that living things are automata, the difference between humans and animals being that the former have a conscious mind, whereas the latter do not.

Francis Bacon, one-time Lord Chancellor of England, drew the less abstract conclusion that the new philosophy gave to humankind immeasurable potential for understanding nature and hence for controlling it; God's promise in the Book of Genesis that people should have dominion over nature now becomes realizable through science, and the dire effects of the Fall can be reversed through humanity's own efforts.

Nicholas Copernicus (1473–1543) set out to reform the calendar by constructing a simpler set of astronomical tables, but ended up by replacing the long established Aristotelian/Ptolemaic model of an earth-centred universe with one which placed the sun at the centre. In spite of his attempt to justify his theory with reference to the ancient Hermetic notions of the sun as 'the visible God', his heleocentric model had enormous intellectual and cultural consequences, for it not only led to the scientific revolution but, by removing humanity from the centre of the universe, upset the whole carefully constructed cosmological edifice in which the roles of God and of humankind could clearly be delineated. His colleague Andreas Osiander (1498–1552) was so shocked by these new ideas that he felt it necessary to add a preface to Copernicus' work claiming that it was really no more than a technical device for making astronomical calculations.

Therefore on long pondering [the] uncertainty of mathematical traditions on the deduction of the motions of the system of the spheres, I began to feel disgusted that no more certain theory on the motions of the mechanisms of the universe, which has been established for us by the best and most systematic craftsman of all, was agreed by the philosophers, who otherwise theorised so minutely with most careful attention to the details of this system . . .

I therefore took this opportunity and also began to consider the possibility that the Earth moved. Although it seemed an absurd opinion, nevertheless because I knew that others before me had been granted the liberty of imagining whatever circles they wished to represent the phenomena of the stars, I thought that I likewise would readily be allowed to test whether, by assuming some motion of the Earth's, more dependable representations than theirs could be found for the revolutions of the heavenly spheres . . .

First and above all lies the sphere of the fixed stars, containing itself and all things, for that very reason immovable; in truth the frame of the universe, to which the motion and position of all other stars are referred. Though some men think it to move in some way, we assign another reason why it appears to do so in our theory of the movement of the earth. Of the moving bodies first comes Saturn, who completes his circuit in thirty years. After him Jupiter, moving in a twelve year revolution. Then Mars, who revolves biennially. Fourth in order an annual cycle takes place, in which we have said is contained the earth, with the lunar orbit as an epicycle. In the fifth place, Venus is carried round in nine months. Then Mercury holds the sixth place, circulating in the space of eighty days. In the middle of all dwells the Sun. Who indeed in this most beautiful temple would place the torch in any other or better place than one whence it can illuminate the whole at the same time? Not ineptly, some call it the lamp of the universe, others its mind, others again its ruler – Trismegistus, the visible God, Sophocles' Electra, the contemplation of all things. And thus rightly in as much as the Sun, sitting on a royal throne, governs the circumambient family of stars. We find, therefore, under this orderly arrangement, a wonderful symmetry in the universe, and a definite relation of harmony in the motion and magnitude of the orbs, of a kind it is not possible to obtain in any other way.

Copernicus: *On the Revolutions of the Heavenly Bodies*

I have no doubt that certain learned men, now that the novelty of the hypotheses of this work has been widely reported – for it establishes that the Earth moves, and indeed that the Sun is motionless in the middle of the universe – are extremely shocked, and think that the scholarly disciplines, rightly established once and for all, should not be upset. But if they are willing to judge the matter thoroughly, they will find that the author of this work has committed nothing which deserves censure. For it is proper for an astronomer to establish a record of the motions of the heavens with diligent and skilful observations, and then to think out and construct laws for them, or rather hypotheses, whatever their nature may be, since the true laws cannot be reached by the use of reason; and from those assumptions the motions can be correctly calculated, both for the future and for the past. Our author has shown himself outstandingly skilful in both these respects. Nor is it necessary that these hypotheses be true, nor indeed even probable, but it is sufficient if they merely produce calculations which agree with the observations . . . for it is clear enough that this subject is completely and simply ignorant of the laws which produce apparently irregular motions. And if it does work out any laws – as certainly it does work out very many – it does not do so in any way with the aim of persuading anyone that they are valid, but only to provide a correct basis for calculation. Since different hypotheses are sometimes available to explain one and the same motion (for instance eccentricity or anepicycle for the motion of the Sun) an astronomer will prefer to seize on the one which is easiest to grasp; a philosopher will perhaps look more for probability; but neither will grasp or convey anything certain, unless it has been divinely revealed to him. Let us therefore allow these new hypotheses also to become known beside the older, which are no more probable, especially since they are remarkable and easy; and let them bring with them the vast treasury of highly learned observations. And let no one expect from astronomy, as far as hypotheses are concerned, anything certain, since it cannot produce any such thing, in case if he seizes on things constructed for any other purpose as true, he departs from this discipline more foolish than he came to it. Farewell.

Osiander: 'Preface' to *On the Revolutions of the Heavenly Bodies*

Francis Bacon (1561–1626), who was not a 'scientist' in any recognizable sense, but was a lawyer and Lord Chancellor of England under King James I, was the first to offer an ideological justification for the 'new philosophy' that was rapidly replacing the ancient philosophies of nature at the beginning of the seventeenth century, and to argue that not only could the new empirical methods of investigation give humankind a true understanding of the workings of nature but could give us unprecedented power over nature for the pursuance of human well-being.

[A] way must be opened for the human understanding entirely different from any hitherto known, and other helps provided, in order that the mind may exercise over the nature of things the authority which properly belongs to it.

... the entire fabric of human reason which we employ in the inquisition of nature is badly put together and built up, and like some magnificent structure without any foundation. For while men are occupied in admiring and applauding the false powers of the mind, they pass by and throw away those true powers, which, if it be supplied with the proper aids and can itself be content to wait upon nature instead of vainly affecting to overrule her, are within its reach. There was but one course left, therefore – to try the whole thing anew upon a better plan, and to commence a total reconstruction of the sciences, arts and all human knowledge, raised upon the proper foundations ...

I would address one general admonition to all – that they consider what are the true ends of knowledge, and that they seek it not either for pleasure of the mind, or for contention, or for superiority to others, of for profit, or fame, or power, or any of these inferior things, but for the benefit and use of life, and that they perfect and govern it in charity ... I am laboring to lay the foundation, not of any sect or doctrine, but of human utility and power ...

I consider induction to be that form of demonstration which upholds the sense, and closes with nature ... Hence it follows that the order of demonstration is likewise inverted. For hitherto the proceeding has been to fly at once from the sense and particulars up to the most general propositions ... Now my plan is to proceed regularly and gradually from one axiom to another, so that the most general are not reached till the last; but then, when you do come to them, you find them to be not empty notions but well defined, and such as nature would really recognize as her first principle, and such as lie at the heart and marrow of things. Now what the sciences stand in need of is a form of induction which shall analyse experience and take it to pieces ... for certain it is that the senses deceive; but then at the same time they supply the means of discovering their own errors; only the errors are here, the means of discovery are to seek ...

To meet these difficulties, I have sought on all sides diligently and faithfully to provide helps for the sense – substitutes to supply its failures, rectifications to correct its errors; and this I endeavour to accomplish not so much by instruments as by experiments.

Bacon: *The Great Instauration*

For man by the fall fell at the same time from his state of innocency and from his dominion over creation. Both of these losses however can even in this life be in some part repaired; the former by religion and faith, the latter by arts and sciences. For creation was not by the curse made altogether and forever a rebel, but in virtue of that charter 'in the sweat of thy face shalt thou eat bread,' it is now by various labors (not certainly by disputations or idle magical ceremonies, but by various labors) at length and in some measure subdued to the supplying of man with bread, that is to the uses of human life.

[The] true and lawful goal of the sciences is none other than this: that human life be endowed with new discoveries and powers.

[Men] have been kept back as by a kind of enchantment from progress in the sciences by reverence for antiquity, by the authority of men accounted great in philosophy, and then by general consent.

There is no life except a new birth of science; that is, in raising it regularly up from experience and building it afresh.

The secrets of nature reveal themselves more directly under the vexations of art than when they go their own way. Good hopes may therefore be conceived of natural philosophy, when natural history, which is the basis and foundation of it, has been drawn up on a better plan.

[If] a man endeavour to establish and extend the power and dominion of the human race itself over the universe, his ambition ... is without doubt both a more wholesome and a more noble thing ... Now the empire of man over things depends wholly on the arts and sciences. For we cannot command nature except by obeying her ... Only let the human race recover that right over nature which belongs to it by divine bequest, and let power be given it; the exercise thereof will be governed by sound reason and true religion.

Bacon: *The New Organon, Aphorisms*

Where Bacon sought to provide the philosophical justification for the new science, Galileo (1564–1642) laid its theoretical foundations and established its empirical and mathematical methods. The old animistic assumptions were ruthlessly expunged, nature must be investigated through observation and experimentation, using new instruments such as the telescope and the thermometer, and employing the exact techniques of mathematics. By adopting this approach Galileo articulated a new image of nature which was devoid of both spiritual and sensual properties.

I say, first: there is no vegetative soul in the heavens. First: because, from Aristotle, third *Metaphysics*, text 15, what requires food is not eternal. The reason for this: because what is nourished must have an organ, and so requires a body that is not simple; it must change food and convert it into its own substance, lest it become weak; but what has these characteristics is corruptible; therefore [the heavens would be corruptible and not eternal]. Second: on the part of the food. If the heavens are nourished they are nourished by something either corruptible or incorruptible; if corruptible, then they themselves would be corruptible; if incorruptible, they could not convert it to their own substance; moreover, the nourishment would finally run out at some time; therefore [the heavens again would not be eternal].

I say, second: in the heavens there is no sensitive soul having either [a] an internal or [b] an external sense. Proof of the conclusion with regard to the second part [b]: first, because the sensitive soul presupposes both the vegetative soul and touch, and from the second *De Anima*, 17; but touch consists in primary qualities which do not exist in the heavens, any more than does the vegetative soul; therefore [the heavens have no sensitive soul] ... Second: if there were a sensitive soul in the heavens there would be organs also, and thus the heavens would be composite bodies, they could move themselves, and they would not require intelligences; and all of these consequences are opposed to the truth. Third: because senses would exist in the heavens to no purpose; for they are not necessary for conservation because the heavens are incorruptible; nor for intellection because ... the heavens do not possess an intellective form; nor for motion or for guidance, because they are moved and governed by intelligences.

Galileo: *Early Notebooks*

Philosophy is written in this grand book, the universe, which stands continually open to our gaze. But the book cannot be understood unless one first learns to comprehend the language and read the letters in which it is composed. It is written in the language of mathematics, and its characters are triangles, circles, and other geometric figures without which it is humanly impossible to understand a single word of it...

I say that whenever I conceive any material or corporeal substance, I immediately feel the need to think of it as bounded, and as having this or that shape; as being large or small in relation to other things, and in some specific place at any given time; as being in motion or at rest; as touching or not touching some other body; and as being one in number, or few, or many. From these conditions I cannot separate such a substance by any stretch of my imagination. But that it must be white or red, bitter or sweet, noisy or silent, and of sweet or foul odor, my mind does not feel compelled to bring in as necessary accompaniments. Without the senses as our guides, reason or imagination unaided would probably never arrive at qualities like these. Hence I think that tastes, odors, colors, and so on are no more than mere names so far as the object in which we place them is concerned, and that they reside only in the consciousness. Hence if the living creature were removed, all these qualities would be wiped away and annihilated.

Galileo: *The Assayer*

Now let us review the observations made during the past two months, once more inviting the attention of all who are eager for true philosophy to the first steps of such important contemplations. Let us speak first of that surface of the moon which faces us. For greater clarity I distinguish two parts of this surface, a lighter and a darker; the lighter part seems to surround and to pervade the whole hemisphere, while the darker part discolors the moon's surface like a kind of cloud, and makes it appear covered with spots. Now these spots which are fairly dark and rather large are plain to everyone and have been seen throughout the ages; these I shall call the 'large' or 'ancient' spots, distinguishing them from others that are smaller in size but so numerous as to occur all over the lunar surface, and especially the lighter part. The latter spots have never been seen by anyone before me. From observations of these spots

repeated many times I have been led to the opinion and con-
viction that the surface of the moon is not smooth, uniform,
and precisely spherical as a great number of philosophers believe
it (and the other heavenly bodies) to be, but is uneven, rough,
and full of cavities and prominences, being not unlike the face of
the earth, relieved by chains of mountains and deep valleys.

Galileo: *The Starry Messenger*

---

*Having made a clear distinction between the physical or material
world on the one hand and the mental or spiritual world on the other,
René Descartes (1596–1650) proceeded to outline a model of the world
of nature in mechanical terms, imagining it to be composed of material
particles which, like the cogs and wheels of a machine, interacted
through contact, thereby excluding the need for any mysterious forces or
spiritual influences. Even living things were to be seen as machines, like
the automata, such as flute-playing dolls, which in his day were constructed for entertainment. Descartes did not go so far as some in his
day, however, to suppose that the universe was made for humankind's
sake.*

I recognise only two *summa genera* of realities: intellectual or
mental realities, i.e. such as belong to a mind or conscious
substance; and material realities, i.e. such as belong to an
extended substance, a body. Cognition, volition, and all cog-
nitive and volitional states are referred to a conscious substance;
to an extended substance are referred size (i.e. actual extension
in length, breadth, and depth), shape, motion, position, divisibility of its parts, and so on.

Descartes: *Principles of Philosophy*

I must begin by observing the great difference between mind
and body. Body is of its nature always divisible; mind is wholly
indivisible. When I consider the mind – that is, myself, in so far
as I am merely a conscious being – I can distinguish no parts
within myself; I understand myself to be a single and complete
thing. Although the whole mind seems to be united to the
whole body, yet when a foot or arm or any other part of the
body is cut off I am not aware that any subtraction has been

made from the mind. Nor can the faculties of will, feeling, understanding and so on be called parts; for it is one and the same mind that wills, feels, and understands. On the other hand, I cannot think of any corporeal or extended object without being readily able to divide it in thought and therefore conceiving of it as divisible. This would be enough to show me the total difference between mind and body.

Descartes: *Meditations on First Philosophy*

The nature of matter, or of body, considered in general, does not consist in its being a thing that has hardness or weight, or colour, or any other sensible quality, but simply in its being a thing that has extension in length, breadth and depth ... Thus it is one and the same matter that exists throughout the universe; its one distinctive characteristic everywhere is extension. All the properties we can clearly and distinctly perceive in it are reducible to divisibility and a capacity for varying motions. From this there follows the potentiality of all states. Motion is the activity whereby a body travels from one place to another.

From what has already been said it is established that all bodies in the universe consist of one and the same matter; that this is divisible arbitrarily into parts, and that this is divided into many pieces with many different motions; that their motion is in a way circular, and the same quantity of motion is constantly preserved in the universe. We cannot determine by reason how big these pieces of matter are, or how quickly they move, or what circles they describe. God might have arranged these things in countless different ways; which way he in fact chose rather than the rest is a thing we must learn from observation. Therefore, we are free to make any assumption we like about them, so long as all the consequences agree with experience. So, by your leave, I shall suppose that all the matter constituting the visible world was originally divided by God into unsurpassably equal particles of medium size ... they had collectively just the same quantity of motion now found in the world; that each turned round its own centre, so that they formed a fluid body ... and thus constituted as many different vortices as there now are stars in the world. These few assumptions are, I think, enough to supply causes from which all effects observed in our universe would arise by the laws of nature previously stated; and

I think one cannot imagine any first principles that are more simple, or easier to understand, or indeed more likely.

Descartes: *Principles of Philosophy*

I have described the Earth and the whole visible universe in the manner of a machine ... The only difference I can see between machines and natural objects is that the workings of machines are mostly carried out by apparatus large enough to be readily perceptible by the senses ... But mechanics, which is a part or species of physics, uses no concepts but belong also to physics; and it is just as 'natural' for a clock composed of such and such wheels to tell the time, as it is for a tree grown from such and such seed to produce a certain fruit. So, just as when men with experience of machinery, when they know what a machine is for, and can see part of it, can readily form a conjecture about the way its unseen parts are fashioned; in the same way, starting from the sensible effects of sensible bodies, I have tried to investigate the insensible causes and particles underlying them.

Descartes: *Principles of Philosophy*

But though I regard it as established that we cannot prove there is any thought in animals, I do not think it is thereby proved that there is not, since the human mind does not reach into their hearts. But when I investigate what is most probable in this matter, I see no argument for animals having thoughts except the fact that since they have eyes, ears, tongues and other sense-organs like ours, it seems likely that they have sensation like us; and since thought is included in our mode of sensation, similar thought seems to be attributable to them. This argument, which is very obvious, has taken possession of the minds of all men from their earliest age. But there are other arguments, stronger and more numerous, but not so obvious to everyone, which strongly urge the opposite. One is that it is more probable that worms and flies and caterpillars move mechanically than that they all have immortal souls.

It is certain that in the bodies of animals, as in ours, there are bones, nerves, muscles, animal spirits, and other organs so disposed that they can by themselves, without any thought, give rise to all the animal motions we observe. This is very clear in convulsive movements in which the machine of the body moves despite the soul, and sometimes more violently and in a more varied manner than when it is moved by the will.

Second, it seems reasonable, since art copies nature, and men can make various automata which move without thought, that nature should produce its own automata, much more splendid than artificial ones. These natural automata are the animals. This is especially likely since we have no reason to believe that thought always accompanies the disposition of organs which we find in animals. It is much more wonderful that a mind should be found in every human body than that one should be lacking in every animal.

But in my opinion the main reason which suggests that the beasts lack thought is the following. Within a single species some of them are more perfect than others, as men are too. This can be seen in horses and dogs, some of whom learn what they are taught much better than others. Yet, although all animals easily communicate to us, by voice or bodily movement, their natural impulses of anger, fear, hunger and so on, it has never yet been observed that any brute animal reached the stage of using real speech, that is to say, of indicating by word or sign something pertaining to pure thought and not to natural impulse. Such speech is the only certain sign of thought hidden in a body. All men use it, however stupid and insane they may be, and though they may lack tongue and organs of voice; but no animals do. Consequently it can be taken as a real specific difference between men and dumb animals.

Descartes: Letter to Henry More

In ethics indeed it is an act of piety to say that God made everything for our sake, that we may be the more impelled to thank him, and the more on fire with love of him ... But it is by no means probable that all things were made for our sake in the sense that they have no other use. In physical theory this supposition would be wholly ridiculous and absurd; for undoubtedly many things exist ... that have never been seen or thought of by any man, and have never been any use to anybody.

Descartes: *Principles of Philosophy*

The mechanistic image of nature as matter in motion became a central philosophical assumption of the leaders of the scientific revolution, including Robert Boyle (1627–1691) who was in many ways the founder of modern chemistry. But it was in the work of Isaac Newton (1642–1717) that the mechanical philosophy received its most powerful and fully articulated expression, providing a theoretical framework and methodology out of which much of modern science has been constructed.

I. Of the principles of things corporeal, none can be more *few*, without being insufficient, or more *primary*, than *matter* and *motion*.

II. The natural genuine effect of variously determined *motion* in portions of *matter* is to divide it into parts of differing sizes and shapes, and to put them into different motions; and the consequences that flow from these, in a world framed as ours is, are, as to the separate fragments, posture, order, and situation; and, as to the conventions of many of them, peculiar compositions and contextures.

III. The parts of matter endowed with these catholic affections are by various associations reduced to natural bodies of several kinds, according to the plenty of the matter, and the various compositions and decompositions of the principles, which all suppose the common matter they diversify; and these several kinds of bodies, by virtue of their motion, rest, and other mechanical affections, which fit them to act on and suffer from one another, become endowed with several kinds of qualities (whereof some are called *manifest* and some *occult*), and those that act upon the peculiarly framed organs of sense, whose perceptions by the animadversive faculty of the soul are sensations.

IV. These principles – *matter, motion* (to which *rest* is related), *bigness, shape, posture, order, texture* – being so *simple, clear* and *comprehensive*, are applicable to all the real phenomena of nature, which seem not explicable by any other not consistent with ours. For if recourse be had to an immaterial principle or agent, it may be such a one as is not intelligible; and however it will not enable us to *explain* the phenomena, because its *way* of working upon things material would probably be more difficult to be physically made out than a Mechanical account of the phenomena. And notwithstanding the immateriality of a *created* agent, we cannot conceive how it should produce changes in a body without the help of Mechanical principles, especially *local motion*; and accordingly, we find not that the reasonable soul in man is able to produce what changes it pleases in the body, but is confined to such as it may produce by determining or guiding the motions of the spirits, and other parts of the body subservient to voluntary motion.

V. And if the agent or active principles resorted to be not immaterial, but of a corporeal nature, they must *either* in effect be the same with the corporeal principles above-named; OR, because of the great universality and simplicity of ours, the new ones proposed must be less general than *they*, and consequently capable of being subordinated or reduced to ours, which by various compositions may afford matter to several hypotheses, and by several coalitions afford minute concretions exceedingly numerous and durable, and consequently fit to become the elementary ingredients of more compounded bodies, being in most trials similar and, as it were, the radical parts, which may after several manners be diversified; as, in Latin, the themes are by prepositions, terminations, &c, and in Hebrew, the roots by the heemantic letters. So that the fear that so much of a *new* physical hypothesis as is *true* will overthrow, or make useless, the Mechanical principles, is as if one should fear that there will be a language proposed that is discordant from, or not reducible to, the letters of the alphabet.

Boyle: *The Excellency of the Mechanical Hypothesis*

Hitherto we have explained the phenomena of the heavens and of our sea by the power of gravity, but have not yet assigned the cause of this power. This is certain, that it must proceed from a cause that penetrates to the very centres of the sun and planets, without suffering the least diminution of its force; that operates not according to the quantity of the surfaces of the particles upon which it acts (as mechanical causes used to do), but according to the quantity of the solid matter which they contain, and propagates its virtue on all sides to immense distances, decreasing always as the inverse square of the distances. Gravitation towards the sun is made up out of the gravitations towards the several particles of which the body of the sun is composed; and in receding from the sun decreases accurately as

the inverse square of the distances as far as the orbit of Saturn
... But hitherto I have not been able to discover the cause of
those properties of gravity from phenomena, and I frame no
hypotheses; for whatever is not deduced from the phenomena is
to be called an hypothesis, and hypotheses, whether metaphysical or physical, whether of occult qualities or mechanical,
have no place in experimental philosophy. In this philosophy
particular propositions are inferred from the phenomena, and
afterwards rendered general by induction. Thus it was the
impenetrability, the mobility, and the impulsive force of bodies,
and the laws of motion and of gravitation, were discovered. And
to us it is enough that gravity does really exist, and acts
according to the laws which we have explained, and abundantly
serves to account for all the motions of the celestial bodies, and
of our sea.

Newton: *Principia Mathematica*

[By] the help of these Principles, all material Things seem to
have been composed of the hard and solid Particles above-
mentioned, variously associated in the first Creation by the
Counsel of an intelligent Agent. For it became him who created
them to set them in order. And if he did so, it's unphilosophical
to seek for any other Origin of the World, or to pretend that it
might arise out of Chaos by the mere Laws of Nature; though
being once form'd, it may continue by those Laws for many
Ages. For while Comets move in very excentrick Orbs in all
manner of Positions, blind Fate could never make all the Planets
move one and the same way in Orbs concentrick, some
inconsiderable Irregularities excepted, which may have risen
from the mutual Actions of Comets and Planets upon one
another, and which will be apt to increase, till the System wants
a Reformation. Such a wonderful Uniformity in the Planetary
System must be allowed the Effect of Choice. And so must the
Uniformity in the Bodies of Animals ...
  [This] can be the effect of nothing else than the Wisdom and
a Skill of a powerful ever-living Agent, who being in all places, is
more able by his Will to move the Bodies within his boundless
uniform Sensorium, and thereby to form and reform the Parts
of the Universe, than we are by our Will to move the parts of
our own Bodies. And yet we are not to consider the World as
the Body of God, or the several Parts thereof, as Parts of God

... And since space is divisible *in infinitum*, and Matter is not necessarily in all places, it may be also allow'd that God is able to create Particles of Matter of several Sizes and Figures, and in several Proportions to Space, and perhaps of different Densities and Forces, and thereby to vary the Laws of Nature, and make Worlds of several sorts in several Parts of the Universe. At least, I see nothing of Contradiction in all this.

Newton: *Opticks*

6

THE ORDER OF NATURE IN
THE AGE OF ENLIGHTENMENT

The new mechanical philosophy did not dispense with God, for although spiritual influences were no longer seen to be operating within nature – the mechanical interaction of its parts was thought to be sufficient to explain its workings – it was deemed necessary by most natural philosophers of that period to retain the deity as creator, originator of motion, and as the intelligence behind, albeit beyond, the natural world. As far as the everyday workings of nature were concerned, God, and indeed the spiritual world as a whole, had become a redundant hypothesis, and it is hardly surprising that during the period following the scientific revolution God and the realm of the spirit became less and less an object of central concern. Thus, while the orderly workings of nature as revealed by the investigations of natural philosophers were often argued to be evidence of the existence of a transcendent cosmic intelligence, the interest increasingly focused on nature and humanity's relation to it rather than to God. 'Nature' indeed became a key concept. In the radical new philosophical climate of the eighteenth century it came to mean, not just all the material stuff that comprised the world 'out there', but the orderly and harmonious workings of the material cosmos where its evident clockwork efficiency became a model of all that was virtuous and beautiful. These ideas had important implications for humanity and society, for these too were seen to be elements integral to the workings of the natural order, and hence legitimate objects for scientific investigation. Thus the whole of nature, the cosmos at large, living creatures, humankind, society, the economy, even the inner realms of mind, became part of the new enterprise whose aim was not just the contemplation of nature but its exploitation for the purposes of human progress. These ideas, which were sketched out in the eighteenth century, became the dominant ideology of the nineteenth, and have only really been fundamentally challenged in the twentieth.

––––––––––––––

In spite of the overthrow of the ancient philosophies, some vestigial aspects of the traditional world-view still haunted the mind of the

*Enlightenment, and are to be found in the poetry of Alexander Pope
(1688–1744), and in the philosophical writings of Leibniz (1646–
1716) who, though in many ways a leading exponent of the new philosophy, perpetuated a holistic view of nature in which every part
mirrors every other part. For both, as indeed for many in the
Enlightenment, nature was viewed as originating in God, as essentially
good, and as the product of what Leibniz called a 'pre-established
harmony'.*

Vast chain of Being, which from God began,
Natures aethereal, human, angel, man,
Beast, bird, fish, insect! what no eye can see,
No glass can reach! from Infinite to thee,
From thee to Nothing! – On superior pow'rs
Were we to press, inferior might on ours:
Or in the full creation leave a void,
Where, one step broken, the great scale's destroy'd:
From Nature's chain whatever link you strike,
Tenth, or ten thousandth, breaks the chain alike ...
All Nature is but Art, unknown to thee;
All Chance, Direction, which thou canst not see;
All Discord, Harmony, not understood;
All partial Evil, universal Good:
And, spite of Pride, in erring Reason's spite,
One truth is clear, 'WHATEVER IS IS RIGHT'.

Pope: *An Essay on Man*

All nature is a plenum. Everywhere there are simple substances,
effectively separated from one another by actions of their own
which are continually altering their relations; and each simple
substance or distinct monad, which forms the centre of a
compound substance (eg of an animal) and the principle of its
oneness, is surrounded by a *mass* composed of an infinity of
other monads which constitute the body belonging to this
central monad; corresponding to the affections of its body it
represents, as in a kind of *centre*, the things which are outside of
it. And this *body* is *organic*, when it forms a kind of automaton
or natural machine, which is a machine not only as a whole but
also in its smallest observable parts. And since because the world
is a plenum everything is connected together, and each body
acts on every other body more or less according to the distance,

and is affected by it by reaction, it follows that every monad is a mirror that is alive or endowed with inner activity, is representative of the universe from its own point of view, and is as much regulated as the universe itself. The perceptions in the monad spring from one another according to the laws of the appetites or the *final causes of good and evil*, which consist in the observable perceptions, regulated or unregulated – in the same way as the changes of bodies and of external phenomena spring from one another according to the laws of *efficient causes*, that is to say of motions. Thus there is a perfect *harmony* between the perceptions of the monad and the motions of the bodies, pre-established at the outset between the system of efficient causes and the system of final causes. Herein consists the concord and the physical union of the soul and the body, which exists without the one being able to change the laws of the other.

Each monad, together with a particular body, makes a living substance. Thus there is not only life everywhere, joined to members or organs, but there are also infinite degrees of it in the monads, some of them more or less dominating over others. But when the monad has its organs adjusted in such a way that by means of them the impressions they receive, and consequently the perceptions which represent them, are distinguished and heightened (as, for example, when by means of the shape of the humours of the eye rays of light are concentrated and act with more force), this may amount to *sensation*, that is to say, to a perception accompanied by *memory* – a perception, to wit, of which a certain echo long remains to make itself heard on occasion. Such a living being is called an *animal*, as its monad is called a *soul*. And when this soul is raised to the level of *reason*, it is something more sublime, and is reckoned as a mind, as will be explained later. It is true that animals are sometimes in the condition of simple living beings and their souls in the condition of simple monads, to wit, when their perceptions are not sufficiently distinguished to be remembered, as occurs in a deep dreamless sleep or in a swoon. But perceptions which have become entirely confused must necessarily be developed again in animals, for reasons I shall give below. Thus it is well to distinguish between *perception*, which is the inner state of the monad representing external things, and *apperception*, which is *consciousness*, or the reflective knowledge of this inner state, and which is not given to all souls, nor at all times to the same soul. It is for want of this distinction that the Cartesians made the mistake of taking no account of perceptions which are not apperceived, as common people take no account of insensible bodies. It is this also which made these same Cartesians believe that minds alone are monads, and that there are no souls in animals, and still less other *principles of life*. And while, in thus denying sensations to animals, they have gone against the common opinion of men too much, so they have, on the other hand, taken too much account of the prejudices of the vulgar, in confusing a *long stupor*, which arises from a great confusion of perceptions, with *actual death*, in which all perception would cease. This teaching of theirs has confirmed the ill-founded belief in the destruction of some souls, and the pernicious view of certain people, self-styled free-thinkers, who have denied the immortality of ours...

It follows from the supreme perfection of God that in producing the universe He chose the best possible plan, containing the greatest variety together with the greatest order; the best arranged situation, place, and time; the greatest effect produced by the simplest means; the most power, the most knowledge, the most happiness and goodness in created things of which the universe admitted. For as all possible things have a claim to existence in the understanding of God in proportion to their perfections, the result of all these claims must be the most perfect actual world which is possible. Otherwise it would not be possible to explain why things have happened as they have rather than otherwise.

The supreme wisdom of God has made Him choose especially the *laws of motion* which are the best adjusted and the most fitted to abstract and metaphysical reasons. According to them there is always conserved the same quantity of total and absolute force or activity; the same quantity of relative force or reaction; the same quantity, finally, of force of direction. Moreover the activity is always equal to the reaction, and the whole effect is always equivalent to its full cause. It is surprising that those laws of motion discovered in our day, some of which I have myself discovered, cannot be explained merely by the consideration of *efficient causes* or of matter. For I have found that it is necessary to have recourse to *final causes*, and that these laws do not depend on the *principle of necessity* as do the truths of logic, arithmetic, and geometry, but on the *principle of fitness*, that is to say on the choice of wisdom. And this is one of the most effective and sensible proofs of the existence of God for those who are able to go deeply into these matters.

It follows, further, from the perfection of the Supreme

Author, that not only is the order of the whole universe the most perfect possible, but also that each living mirror which represents the universe from its own point of view, that is to say each monad, each substantial centre, must have its perceptions and appetites regulated in the best way which is compatible with all the rest. From which it follows that *souls*, that is to say the most dominant monads, or rather animals themselves, cannot fail to wake up from the state of stupor in which they may be placed by death or by some other accident.

For everything is regulated in things once for all with as much order and agreement as possible, since supreme wisdom and goodness cannot act without perfect harmony: the present is big with the future, what is to come could be read in the past, what is distant is expressed in what is near. The beauty of the universe could be learnt in each soul, could one unravel all its folds which develop perceptibly only with time. But as each distinct perception of the soul includes an infinity of confused perceptions which embrace all the universe, the soul itself does not know the things which it perceives, except in so far as it has perceptions of them which are distinct and heightened: and it has perfection in proportion to its distinct perceptions. Each soul knows the infinite, knows everything, but confusedly. Just as when I am walking along the shore of the sea and hear the great noise it makes, though I hear the separate sounds of each wave of which the total sound is made up, I do not discriminate them one from another; so our confused perceptions are the result of the impressions which the whole universe makes on us. It is the same with each monad. God alone has a distinct knowledge of everything, for he is the source of everything.

Leibniz: *Principles of Nature and of Grace, Founded on Reason*

The scientific revolution did not produce instant atheism or materialism, but rather from its early days in the seventeenth century until the late nineteenth century gave support to traditional religious belief. The argument from design, according to which the orderliness of nature was seen as evidence of the work of an intelligent Providence, became a favourite amongst philosophers, theologians, and preachers, and was often seen as the justification for investigating the natural world. There follow some examples from the writings of John Ray (1627–1705), the foremost naturalist of his day, and William Derham (1627–1705), John Wilkins (1614–1672), and William Paley (1743–1805), all Anglican clergy well versed in developments in natural philosophy.

For if in the works of art, as for example, a curious edifice or machine, counsel, design, and direction to an end appearing in the whole frame, and in all the several pieces of it, do necessarily infer the being and operation of some intelligent architect or engineer, why shall not also in the works of nature, that grandeur and magnificence, that excellent contrivance for beauty, order, use, etc. which is observable in them, wherein they do as much transcend the effects of human art as infinite power and wisdom exceeds finite, infer the existence and efficiency of an omnipotent and All-Wise Creator.

Ray: *The Wisdom of God as Manifested in the Works of the Creation*

The whole surface of our globe can afford room and support only to such a number of all sorts of creatures. And if by their doubling, trebling, or any other multiplication of their kind, they should increase to double or treble that number, they must starve, or devour one another. The keeping therefore the balance even, is manifestly a work of the Divine wisdom and providence. To which end, the great author of life hath determined the life of all creatures to such a length, and their increase to such a number, proportional to their use in the world. The life of some creatures is long, and their increase but small, and by that means they do not over-stock the world. And the same benefit is effected, where the increase is great, by the brevity of such creatures' lives, by their great use, and the frequent occasions there are of them for food to man or other animals. It is a very remarkable act of the Divine providence, that useful creatures are produced in great plenty, and others in less. The prodigious and frequent increase of insects, both in and out of the waters, may exemplify the one; and it is observable in the other, that creatures less useful, or by their voracity pernicious, have commonly fewer young, or do seldomer bring forth: of which many instances might be given in the voracious beasts and birds. But there is one so peculiar an animal, as if made for a particular instance in our present case, and that is the condor of

Peru, a fowl of that magnitude, strength, and appetite, as to seize not only on the sheep, and lesser cattle, but even the larger beasts, yea, the very children too. Now these, as they are not most pernicious of birds, so are they the most rare, being seldom seen, or only one, or a few in large countries; enough to keep up the species; but not to overcharge the world.

Thus the balance of the animal world, is, throughout all ages, kept even; and by a curious harmony and just proportion between the increase of all animals and the length of their lives, the world is through all ages well, but not over stored: *One generation passeth away, and another generation cometh*; so equally in its room, to balance the stock of the terraqueous globe in all ages, and places and among all creatures; that is an actual demonstration of our Saviour's assertion, *Mat.* x. 29. that the most inconsiderable, common creature, *Even a sparrow (two of which are sold for a farthing) doth not fall on the ground without our heavenly Father* . . .

And now upon the whole matter, What is all this but admirable and plain management? What can the maintaining, throughout all ages and places, these proportions of mankind, and all other creatures; this harmony in the generations of men be, but the work of One that ruleth the world? Is it possible that every species of animals should so evenly be preserved, proportionate to the occasions of the world? That they should be so well balanced in all ages and places, without the help of Almighty wisdom and power? How is it possible by the bare rules and blind acts of Nature, that there should be any tolerable proportion; for instance, between males and females, either of mankind, or of any other creature; especially such as are of a ferine, not of a domestic nature, and consequently out of the command and management of man? How could life and death keep such an even pace through all the animal world? If we should take it for granted, that, according to the scripture history, the world had a beginning, as who can deny it? or if we should suppose the destruction thereof by Noah's flood: how is it possible, after the world was replenished, that in a certain number of years, by the greater increases and doublings of each species of animals; that, I say, this rate of *doubling* should cease; or that it should be compensated by some other means? That the world should be as well, or better stocked than now it is, in 1656 years, (the time between the creation and the flood; this,) we will suppose may be done by the natural methods of each species doubling or increase: but in double that number of years, or at this distance from the flood, of 4000 years, that the world should not be over-stocked, can never be made out, without allowing an infinite Providence...

The *Creator* doubtless did not bestow so much curiosity, and exquisite workmanship and skill upon his creatures, to be looked upon with a careless, incurious eye, especially to have them slighted or contemned; but to be admired by the rational part of the world, to magnify his own power, wisdom, and goodness throughout all the world, and the ages thereof: and therefore we may look upon it as a great error not to answer those ends of the infinite *Creator*, but rather to oppose and affront them. On the contrary, my text commends God's works, not only for being great, but also approves of those curious and ingenious inquirers, that seek them out, or pry into them. And the more we pry into and discover of them, the greater and more glorious we find them to be, the more worthy of, and the more expressly to proclaim their great *Creator*.

Derham: *Physico-Theology*

The observations which have been made in these latter Times by the Help of the Microscope, since we had the Use and Improvement of it, discover a vast Difference between Natural and Artificial Things. Whatever is natural, beheld thro' that, appears exquisitely form'd and adorn'd with all imaginable Elegancy and Beauty. There are such inimitable Glidings in the smallest Seeds of Plants, but especially in the parts of animals, in the Head or Eye of a small Fly; such Accuracy, Order, and Symmetry in the Frame of the most minute Creatures, a Louse, for example, or a Mite, as no Man were able to conceive without seeing of them. Whereas the most curious Works of Art, the sharpest and finest Needle, doth appear as a blunt rough Bar of Iron, coming from the Furnace or the Forge: The most accurate Engravings or Embossments seem such rude, bungling and deform'd Work, as if they had been done with a Mattock or Trowel: so vast a Difference is there betwixt the Skill of Nature, and the Rudeness and Imperfections of Art.

Wilkins: *Of the Principles and Duties of Natural Religion*

In crossing a heath, suppose I pitched my foot against a *stone*, and were asked how the stone came to be there, I might possibly answer, that, for anything I knew to the contrary, it had lain there for ever; nor would it, perhaps, be very easy to show the absurdity of this answer. But suppose I found a *watch* upon the ground, and it should be inquired how the watch happened to be in that place, I should hardly think of the answer which I had before given – that, for anything I knew, the watch might have always been there. Yet why should not this answer serve for the watch as well as for the stone? Why is it not as admissible in the second case as in the first? For this reason, and for no other, viz, that, when we come to inspect the watch, we perceive (what we could not discover in the stone) that its several parts are framed and put together for a purpose, eg that they are so formed and adjusted as to produce motion, and that motion so regulated as to point out the hour of the day; that, if the different parts had been differently shaped from what they are, if a different size from what they are, or placed after any other manner, or in any other order than that in which they are placed, either no motion at all would have been carried on in the machine, or none which would have answered the use that is now served by it. To reckon up a few of the plainest of these parts, and of their offices, all tending to one result. We see a cylindrical box containing a coiled elastic spring, which, by its endeavour to relax itself, turns round the box. We next observe a flexible chain (artificially wrought for the sake of flexure) communicating the action of the spring from the box to the fusee. We then find a series of wheels, the teeth of which catch in, and apply to, each other, conducting the motion from the fusee to the balance, and from the balance to the pointer, and, at the same time, by the size and shape of those wheels, so regulating that motion as to terminate in causing an index, by an equable and measured progression, to pass over a given space in a given time. We take notice that the wheels are made of brass, in order to keep them from rust; the springs of steel, no other metal being so elastic; that over the face of the watch there is placed a glass, a material employed in no other part of the work, but in the room of which, if there had been any other than a transparent substance, the hour could not be seen without opening the case. This mechanism being observed (it requires indeed an examination of the instrument, and perhaps some previous knowledge of the subject, to perceive and understand it: but being once, as we have said, observed and understood), the inference, we think, is inevitable, that the watch must have had a maker: that there must have existed, at some time, and at some place or other, an artificer or artificers who formed it for the purpose which we find it actually to answer; who comprehended its construction, and designed its use . . .

Every indication of contrivance, every manifestation of design, which existed in the watch, exists in the works of nature; with the difference, on the side of nature, of being greater and more, and that in a degree which exceeds all computation. I mean that the contrivances of nature surpass the contrivances of art, in the complexity, subtlety, and curiosity of the mechanism; and still more, if possible, do they go beyond them in number and variety; yet in a multitude of cases, are not less evidently mechanical, not less evidently contrivances, not less evidently accommodated to their end, or suited to their office than are the most perfect productions of human ingenuity.

Paley: *Natural Theology*

Something of the enthusiasm of the Enlightenment for the sublime harmony and orderliness of nature is captured in the following quotations from the English philosopher Anthony Ashley Cooper, Earl of Shaftesbury (1671–1713), whose style anticipates that of the Romantics a century later, and from the essayist Joseph Addison (1672–1719).

All things in this world are united, for as the branch is united with the tree, so is the tree as immediately with the earth, air and water which feed it. As much as the fertile mould is fitted to the tree, as much as the strong and upright trunk of the oak or elm is fitted to the twinning branches of the vine or ivy; so much are the very leaves, the seed, and fruits of these trees fitted to the various animals: these again to one another and to the elements where they live, and to which they are, as appendices, in a manner fitted and joined, as either by wings for the air, fins for the water, feet for the earth, and by other correspondent parts of a more curious frame and texture. Thus in contemplating the earth we must of necessity view it all as one, holding to one common stock. Thus too in the bigger world [the macrocosmos]. See there the mutual dependency of things! the relation of one to another; of the sun to this inhabited earth, and of the earth and the other planets to the sun! the order, union, and coherence of the whole . . .

Ye Fields and Woods, my refuge from the toilsome world of business, receive me in your quieter sanctuaries, and favour my retreat and thoughtful solitude. Ye verdant plains, how gladly I salute ye! – Hail all ye blissful mansions! known seats! delightful prospects! majestic beauties of this earth, and all ye rural powers and graces! Blessed be ye chaste abodes of happiest mortals, who here in peaceful innocence enjoy a life unenvied, though divine; whilst with its blessed tranquillity it affords a happy leisure and retreat for man, who, made for contemplation, and to search his own and other natures, may here best meditate the cause of things; and placed amidst the various scenes of Nature, may nearer view her works.

O glorious nature! supremely fair, and sovereignly good! all-loving and all-lovely, all-divine! whose looks are so becoming, and of such infinite grace; whose study brings such wisdom, and whose contemplation such delight; whose every single work affords an ampler scene, and is a nobler spectacle than all that ever art presented! O mighty Nature! wise substitute of Providence! impowered Creatress! O thou impowering Deity, supreme creator! Thee I invoke, and thee alone adore. To thee this solitude, this place, these rural meditations are sacred; whilst thus inspired with harmony of thought, tho unconfined by words, and in loose numbers, I sing of Nature's order in created beings, and celebrate the beauties which resolve in thee, the source and principle of all beauty and perfection.

Shaftesbury: *The Moralists*

When we survey the whole earth at once, and the several planets that lie within its neighbourhood, we are filled with a pleasing astonishment, to see so many worlds, hanging one above another, and sliding round their axles in such an amazing pomp and solemnity. If, after this, we contemplate those wild fields of ether, that reach in height as far as from Saturn to the fixed stars, and run abroad almost to an infinitude, our imagination finds its capacity filled with so immense a prospect, and puts itself upon the stretch to comprehend it. But if we rise yet higher, and consider the fixed stars as so many vast oceans of flame, that are each of them attended with a different set of planets, and still discover new firmaments and new lights that are sunk further into those unfathomable depths of ether, so as not to be seen by the strongest of our telescopes, we are lost in such a labyrinth of suns and worlds, and confounded with the immensity and magnificence of nature.

Addison: 'The Harmony of the World'

Enlightenment thought in the eighteenth century revolved round a group of radical thinkers centred on Paris, and known as 'Les Philosophes'. Baron d'Holbach (1723–1789) was a key figure in this group, and in his book The System of Nature *of 1770 he derided religious and metaphysical beliefs and expounded an extreme form of atheism and materialism, viewing the human being as nothing more than a machine and hence devoid of free will.*

These facts prove, beyond a doubt, that motion is produced, is augmented, is accelerated in matter, without the help of any exterior agent: therefore it is reasonable to conclude that motion is the necessary consequence of immutable laws, resulting from the essence, from the properties existing in the different elements, and the various combinations of these elements. Are we not justified, then, in concluding, from these precedents, that there may be an infinity of other combinations, with which we are unacquainted, competent to produce a great variety of motion in matter, without being under the necessity of having recourse, for the explanation, to agents who are more difficult to comprehend than even the effects which are attributed to them?

Had man but paid proper attention to what passed under his review, he would not have sought out of Nature, a power distinguished from herself, to set her in action, and without which he believes she cannot move. If, indeed, by Nature is meant a heap of dead matter, destitute of peculiar qualities purely passive, we must unquestionably seek out of this Nature the principle of her motion. But if by Nature be understood, what it really is, a whole, of which the numerous parts are endowed with various properties; which oblige them to act according to these properties which are in a perpetual ternateness of action and re-action; which press, which gravitate towards a common center, whilst others depart from and fly off towards the periphery, or circumference; which attract and repel; which by continual approximation and constant collision, produce and decompose all the bodies we behold; then, I say, there is no necessity to have recourse to supernatural powers, to account for the formation of things, and those extraordinary appearances which are the result of motion . . .

If, therefore, it be asked, whence came matter? it is very reasonable to say it has always existed. If it be inquired, whence proceeds the motion that agitates matter? the same reasoning furnishes the answer; namely, that as motion is coeval with matter, it must have existed from all eternity, seeing that motion is the necessary consequence of its existence – of its essence – of its primitive properties, such as its extent, its gravity, its impenetrability, its figure, &c. By virtue of these essential constituent properties, inherent in all matter, and without which it is impossible to form an idea of it, the various matter of which the universe is composed must from all eternity have pressed against each other – have gravitated towards a center – have clashed – have come in contact – have been attracted – have been repelled – have been combined – have been separated: in short, must have acted and moved according to the essence and energy peculiar to each genus, and to each of its combinations.

In short, Nature is but an immense chain of causes and effects, which unceasingly flow from each other. The motion of particular beings depends on the general motion, which is itself maintained by individual motion. This is strengthened or weakened, accelerated or retarded, simplified or complicated, procreated or destroyed, by a variety of combinations and circumstances, which every moment change the directions, the tendency, the modes of existing, and of acting, of the different beings that receive its impulse.

If it were true, as has been asserted by some philosophers, that every thing has a tendency to form one unique or single mass, and in that unique mass the instant should arrive when all was in *nisus*, all would eternally remain in this state; to all eternity there would be no more than one Being and one effort: this would be eternal and universal death.

If we desire to go beyond this, to find the principle of action in matter, to trace the origin of things, it is for ever to fall back upon difficulties; it is absolutely to abridge the evidence of our senses; by which only we can understand, by which alone we can judge of the causes acting upon them, or the impulse by which they are set in action.

Let us, therefore, content ourselves with saying what is

supported by our experience, and by all the evidence we are capable of understanding; against the truth of which not a shadow of proof, such as our reason can admit, has ever been adduced – which has been maintained by philosophers in every age – which theologians themselves have not denied, but which many of them have upheld; namely, that matter always existed; that it moves by virtue of its essence; that all the phenomena of Nature are ascribable to the diversified motion of the variety of matter she contains; and which, like the phoenix, is continually regenerating out of its own ashes...

In Nature, however, there can be only natural causes and effects; all motion excited in this Nature, follows constant and necessary laws: the natural operations, to the knowledge of which we are competent, of which we are in a capacity to judge, are of themselves sufficient to enable us to discover those which elude our sight; we can at least judge of them by analogy. If we study Nature with attention, the modes of action which she displays to our senses will teach us not to be disconcerted by those which she refuses to discover. Those causes which are the most remote from their effects, unquestionably act by inter-mediate causes; by the aid of these, we can frequently trace out the first. If in the chain of these causes we sometimes meet with obstacles that oppose themselves to our research, we ought to endeavour by patience and diligence to overcome them; when it so happens we cannot surmount the difficulties that occur, we still are never justified in concluding the chain to be broken, or that the cause which acts is *super-natural*. Let us, then, be content with an honest avowal, that Nature contains resources of which we are ignorant; but never let us substitute phantoms, fictions, or imaginary causes, senseless terms for those causes which escape our research; because, by such means we only confirm ourselves in ignorance, impede our enquiries, and obstinately remain in error.

d'Holbach: *The System of Nature*

The German philosopher Immanuel Kant (1724–1804) in many ways both summed up the Enlightenment and anticipated the later Romantic movement. In spite of his belief that human reason is limited by the bounds of the five senses and therefore cannot make claims to go beyond physical phenomena, he was not content with the prevailing mechanistic view which seemed to deprive nature of any sense of purpose, and he therefore suggested that we must inevitably view nature 'as if' it was purposeful, even if we can never know that this is true of nature 'in itself'. And in spite of his admiration for Newton, he outlined in his early days a dynamic cosmological theory which has more in common with recent speculation concerning the creative propensity of the cosmos than with the somewhat static cosmology favoured in his day.

But if we go through the whole of nature we find in it, as nature, no being which could make claim to the eminence of being the final purpose of creation; and we can even prove *a priori* that what might be for nature an *ultimate purpose*, according to all the thinkable determinations and properties wherewith one could endow it, could yet as a natural thing never be a *final purpose*.

If we consider the vegetable kingdom we might at first sight, on account of the immeasurable fertility with which it spreads itself almost on every soil, be led to take it for a mere product of that mechanism which nature displays in the formations of the mineral kingdom. But a more intimate knowledge of its indescribably wise organisation does not permit us to hold to this thought, but prompts the question: What are these things created for? If it is answered: For the animal kingdom, which is thereby nourished and has thus been able to spread over the earth in genera so various, then the further question comes: What are these plant-devouring animals for? The answer would be something like this: For beasts of prey, which can only be nourished by that which has life. Finally we have the question: What are these last, as well as the first-mentioned natural kingdoms, good for? For man, in reference to the manifold use of which his Understanding teaches him to make all these creatures. He is the ultimate purpose of creation here on earth, because he is the only being upon it who can form a concept of purposes, and who can by his Reason make out of an aggregate of purposively formed things a system of purposes.

We might also with the chevalier *Linnaeus* go the apparently opposite way and say: The herbivorous animals are there to moderate the luxurious growth of the vegetable kingdom, by which many of its species are choked. The carnivora are to set bounds to the voracity of the herbivora. Finally man, by his pursuit of these and his diminution of their numbers, preserves a certain equilibrium between the producing and the destructive powers of nature. And so man, although in a certain reference he might be esteemed a purpose, yet in another has only the rank of a means.

Kant: *Critique of Judgement*

It seems that this end which is to be the fate of the worlds, as of all natural things, is subject to a certain law whose consideration gives our theory a new feature to recommend it. According to that law the heavenly bodies that perish first, are those which are situated nearest the centre of the universe, even as the production and formation did begin near this centre; and from that region deterioration and destruction gradually spread to further distances till they come to bury all the world that has finished its period, through a gradual decline of its movements, in a single chaos at last. On the other hand, Nature unceasingly occupies herself at the opposite boundary of the developed world, in forming worlds out of the raw material of the scattered elements; and thus, while she grows old on one side near the centre, she is young on the other, and is fruitful in new productions. According to this law the developed world is bounded in the middle between the ruins of the nature that has been destroyed and the chaos of the nature that is still unformed; and if we suppose, as is probable, that a world that has already attained to perfection may last a longer time than what it required to become formed, then, notwithstanding all the devastations which the perishableness of things incessantly brings about, the range of the universe will still generally increase...

[Therefore] we ought not to lament the perishing of a world as a real loss of Nature. She proves her riches by a sort of prodigality which, while certain parts pay their tribute to mortality, maintains itself unimpaired by numberless new generations in the whole range of its perfection. What an innumerable multitude of flowers are destroyed by a single cold day! And how little are they missed, although they are glorious products of the art of nature and demonstrations of the Divine Omnipotence ... The infinitude of the creation is great enough to make a world, or a Milky Way of worlds, look in comparison with it, what a flower or an insect does in comparison with the earth. But while nature thus adorns eternity with changing scenes,

God continues engaged in incessant creation in forming the matter for the construction of still greater worlds.

Kant: *Natural History and Theory of the Heavens*

The language used by the Portuguese–Jewish philosopher Spinoza (1632–1677) is still that of traditional theology, but his style derives from Euclidean geometry, and his view that all things are modifications of the divine substance is anything but orthodox. In the eighteenth century he was often viewed as a dangerous atheist, but the Romantics embraced his ideas as a form of pantheism – in effect the divinization of nature.

PROP. XV. Whatever is, is in God, and nothing can exist or be conceived without God.
Proof. – Save God no substance is granted or can be conceived (Prop. 14), that is, a thing which is in itself and through itself is conceived. But modifications cannot exist or be conceived without substance, wherefore these can only exist in divine nature, and through that alone be conceived. But nothing is granted save substances and their modifications. Therefore nothing can exist or be conceived without God.
PROP. XVIII. God is the indwelling and not the transient cause of all things.
Proof. – All things that are, are in God, and through God must be conceived, and therefore God is the cause of all things which are in him: which is the first point. Again, beyond God no substance, that is, a thing which outside God is in itself, can be granted: which was the second point. Therefore God is the indwelling and not the transient cause of all things.
PROP. XXV. God is not only the effecting cause of the existence of things, but also of their essence.
Proof. – If you deny it, then let God be not the cause of the essence of things: therefore the essence of things can be conceived without God. But this is absurd. Therefore God is the cause of the essence of things.

Spinoza: *Ethics*

7

THE ROMANTICIZATION OF NATURE

Construing nature as a machine and applying to it all the latest experimental and mathematical techniques was immensely fruitful in enabling humankind over the following centuries to understand and control the natural world in all its aspects and at all its levels. But a price had to be paid: the world of spirit, of meaning, and value, the world characterized by imagination rather than reason, by feeling rather than logic, became detached from the world of nature and alien to the new methods of natural philosophy. It is hardly surprising, then, that since the time of the Enlightenment we have seen several waves of reaction against this worldview, the first of which can be identified in the Romantic movement of the late eighteenth and early nineteenth centuries. Not that Romanticism was completely hostile to science (as it became known at this time); out-and-out anti-science is a phenomenon of the twentieth century. Rather, the Romantics, especially in Germany and England which were the main centres of the movement, believed that the new philosophy was too limited, too narrow in its vision, and failed, with its emphasis on mathematical abstraction, to account either for the full richness of the natural world or for the deep imaginative powers of the human understanding. For them nature still remained a mysterious place, one which cannot be captured by the rule and compass of science. At one level this led, in Germany especially, to the building of new metaphysical systems in which the material and the spiritual were reintegrated within grand new schemes which harked back to the philosophical speculations of old. At another level it manifested itself in highly expressive forms of poetry, art and music which displayed a heightened sense of awareness of humanity's affinity with the natural world. In both cases it led to a new appreciation, one might say exaltation, of nature, one which saw nature as home, as mother, as healer, and as teacher and inspiration, and which sometimes sought actually to identify the natural world with God – the idea called 'pantheism'.

Jean-Jacques Rousseau (1712–1778) is usually identified with the Enlightenment, in spite of certain disagreements with fellow Philo-

Let us conclude then that man in a state of nature, wandering up and down the forests, without industry, without speech, and without home, an equal stranger to war and to all ties, neither standing in need of his fellow-creatures nor having any desire to hurt them, and perhaps even not distinguishing them one from another; let us conclude that, being self-sufficient and subject to so few passions, he could have no feelings or knowledge but such as befitted his situation; that he felt only his actual necessities, and disregarded everything he did not think himself immediately concerned to notice, and that his understanding made no greater progress than his vanity. If by accident he made any discovery, he was the less able to communicate it to others, as he did not know even his own children. Every art would necessarily perish with its inventor, where there was no kind of education among men, and generations succeeded generations without the least advance; when, all setting out from the same point, centuries must have elapsed in the barbarism of the first ages; when the race was already old, and man remained a child.

Rousseau: *A Discourse on the Origin of Inequality*

Men are not made to be crowded together in ant-hills, but scattered over the earth to till it. The more they are massed together, the more corrupt they become. Disease and vice are the sure results of over-crowded cities. Of all creatures man is least fitted to live in herds. Huddled together like sheep, men would very soon die. Man's breath is fatal to his fellows. This is literally as well as figuratively true.

Men are devoured by our towns. In a few generations the race dies out or becomes degenerate; it needs renewal, and it is always renewed from the country. Send your children to renew themselves, so to speak, send them to regain in the open fields the strength lost in the foul air of our crowded cities. Women hurry home that their children may be born in the town; they *ought* to do just the opposite, especially those who mean to nurse their own children. They would lose less than they think, and in more natural surroundings the pleasures associated by nature with maternal duties would soon destroy the taste for other delights.

Rousseau: *Émile*

All is in a continuous flux upon earth. Nothing keeps a constant and fixed form, and our affections which attach themselves to exterior things pass away and change necessarily like them. Always in advance or behind us, they recall the past, which is no more, or presage the future, which often is not to be; there is nothing solid there to which the heart can attach itself. Therefore one has scarcely here below anything but passing pleasures; for the happiness which lasts, I doubt if it is known. Scarcely is there, in our most living delights, a moment where the heart can truly say to us: I wish that this moment should last forever. And how can one call that happiness which is a fugitive state which leaves our heart unquiet and empty, which makes us regret something beforehand or desire something after?

But if there is a state where the soul finds a position sufficiently solid to repose thereon, and to gather together all its being, without having need for recalling the past, nor to climb on into the future; where time counts for nothing, where the present lasts forever, without marking its duration in any way, and without any trace of succession, without any other sentiment of privation, neither of enjoyment, of pleasure nor pain, of desire nor of fear, than this alone of our existence, and which this feeling alone can fill entirely: so long as this state lasts, he who finds it may be called happy, not with an imperfect happiness, poor and relative, such as that which one finds in the pleasures of life, but with a sufficing happiness, perfect and full, which does not leave in the soul any void which it feels the need of filling. Such is the state in which I found myself often at the island of St Peter, in my solitary reveries, either resting in my boat which I let drift at the will of the water, or seated on the banks of the agitated lake, or elsewhere at the border of a beautiful river, or of a brooklet murmuring on the sand.

Rousseau: *Reveries of a Solitary Stroller*

In the following passage Mary Wollstonecraft (1759–1797), best known for her book A Vindication of the Rights of Woman, *and an admirer of Rousseau, laments the tendency of her age to observe nature through a veil of poetic artifice, and, in a spirit that was becoming identified as Romanticism in her last years, advocated the importance of spontaneity and of approaching nature through direct experience.*

A taste for rural scenes, in the present state of society, appears to be very often an artificial sentiment, rather inspired by poetry and romances, than a real perception of the beauties of nature. But, as it is reckoned a proof of refined taste to praise the calm pleasures which the country affords, the theme is never exhausted. Yet it may be made a question, whether this romantic kind of declaration, has much effect on the conduct of those, who leave, for a season, the crowded cities in which they were bred.

I have been led to these reflections, by observing, when I have resided for any length of time in the country, how few people seem to contemplate nature with their own eyes. I have 'brushed the dew away' in the morning; but, pacing over the printless grass, I have wondered that, in such delightful situations, the sun was allowed to rise in solitary majesty, whilst my eyes alone hailed its beautifying beams. The webs of the evening have still been spread across the hedged path, unless some labouring man, trudging to work disturbed the fairy structure; yet, in spite of this supineness, when I joined the social circle, every tongue rang changes on the pleasures of the country.

Having frequently had occasion to make the same observations, I was led to endeavour, in one of my solitary rambles, to trace the cause, and likewise to enquire why the poetry written in the infancy of society, is most natural: which, strictly speaking (for *natural* is a very indefinite expression) is merely to say, that it is the transcript of immediate sensations, in all their native wildness and simplicity, when fancy, awakened by the sight of interesting objects, was most actively at work. At such moments, sensibility quickly furnishes smiles, and the sublimated spirits combine images, which rising spontaneously, it is not necessary coldly to ransack the understanding or memory, till the laborious efforts of judgement exclude present sensations, and damp the fire of enthusiasm ...

In a more advanced state of civilization, a poet is rather the creature of art, than of nature. The books that he reads in his youth, become a hot-bed in which artificial fruits are produced, beautiful to the common eye, though they want the true hue and flavour. His images do not arise from sensations; they are copies; and, like the works of the painters who copy ancient statues when they draw men and women of their own times, we acknowledge that the features are fine, and the proportions just; yet they are men of stone; insipid figures, that never convey to the mind the idea of a portrait taken from life, where the soul gives spirit and homogeneity to the whole. The silken wings of fancy are shrivelled by rules; and a desire of attaining elegance of diction, occasions an attention to words, incompatible with sublime, impassioned thoughts...

These hints will assist the reader to trace some of the causes why the beauties of nature are not forcibly felt, when civilization, or rather luxury, has made considerable advances – those calm sensations are not sufficiently lively to serve as a relaxation to the voluptuary, or even to the moderate pursuer of artificial pleasures. In the present state of society, the understanding must bring back the feelings to nature, or the sensibility must have such native strength, as rather to be whetted than destroyed by the strong exercises of passion.

Wollstonecraft: 'On Poetry and Our Relish for the Beauties of Nature'

The life of Johann von Goethe (1749–1832) spanned the whole of the Romantic period, but his relation to it, like that of Rousseau, was ambivalent, for though works like The Sufferings of Young Werther *helped to inspire the early Romantic movement known as* Sturm und Drang *('Storm and Stress'), he later veered away from Romanticism and called it a 'sickness', by contrast with 'healthy' classicism. In both the following passages we get a good flavour, not only of the exalted place accorded to nature, which is looked upon with an undisguised religious reverence, but also something of the inflated style which was characteristic of the period. Freud tells us that the* Aphorisms on Nature *helped to decide him to pursue a career in the natural sciences.*

Was it necessary, I wonder, that that which makes the happiness of a man should also become the source of his misery? The warm, rich feeling of my heart for living nature, which flooded me with so much rapture, which turned the world around me into a paradise, is now becoming an unendurable tormentor to me, a torturing spirit that pursues me on all my ways. Whereas formerly I would survey the fruitful valley from the cliffs, looking across the river toward yonder heights, and seeing everything around me sprouting and swelling; whereas I saw those mountains, from the foot all the way to the summit, clad with a dense growth of tall trees, and those valleys in their manifold windings shaded by the loveliest groves, while the gentle stream flowed along among the whispering reeds and mirrored the beloved clouds that the light breeze wafted across the evening sky; and then I would hear the birds around me bring the woods to life, and the millions of swarming mites danced bravely in the last red rays of the sun, whose last quivering glance freed the buzzing beetle from its grass, and the humming and stirring about me drew my attention to the earth, and the moss, which wrests its nourishment from my resistant rocks, and the underbrush that creeps down the sandy slope would reveal to me the glowing inner holy life of nature – how I would take all that into my warm heart, feeling myself as it were deified in the overflowing abundance, and all the glorious forms of this infinite world come to life within my soul. Monstrous mountains invested me, abysses lay before me, and mountain torrents plunged downward, the rivers flowed below me, and the woods and wilds resounded; and I saw all the unfathomable forces in the depths of the earth working and creating within each other; and now above the ground and under the sky swarm the living creatures in their untold diversity. Everything, everything peopled with myriads of forms; and then the people seeking joint security in their little houses, and building their nests, and ruling in their minds over the wide world! Poor fool that you are! deeming everything so insignificant because *you* are so small. – From the inaccessible mountains across the desert that no foot has trodden, and on to the end of the unknown ocean, breathes the spirit of the eternally creating One, rejoicing in every speck of dust that hears Him and is alive. – Ah, in those days, how often did my longing take the wings of a crane that flew overhead and carry me to the shore of the uncharted sea, to drink from the foaming cup of the infinite that swelling rapture of life, and to taste but for an instant, despite the limited force of my soul, one drop of the bliss of that being which produces all things in and by means of itself.

Goethe: *The Sufferings of Young Werther*

Nature! We are surrounded and embraced by her: powerless to separate ourselves from her, and powerless to penetrate beyond her.

Without asking, or warning, she snatches us up into her circling dance, and whirls us on until we are tired, and drop from her arms.

She is ever shaping new forms: what is, has never yet been; what has been, comes not again. Everything is new, and yet nought but the old.

We live in her midst and know her not. She is incessantly speaking to us, but betrays not her secret. We constantly act upon her, and yet have no power over her.

The one thing she seems to aim at is Individuality; yet she cares nothing for individuals. She is always building up and destroying; but her workshop is inaccessible.

Her life is in her children; but where is the mother? She is the only artist; working-up the most uniform material into utter opposites; arriving, without a trace of effort, at perfection, at the most exact precision, though always veiled under a certain softness.

Each of her works has an essence of its own; each of her phenomena a special characterisation: and yet their diversity is in unity.

She performs a play; we know not whether she sees it herself, and yet she acts for us, the lookers-on.

Incessant life, development, and movement are in her, but she advances not. She changes for ever and ever, and rests not a moment. Quietude is inconceivable to her, and she has laid her curse upon rest. She is firm. Her steps are measured, her exceptions rare, her laws unchangeable.

She has always thought and always thinks; though not as a man, but as Nature. She broods over an all-comprehending idea, which no searching can find out.

Mankind dwell in her and she in them. With all men she plays a game for love, and rejoices the more they win. With many, her moves are so hidden, that the game is over before they know it.

That which is most unnatural is still Nature; the stupidest philistinism has a touch of her genius. Whoso cannot see her everywhere, sees her nowhere rightly.

She loves herself, and her innumerable eyes and affections are fixed upon herself. She has divided herself that she may be her own delight. She causes an endless succession of new capacities for enjoyment to spring up, that her insatiable sympathy may be assuaged.

She rejoices in illusion. Whoso destroys it in himself and others, him she punishes with the sternest tyranny. Whoso follows her in faith, him she takes as a child to her bosom.

Her children are numberless. To none is she altogether miserly; but she has her favourites, on whom she squanders much, and for whom she makes great sacrifices. Over greatness she spreads her shield.

She tosses her creatures out of nothingness, and tells them not whence they came, nor whither they go. It is their business to run, she knows the road.

Her mechanism has few springs – but they never wear out, are always active and manifold.

The spectacle of Nature is always new, for she is always renewing the spectators. Life is her most exquisite invention; and death is her expert contrivance to get plenty of life.

She wraps man in darkness, and makes him for ever long for light. She creates him dependent upon the earth, dull and heavy; and yet is always shaking him until he attempts to soar above it.

She creates needs because she loves action. Wondrous! that she produces all this action so easily. Every need is a benefit, swiftly satisfied, swiftly renewed. – Every fresh want is a new source of pleasure, but she soon reaches an equilibrium.

Every instant she commences an immense journey, and every instant she has reached her goal.

She is vanity of vanities; but not to us, to whom she has made herself of the greatest importance. She allows every child to play tricks with her; every fool to have judgement upon her; thousands to walk stupidly over her and see nothing; and takes her pleasure and finds her account in them all.

We obey her laws even when we rebel against them; we work with her even when we desire to work against her.

She makes every gift a benefit by causing us to want it. She delays, that we may desire her; she hastens, that we may not be weary of her.

She has neither language nor discourse; but she creates tongues and hearts, by which she feels and speaks.

Her crown is love. Through love alone dare we come near her. She separates all existences, and all tend to intermingle. She has isolated all things in order that all may approach one another. She holds a couple of draughts from the cup of love to be fair payment for the pains of a lifetime.

She is all things. She rewards herself and punishes herself; is her own joy and her own misery. She is rough and tender, lovely and hateful, powerless and omnipotent. She is an eternal present. Past and future are unknown to her. The present is her eternity. She is beneficent. I praise her and all her works. She is silent and wise.

No explanation is wrung from her; no present won from her, which she does not give freely. She is cunning, but for good ends; and it is best not to notice her tricks.

She is complete but never finished. As she works now, so can she always work. Everyone sees her in his own fashion. She hides under a thousand names and phrases, and is always the same. She has brought me here and will also lead me away. I trust her. She may scold me, but she will not hate her work. It was not I who spoke of her. No! What is false and what is true, she has spoken it all. The fault, the merit, is all hers.

Goethe: *Aphorisms on Nature*

Johann Gottlieb Fichte (1762–1814) and Friedrich von Schelling (1775–1854), though starting from different premises, both belonged to a line of great German philosophers who, essentially part of the Romantic movement, attempted to construct comprehensive metaphysical systems in which the natural world was integrated within a spiritual view of nature, one which was at odds with the mechanistic and materialistic outlook of the preceding period. Their philosophies of nature were characterized by a sense of dynamic, even evolutionary, development, of organic wholeness, and of purpose, a conception in which matter and spirit cannot in the final analysis be distinguished from each other.

When I contemplate all things as one whole, one Nature, there is but one power; – when I regard them as separate existences, there are many powers, which develop themselves according to their inward laws, and pass through all the possible forms of which they are capable; and all objects in Nature are but those powers under certain determinate forms. The manifestations of each individual power of Nature are determined, become what they are, partly by its own essential character, partly through its own previous manifestations, and partly through the manifestations of all the other powers of Nature with which it is connected. But it is connected with them all – for Nature is one connected whole – and its essential character remains what it is, and while it continues to manifest itself under these particular circumstances, its manifestations must necessarily be what they are; – and it is absolutely impossible that they should be in the smallest degree different from what they are.

In every moment of her duration Nature is one connected whole; in every moment each individual part must be what it is, because all the others are what they are; and you could not remove a single grain of sand from its place, without thereby, although perhaps imperceptibly to you, changing something throughout all parts of the immeasurable whole. But every moment of this duration is determined by all past moments, and will determine all future moments; and you cannot conceive the whole indefinite Past to have been other than what it has been, and the whole indefinite Future other than what it will be . . .

What high satisfaction this system affords to my understanding! What order, what firm connexion, what comprehensive supervision does it introduce into the whole fabric of my knowledge! Consciousness is here no longer a stranger in Nature, whose connexion with existence is so incomprehensible; it is native to it, and indeed one of its necessary manifestations. Nature herself ascends gradually in the determinate series of her creations. In rude matters she is a simple existence; in organized matter she returns within herself to internal activity, – in the plant to produce form, in the animal motion; – in man, as her highest masterpiece, she turns inward that she may perceive and contemplate herself, – in him she, as it were, doubles herself, and from being mere existence, becomes existence and consciousness in one.

Fichte: *The Vocation of Man*

Philosophy, accordingly, is nothing other than a *natural history of our mind*. From now on all dogmatism is overturned from its foundations. We consider the system of our ideas, not in its *being*, but in its *becoming*. Philosophy becomes *genetic*; that is, it allows the whole necessary series of our ideas to arise and take its course, as it were, before our eyes. From now on there is no longer any separation between experience and speculation. The system of Nature is at the same time the system of our mind, and only now, once the great synthesis has been accomplished, does our knowledge return to analysis (to *research* and *experiment*). But this system does not yet exist. Many faint-hearted spirits have misgivings at the outset, for they speak of a system of *our nature* (the magnitude of which they do not know), no otherwise than as if they were speaking about a *syllabus* of our *concepts*.

The dogmatist, who assumes everything to be originally *present* outside us (not as *coming to be* and *springing forth from us*) must surely commit himself at least *to this*: that what is *external* to us is also to be explained by *external* causes. He succeeds in doing this, as long as he remains within the nexus of cause and effect, despite the fact that he can never make it intelligible how this nexus of causes and effects has *itself* arisen. As soon as he raises himself above the individual phenomenon, his whole philosophy is at an end; the limits of mechanism are also the limits of his system.

But now mechanism alone is far from being what constitutes Nature. For as soon as we enter the realm of *organic nature*, all mechanical linkage of cause and effect ceases for us. Every organic product exists *for itself*; its being is dependent on no other being. But now the cause is never the *same as* the effect; only between quite *different* things is a relation of cause and effect possible. The organic, however, produces *itself*, arises *out of itself*, every single plant is the product only of an individual *of its own kind*, and so every single organism endlessly produces and reproduces only *its own species*. Hence no organization progresses *forward*, but is forever turning back always into *itself*. Accordingly, an organization as such is neither *cause* nor *effect* of anything outside it, and so is nothing that intrudes into the nexus of mechanism . . .

This philosophy must accept, therefore, that there is a hierarchy of life in Nature. Even in mere organized matter there is *life*, but a life of a more restricted kind. This idea is so old, and has hitherto persisted so constantly in the most varied forms, right up to the present day – (already in the most ancient times it was believed that the whole world was pervaded by an animating principle, called the world-soul, and the later period of Leibniz gave every plant its soul) – that one may very well surmise from the beginning that there must be some reason latent in the human mind itself for this natural belief. And so it is. The sheer wonder which surrounds the problem of the origin of organic bodies, therefore, is due to the fact that in these things necessity and contingency are most intimately united. *Necessity*, because their very *existence* is *purposive*, not only their form (as in the work of art), *contingency*, because this purposiveness is nevertheless actual only for an intuiting and reflecting being. For that reason, the human mind was early led to the idea of a *self*-organizing matter, and because organization is conceivable only in relation to a mind, to an original union of mind and matter in these things. It was itself compelled to seek the reason for these things, on the one hand, in Nature herself, and on the other, in a principle exalted above Nature; and hence it very soon fell into thinking of mind and Nature as one. Here for the first time there emerged from its sacred obscurity that ideal being in which the mind supposes concept and deed, design and execution, to be one. Here first a premonition came over man of his own nature, in which intuition and concept, form and object, ideal and real, are originally one and the same. Hence the peculiar aura which surrounds this problem, an aura which the philosophy of mere reflection, which sets out only to *separate*, can never develop, whereas the pure intuition, or rather, the creative imagination, long since discovered the symbolic language, which one has only to construe in order to discover that Nature speaks to us the more intelligibly the less we think of her in a merely reflective way.

Schelling: *Ideas for a Philosophy of Nature*

The influence of Kant and of the German nature philosophers such as Schelling is to be seen in the thinking of Samuel Taylor Coleridge (1772–1834) who took a strong stand against the materialist and mechanistic theories that had developed in the eighteenth century. He argued both against Cartesian dualism and against the suggestion that life and mind can be reduced to the mechanical arrangement of material parts, and proposed an organicist philosophy in which the human imagination was able to combine together both spirit and matter.

How matter can ever unite with perception – how *being* can ever transform itself into *knowing*, is conceivable only on one condition; that is if it can be shewn that the *vis prepresentativa*, or the sentient, is itself a species of matter; ie either as a property, or attribute, or self-subsistence. Now that it is a property is an assumption of materialism; of which permit me to say thus much in praise, that it is a system which could not but be patronized if it performed what it promises. But how any affection from without could metamorphose itself into perception or will, the materialist has not only left incomprehensible as he found it, but has made it a comprehensible absurdity. For, grant that an object from without could act upon the conscious self as on a consubstantial object; yet such an affection as could only engender something homogeneous with itself. Motion could only propagate motion. Matter has no inward. We remove one surface, but to meet with another. We can but divide a particle into particles; and each particle has the power of being again divided ...

The most consistent proceeding of the dogmatic materialist would be to fall back into the common rank of [Cartesian] *soul-and-bodyists*, to affect the mysterious, and to declare the whole process a revelation *given* and not to be *understood*, which it would be profane to examine too closely. But a revelation unconfirmed by miracles, and a faith not commanded by the conscience, a philosopher may venture to pass by, without suspecting himself of any irreligious tendency. Thus, as materialism has generally been taught, it is utterly unintelligible, and owes all its proselytes to the propensity so common among men, to mistake distinct images for clear conceptions; and vice versa, to reject as inconceivable whatever from its own nature is unimaginable. But as soon as it becomes intelligible, it ceases to be materialism. In order to explain *thinking*, as a material phenomenon, it is necessary to refine matter into a mere modification of intelligence, with the two-fold function of *appearing* and *perceiving* ...

[We] have been assured, not in old times but even in our own, that mind is a function of the brain, that all our moral and intellectual being are the effects of organization; which I confess has always had much the same effect on my mind as if a man should say, that building with all the included handicraft of plastering, sawing, planing, etc, was the offspring of the house and that the mason and carpenter were the [result of a suite of chambers, with the passages and staircases that lead to them]. For to make A the offspring of B, where the very existence of B as B presupposes the existence of A, [is preposterous] ... For what, again, I say, is [organic] organization? Not the mere arrangement of parts as means to an end, for in that sense I should call my watch organization, or a steam engine organization. But we agree these are machines, not organizations. It appears, then, that if I am to attach any meaning at all to the word organization, it must be distinct from mechanism in this, that in all machines I suppose the power to be from without, that if I take my watch there is nothing in the component parts of this watch that constitutes it peculiarly fit for a watch, or produces it. There is nothing in the steam engine which of itself, independent of its position, would account for that position at all. Organization therefore must not only be an arrangement of parts together, as means to an end, but it must be such an interdependence of parts, each of which in its turn being means to an end, as arises from within. The moment a man dies we can scarcely say he remains organized in the proper sense. The powers of chemistry are beginning to show us that no force, not even mechanical power, can *make* life. To say therefore that life is the result of organization, and yet at the same time to admit that organization is distinguished from mechanism only by life, is assuredly what I before said, to affirm a thing to be its own parent.

Coleridge: *Philosophical Lectures*

126

Schelling suggests at the end of the above passage (page 125) that nature can best be approached, not by reflective reason but by 'intuition' and 'creative imagination', modes of awareness more familiar to poets than to philosophers. All the great themes of Romanticism are to be found in the English poets of the period: William Blake (1757–1827) expresses a deeply personal view of nature in which the atoms of the new philosophy can only be part of a much wider vision; in John Keats (1795–1821) we see hostility to the overly-simplified view of nature which is the product of Newton's analytical approach; and in William Wordsworth (1770–1850) we find a marvellously poetic statement of a form of pantheism.

Mock on mock on, Voltaire, Rousseau!
Mock on, mock on – 'Tis all in vain!
You throw the sand against the wind,
And the wind blows it back again.

And every sand becomes a gem
Reflected in the beams divine;
Blown back they blind the mocking eye,
But still in Israel's paths they shine.

The atoms of Democritus
And Newton's particles of light
Are sands upon the Red Sea shore,
Where Israel's tents do shine so bright.

Blake: 'Mock on, Voltaire'

Do not all charms fly at the mere touch of cold philosophy?
There was an awful rainbow once in heaven:
We know her woof, her texture; she is given
In the dull catalogue of common things.
Philosophy will clip an angel's wings,
Conquer all mysteries by rule and line,
Empty the haunted air, and gnomed mine –
Unweave a rainbow, as it erewhile made
The tender-personed Lamia melt into a shade.

Keats: 'Lamia'

The sounding cataract
Haunted me like a passion; the tall rock,
The mountain, and the deep and gloomy wood,
Their colours and their forms, were then to me
An appetite; a feeling and a love,
That had no need of a remoter charm,
By thought supplied, nor any interest
Unborrowed from the eye. – That time is past,
And all its aching joys are now no more,
And all its dizzy raptures. Not for this
Faint I, nor mourn nor murmur; other gifts
Have followed; for such loss, I would believe,
Abundant recompense. For I have learned
To look on nature, not as in the hour
Of thoughtless youth; but hearing often-times
The still, sad music of humanity,
Nor harsh nor grating, though of ample power
To chasten and subdue. And I have felt
A presence that disturbs me with the joy
Of elevated thoughts; a sense sublime
Of something far more deeply interfused,
Whose dwelling is the light of setting suns,
And the round ocean and the living air,
And the blue sky, and in the mind of man;
A motion and a spirit, that impels
All thinking things, all objects of all thought,
And rolls through all things. Therefore am I still
A lover of the meadows and the woods,
And mountains; and of all that we behold
From this green earth; of all the mighty world
Of eye, and ear, – both what they half create,
And what perceive; well pleased to recognize
In nature and the language of the sense
The anchor of my purest thoughts, the nurse,
The guide, the guardian of my heart, and soul
Of all my moral being.

Wordsworth: 'Lines Written a Few Miles above Tintern Abbey'

It would be wrong to imagine that the Romantics were hostile to science. What they objected to was the restrictive mechanical model which had dominated thinking about nature for over a century. The study of nature could indeed be a liberating, even a spiritual, experience, and in his multi-volume work, Cosmos, *the German explorer Alexander von Humboldt (1769–1859) presented a generally comprehensible account of the universe as then known, in terms which conveyed the excitement and aesthetic delight of his investigations into the natural world.*

Nature is a free domain; and the profound conceptions and enjoyments she awakens within us can only be vividly delineated by thought clothed in exalted forms of speech, worthy of bearing witness to the majesty and greatness of the creation.

In considering the study of physical phenomena, not merely in its bearings on the material wants of life, but in its general influence on the intellectual advancement of mankind, we find its noblest and most important result to be a knowledge of the chain of connection, by which all natural forces are linked together, and made mutually dependent upon each other; and it is the perception of these relations that exalts our views and ennobles our enjoyments. Such a result can, however, only be reaped as the fruit of observation and intellect, combined with the spirit of the age, in which are reflected all the varied phases of thought. He who can trace, through by-gone times, the stream of our knowledge to its primitive source, will learn from history how, for thousands of years, man has laboured, amid the ever-recurring changes of form, and has thus by the force of mind gradually subdued a greater portion of the physical world to his domination. In interrogating the history of the past, we trace the mysterious course of ideas yielding the first glimmering perception of the same image of a Cosmos, or harmoniously ordered whole, which, dimly shadowed forth to the human mind in the primitive ages of the world, is now fully revealed to the maturer intellect of mankind as the result of long and laborious observation ...

When the human mind first attempts to subject to its control the world of physical phenomena, and strives by meditative contemplation to penetrate the rich luxuriance of living nature, and the mingled web of free and restricted natural forces, man feels himself raised to a height from whence, as he embraces the vast horizon, individual things blend together in varied groups, and appear as if shrouded in a vapoury veil. These figurative expressions are used in order to illustrate the point of view from whence we would consider the universe both in its celestial and terrestrial sphere. I am not insensible of the boldness of such an undertaking. Among all the forms of exposition to which these pages are devoted, there is none more difficult than the general delineation of nature, which we purpose sketching, since we must not allow ourselves to be overpowered by a sense of the stupendous richness and variety of the forms presented to us, but must dwell only on the consideration of masses, either possessing actual magnitude or borrowing its semblance from the associations awakened within the subjective sphere of ideas. It is by a separation and classification of phenomena, by an intuitive insight into the play of obscure forces, and by animated expressions, in which the perceptible spectacle is reflected with vivid truthfulness, that we may hope to comprehend and describe the *universal all* in a manner worthy of the dignity of the word *cosmos* in its signification of *universe, order of the world* and *adornment* of this universal order. May the immeasurable diversity of phenomena which crowd into the picture of nature in no way detract from that harmonious impression of rest and unity, which is the ultimate object of every literary or purely artistical composition.

Humboldt: *Cosmos: A Sketch of a Physical Description of the Universe*

8

THE NINETEENTH CENTURY: ROMANTIC TWILIGHT

Although the Romantic era is usually confined historically to the period 1770 to 1830, its influence was felt throughout the nineteenth century both in Europe and in America. This century saw a rapid growth in scientific exploration and technological achievement, which in turn was associated with the take-off of the Industrial Revolution and its accompanying disruption of traditional social patterns and values. The mechanical conception of nature was ceasing to be merely a philosopher's speculation and was becoming an all-too visible reality, and indeed the social critic Thomas Carlyle actually described his epoch as the 'Age of the Machine'. This period was in part a re-enactment of an earlier engagement fought by the Romantics against the Enlightenment, and we can see in the writings of Englishmen such as Ruskin and Morris, and Americans such as Emerson and Thoreau, a determination to hold the burgeoning materialism at bay and to re-endow nature with value, spirit, and even divinity. In their view nature was not an object to be investigated and exploited merely for economic purposes, an attitude increasingly prevalent in the nineteenth century, but rather a home which accommodated and enhanced our most spiritual aspirations, and although the extension of moral duties from the human to the animal realm had already been urged by the philosopher John Locke amongst others, the nineteenth century saw the first concerted challenge to established belief in the rights of humans over animals. Like the earlier Romantics these writers frequently looked back to, and even sought to recapture, an age when, as they saw it, humanity was in harmony with nature and when the cosmos was believed to be invested with divinity, and in this regard they foreshadowed a certain tendency of thought within the green movement today.

———————

The thinking of Arthur Schopenhauer (1788–1860) had roots in both the philosophers of the Romantic period and in the ancient philosophies of India for which he had a profound reverence. His philosophy of

*nature combines a pervasive pessimism which sees the world as driven by
a dynamic but blind and pointless principle he called the 'will-to-live',
with a belief in the ultimate unity of all things. He was one of the first
modern philosophers to attack the orthodox view that humanity is
superior to the animal kingdom and enjoys certain rights over it,
advocating a Buddhist-like ethic of universal compassion.*

Every glance at the world, to explain which is the task of the
philosopher, confirms and establishes that the *will-to-live*, far
from being an arbitrary hypostasis or even an empty expression,
is the only true description of the world's innermost nature.
Everything presses and pushes towards *existence*, if possible
towards *organic existence*, ie, *life*, and then to the highest
possible degree thereof. In animal nature, it then becomes
obvious that the *will-to-live* is the keynote of its being, its only
unchangeable and unconditioned quality. Let us consider this
universal craving for life, and see the infinite eagerness, ease,
and exuberance with which the will-to-live presses impetuously
into existence under millions of forms everywhere and at every
moment by means of fertilizations and germs ... seizing every
opportunity, greedily grasping for itself every material capable
of life; and then again, let us cast a glance at this awful alarm and
wild rebellion, when in any individual phenomenon it is to pass
out of existence, especially where this occurs with distinct
consciousness. Then it is precisely the same as if in this single
phenomenon the whole world were to be annihilated for ever;
and the entire inner nature of a living being thus threatened is at
once transformed into the most desperate struggle against, and
resistance to, death ... Therefore in such phenomena it
becomes evident that I have rightly declared the *will-to-live* to
be that which is incapable of further explanation, but is the basis
of every explanation; and that, far from being an empty-
sounding word, like the Absolute, the infinite, the idea, and
other similar expressions, it is the most real thing we know, in
fact the kernel of reality itself.

Schopenhauer: *The World as Will and Representation*

[That] 'man can have no duty to any beings except human' ...
that 'cruelty to animals is contrary to man's duty *to himself*,
because it deadens in him the feeling of sympathy for their

sufferings, and thus a natural tendency that is very useful to morality in relation to *other human beings* is weakened.' Thus only for practice are we to have sympathy for animals, and they are, so to speak, the pathological phantom for the purpose of practicing sympathy for human beings. In common with the whole of Asia not tainted with Islam (that is, Judaism), I regard such propositions as revolting and abominable. At the same time, we see here once more how entirely this philosophical morality, which as previously shown is only a theological one in disguise, depends in reality on the biblical one. Thus, because Christian morality leaves animals out of account (of this, more later on), they are at once outlawed in philosophical morals; they are mere 'things', mere *means* to any ends whatsoever. They can therefore be used for vivisection, hunting, coursing, bullfights, and horse racing, and can be whipped to death as they struggle along with heavy carts of stone. Shame on such a morality that is worthy of pariahs ... and that fails to recognize the eternal essence that exists in every living thing, and shines forth with inscrutable significance from all eyes that see the sun! But that morality knows and respects only its own worthy species, whose characteristic *reason [Vernunft]* is the condition on which a being can be an object of moral consideration and respect...

The moral incentive advanced by me as the genuine, is further confirmed by the fact that *the animals* are also taken under its protection. In other European systems of morality they are badly provided for, which is most inexcusable. They are said to have no rights, and there is the erroneous idea that our behavior to them is without moral significance, or, as it is said in the language of that morality, there are no duties to animals. All this is revoltingly crude, a barbarism of the West, the source of which is to be found in Judaism. In Philosophy it rests, despite all evidence to the contrary, on the assumed total difference between man and animal. We all know that such difference was expressed most definitely and strikingly by Descartes as necessary consequence of his errors. Thus when the philosophy of Descartes, Leibniz, and Wolff built up rational psychology out of abstract concepts and constructed an immortal *anima rationalis*, the natural claims of the animal world obviously stood up against this exclusive privilege, this patent of immortality of the human species, and nature, as always on such occasions, entered her silent protest. With an uneasy intellectual conscience, the philosophers then had to try to support rational psychology by means of the empirical. They were therefore concerned to open up a vast chasm, an immeasurable gulf between man and animal in order to represent them as fundamentally different, in spite of all evidence to the contrary. Such efforts were ridiculed even by Boileau:

Les animaux ont-ils des universités?
Voit-on fleuri chez eux des quatre facultés?

In the end animals would be quite incapable of distinguishing themselves from the external world and would have no consciousness of themselves, no ego! To answer such absurd statements, we can point simply to the boundless egoism inherent in every animal, even the smallest and lowest, which shows clearly enough how very conscious they are of their ego in face of the world or the non-ego. If any Cartesian were to find himself clawed by a tiger, he would become aware in the clearest possible manner of the sharp distinction such a beast draws between its ego and the non-ego . . .

If we entirely disregard for once all possible metaphysical examination of the ultimate ground of that compassion, from which alone non-egoistical actions can result; and if we consider it from the empirical point of view, merely as a natural arrangement, it will be clear to everyone that, for the greatest possible alleviation of the countless sufferings of every kind to which our life is exposed and from which no one entirely escapes, and at the same time as a counterbalance to the burning egoism that fills all beings and often develops into malice, nature could not have done anything more effective than plant that wonderful disposition in the human heart. By virtue of it, one man shares the sufferings of another, and we hear the voice that calls firmly and clearly to one, 'show forbearance!' and to another, 'Give help!' according to the occasion. From the resultant mutual assistance one could certainly expect more for the welfare of all than from a strict command of duty couched in general and abstract terms and resulting from certain rational considerations and combinations of concepts. From such a command the expected result would be less, since universal propositions and abstract truths are quite unintelligible to the untutored, for whom only the concrete has any meaning. But with the exception of an extremely small part, the whole of mankind was always rough and uncultured and must remain so, since the large amount of physical work, inevitably necessary for the race as a whole, leaves no time for the cultivation of the mind. On the other hand, to awaken that compassion which is shown to be the *sole source of disinterested actions and hence the true basis of morality*, there is no need for abstract knowledge, but only for that of intuitive perception, for the mere apprehension of the concrete case to which compassion at once appeals without any further mediation of ideas.

Schopenhauer: *On the Basis of Morality*

Jeremy Bentham (1747–1832) was the founder of the Utilitarian movement which, with its emphasis on empirical facts and its principle of the greatest happiness of the greatest number, had little in common with either Romanticism or Schopenhauer, but, like the latter, he was concerned to extend the principle of benevolence from human beings to animals.

The day has been, I grieve to say in many places it is not yet past, in which the greater part of the [human] species, under the denomination of slaves, have been treated by the law exactly upon the same footing, as, in England for example, the inferior races of animals are still. The day *may* come, when the rest of the animal creation may acquire those rights which never could have been withholden from them but by the hand of tyranny. The French have already discovered that the blackness of the skin is no reason why a human being should be abandoned without redress to the caprice of a tormentor. It may come one day to be recognized, that the number of legs, the villosity of the skin, or the termination of the *os sacrum* [spine], are reasons equally insufficient for abandoning a sensitive being to the same fate. What else is it that should trace the insuperable line? Is it the faculty of reason, or, perhaps, the faculty of discourse? But a full-grown horse or dog, is beyond comparison a more rational, as well as a more conversible animal, than an infant of a day, or a week, or even a month, old. But suppose the case were otherwise, what would it avail? The question is not, Can they *reason?* nor, Can they *talk?* but, Can they *suffer?*

Bentham: *An Introduction to the Principles of Morals and Legislation*

Ralph Waldo Emerson (1803–1882) and Henry David Thoreau (1817–1862) were leading members of the American Transcendentalist movement, a group of writers and philosophers, influenced by Neoplatonism, by European Romanticism and by Indian philosophy, who rejected materialism and utilitarianism, and believed in the essential harmony between humankind and nature and in the unity and essential spirituality of all creation. The poet Walt Whitman (1818–1892), though not a member of this group, shared much of their outlook.

The Supreme Critic on all the errors of the past and the present, and the only prophet of that which must be, is that great nature in which we rest, as the earth lies in the soft arms of the atmosphere; that Unity, that Over-Soul, within which every man's particular being is contained and made one with all other; that common heart, of which all sincere conversation is the worship, to which all right action is submission; that over-powering reality which confutes our tricks and talents, and constrains every one to pass for what he is, and to speak from his character and not from his tongue; and which evermore tends and aims to pass into our thought and hand, and become wisdom, and virtue, and power, and beauty. We live in succession, in division, in parts, in particles. Meantime, within man is the soul of the whole; the wise silence; the universal beauty, to which every part and particle is equally related; the eternal *One*. And this deep power in which we exist, and whose beatitude is all accessible to us, is not only self-sufficing and perfect in every hour, but the act of seeing and the thing seen, the seer and the spectacle, the subject and the object, are one. We see the world piece by piece, as the sun, the moon, the animal, the tree; but the whole, of which these are the shining parts, is the soul.

Emerson: 'The Over-Soul'

This is a delicious evening, when the whole body is one sense, and imbibes delight through every pore. I go and come with a strange liberty in Nature, a part of herself. As I walk along the stoney shore of the pond in my shirt sleeves, though it is cool as well as cloudy and windy, and I see nothing special to attract me, all the elements are unusually congenial to me. The bull-frogs trump to usher in the night, and the note of the whip-poorwill is borne on the rippling wind from over the water. Sympathy with the fluttering alder and poplar leaves almost takes away my breath; yet, like the lake, my serenity is rippled but not ruffled. These small waves raised by the evening wind are as remote from storm as the smooth and reflecting surface. Though it is now dark, the wind still blows and roars in the wood, the waves still dash, and some creatures lull the rest with their notes. The repose is never complete. The wildest animals do not repose, but seek their prey now; the fox, and skunk, and rabbit, now roam the fields and woods without fear. They are Nature's watchmen – links which connect the days of animated life . . .

Yet I experienced sometimes that the most sweet and tender, the most innocent and encouraging society may be found in any natural object, even for the poor misanthrope and most melancholy man. There can be no very black melancholy to him who lives in the midst of Nature and has his senses still . . .

The indescribable innocence and beneficence of Nature, – of sun and wind and rain, of summer and winter, – such health, such cheer, they afford forever! and such sympathy they have ever with our race, that all Nature would be affected, and the sun's brightness fade, and the winds would sigh humanely, and the clouds rain tears, and the woods shed their leaves and put on mourning in midsummer, if any man should ever for a just cause grieve. Shall I not have intelligence with the earth? Am I not partly leaves and vegetable mould myself?

Thoreau: *Walden*

Living down in the country again. A wonderful conjunction of all that goes to make those sometime miracle-hours after sunset – so near and yet so far. Perfect, or nearly perfect days, I notice, are not so very uncommon; but the combinations that make perfect nights are few, even in a lifetime. We have one of those perfections tonight. Sunset left things pretty clear; the larger stars were visible soon as the shades allow'd. A while after 8, three or four great black clouds suddenly rose, seemingly from different points, and sweeping with broad swirls of wind but no thunder, underspread the orbs from view everywhere, and indicated a violent heat-storm. But without storm, clouds, blackness, and all, sped and vanish'd as suddenly as they had risen; and from a little after 9 till 11 the atmosphere and the whole show above were in that state of exceptional clearness and glory just alluded to. In the northwest turned the Great Dipper with its pointers round the Cynosure. A little south of east the constellation of the Scorpion was fully up, with red Antares glowing in its neck; while dominating, majestic Jupiter swam, an hour and a half risen, in the east (no moon till after 11). A large part of the sky seem'd just laid in great splashes of phosphorus. You could look deeper in, farther through, than usual; the orbs thick as heads of wheat in a field. Not that there was any special brilliancy either – nothing near as sharp as I have seen of keen winter nights, but a curious general luminousness throughout to sight, sense, and soul. The latter had much to do with it. (I am convinced there are hours of Nature, especially of the atmosphere, mornings and evenings, address'd to the soul. Night transcends, for that purpose, what the proudest day can do.) Now, indeed, if never before, the heavens declared the glory of God. It was to the full the sky of the Bible, of Arabia, of the prophets, and of the oldest poems. There, in abstraction and stillness, (I had gone off by myself to absorb the scene, to have the spell unbroken), the copiousness, the removedness, vitality, loose-clear-crowdedness, of that stellar concave spreading overhead, softly absorb'd into me, rising so free, interminably high, stretching east, west, north, south – and I, though but a point in the center below, embodying all.

As if for the first time, indeed, creation noiselessly sank into and through me its placid and untellable lesson, beyond – O, so infinitely beyond! – anything from art, books, sermons, or from science, old or new. The spirit's hour – religion's hour – the visible suggestion of God in space and time – now once definitely indicated, if never told again. The untold pointed at – the heavens all paved with it. The Milky Way, as if some superhuman symphony, some ode of universal vagueness, disdaining syllable and sound – a flashing glance of Deity, address'd to the soul. All silently – the indescribable night and stars – far off and silently.

Whitman: *Specimen Days*

The American poet Emily Dickinson (1830–1886) shared with the Transcendentalists an almost mystical sense of the intimate bond between humanity and nature, a bond which is expressed in the poem below, but at the same time she often went against the Romantic current by emphasizing the inscrutability of nature and its indifference towards human interests.

Nature, the gentlest mother,
Impatient of no child,
The feeblest or the waywardest, –
Her admonition mild

In forest and the hill
By traveller is heard,
Restraining rampant squirrel
Or too impetuous bird.

How far her conversation,
A summer afternoon, –
Her household, her assembly;
And when the sun goes down

Her voice among the aisles
Incites the timid prayer
Of the minutest cricket,
The most unworthy flower.

When all the children sleep
She turns as long away
As will suffice to light her lamps;
Then, bending from the sky,

With infinite affection
And infiniter care,
Her golden finger on her lip,
Wills silence everywhere.

Dickinson: 'Nature, the Gentlest Mother'

The American naturalist John Muir (1838–1914) shared with the Transcendentalists the idea that a divine spirit flows through the whole of nature. In his concern for the wilderness, he initiated the ideas of forestry conservation and national parks, and was one of the first to develop a conscious environmental ethic.

When we are with Nature we are awake, and we discover many interesting things and reach many a mark we were not aiming at; some new flower or bird or waterfall comes to our eyes, and we gladly step aside to study it; or some tree of surpassing beauty attracts our attention, or some grove, though the species may be well known, or we come upon a specimen that has been riven and scattered by lightning stroke, or bent into an arch by snow, or one or many over which an avalanche has passed. Or we come upon the wild inhabitants of the region – a bear at breakfast beneath the nut-bearing trees, or in the thickets of berry bushes, or deer feeding among the chaparral, or squirrels and marmots at work or play. Birds, too, come forward and sing for us and display their pretty housekeeping. All these and a thousand other attractions enrich our walks beyond the attainment of the main object, and make our paths unconsciously crooked and charming. It is as if Nature were saying: 'The way is long and rough and the poor fellow is weary and lonesome. Birds, sing him a song; Squirrels, show him your pretty ways; Flowers, beguile the steep ascent with your beauty; sparkle and bloom and shine, ye Lakes and Streams; and wave and chant and shimmer in the sunlight, all ye Pines and Firs, that the wanderer faint not by the way.'

And thus we find in the fields of Nature no place that is blank or barren; every spot on land or sea is covered with harvests, and these harvests are always ripe and ready to be gathered, and no toiler is ever underpaid. Not in these fields, God's wilds, will you ever hear the sad moan of disappointment: 'All is vanity.' No, we are overpaid a thousand times for all our toil, and a single day in so divine an atmosphere of beauty and love would be well worth living for, and at its close, should death come, without any hope of another life, we could still say 'Thank you, God, for the glorious gift!' and pass on. Indeed, some of the days I have spent alone in the depths of the wilderness have shown me that immortal life beyond the grave is not essential to perfect happiness, for these diverse days were so complete there was no sense of time in them, they had no definite beginning or ending, and formed a kind of terrestrial immortality.

Muir: 'A Voyage to Alaska'

Thousands of tired, nerve-shaken, over-civilized people are beginning to find out that going to the mountains is going home; that wildness is a necessity and that mountain parks and reservations are useful not only as fountains of timber and irrigating rivers but as fountains of life. Awakening from the stupefying effects of the vice of over-industry and the deadly apathy of luxury they are trying as best they can to mix and enrich their own little ongoings with those of Nature, and to get rid of rust and disease ... some are washing off sins and cobweb cares of the devil's spinning in all-day storms on mountains.

Muir: 'The Wild Parks and Forest Reservations of the West'

Like Muir, the English writer Richard Jefferies (1848–1887) was able to evoke a sense of kinship with nature which often has the quality of a mystical experience.

I was utterly alone with the sun and the earth. Lying down on the grass, I spoke in my soul to the earth, the sun, the air, and the distant sea far beyond sight. I thought of the earth's firmness – I felt it bear me up; through the grassy couch there came an influence as if I could feel the great earth speaking to me. I thought of the wandering air – its pureness, which is its beauty; the air touched me and gave me something of itself. I spoke to the sea: though so far, in my mind I saw it, green at the rim of the earth and blue in deeper ocean; I desired to have its strength, its mystery and glory. Then I addressed the sun, desiring the soul equivalent of his light and brilliance, his endurance and unwearied race. I turned to the blue heaven over, gazing into its depth, inhaling its exquisite colour and sweetness. The rich blue of the unattainable flower of the sky drew my soul towards it, and there it rested, for pure colour is rest of heart. By all these I prayed; I felt an emotion of the soul beyond all definition; prayer is a puny thing to it, and the word is a rude sign to the feeling, but I know no other.

By the blue heaven, by the rolling sun bursting through untrodden space, a new ocean of ether every day unveiled. By the fresh and wandering air encompassing the world; by the sea sounding on the shore – the green sea white-flecked at the

141

margin and the deep ocean; by the strong earth under me. Then, returning, I prayed by the sweet thyme, whose little flowers I touched with my hand; by the slender grass; by the crumble of dry chalky earth I took up and let fall through my fingers. Touching the crumble of earth, the blade of grass, the thyme flower, breathing the earth-encircling air, thinking of the sea and the sky, holding out my hand for the sunbeams to touch it, prone on the sward in token of deep reverence, thus I prayed that I might touch to the unutterable existence infinitely higher than deity.

With all the intensity of feeling which exalted me, all the intense communion I held with the earth, the sun and sky, the stars hidden by the light, with the ocean – in no manner can the thrilling depth of these feelings be written – with these I prayed, as if they were the keys of an instrument, of an organ, with which I swelled forth the notes of my soul, redoubling my own voice by their power. The great sun burning with light; the strong earth, dear earth; the warm sky; the pure air; the thought of ocean; the inexpressible beauty of all filled me with a rapture, an ecstasy, an inflatus. With this inflatus, too, I prayed. Next to myself I came and recalled myself, my bodily existence. I held out my hand, the sunlight gleamed on the skin and the irides-cent nails; I recalled the mystery and beauty of the flesh. I thought of the mind with which I could see the ocean sixty miles distant, and gather to myself its glory. I thought of my inner existence, that consciousness which is called the soul. These, that is, myself – I threw into the balance to weigh the prayer the heavier. My strength of body, mind, and soul, I flung into it; I put forth my strength; I wrestled and laboured, and toiled in might of prayer. The prayer, this soul-emotion was in itself – not for an object – it was a passion. I hid my face in the grass, I was wholly prostrated, I lost myself in the wrestle, I was rapt and carried away.

Jefferies: *The Story of My Heart*

John Ruskin (1819–1900), who is best known as a leading Victorian art critic, had a deep sense of the emotional and spiritual significance of nature, which he linked to the Gothic style, and in his writings he sought to combat the rising materialism and Utilitarianism of his day.

Now, therefore, I think that, without the risk of any farther serious objection occurring to you, I may state what I believe to be the truth, – that beauty has been appointed by the Deity to be one of the elements by which the human soul is continually sustained; it is therefore to be found more or less in all natural objects, but in order that we may not satiate ourselves with it, and weary of it, it is rarely granted to us in its utmost degrees. When we see it in those utmost degrees, we are attracted to it strongly, and remember it long, as in the case of singularly beautiful scenery, or a beautiful countenance. On the other hand, absolute ugliness is admitted as rarely as perfect beauty; but degrees of it more or less distinct are associated with whatever has the nature of death and sin, just as beauty is associated with what has the nature of virtue and of life.

This being so, you see that when the relative beauty of any particular forms has to be examined, we may reason, from the forms of Nature around us, in this manner: – what Nature does generally, is sure to be more or less beautiful; what she does rarely, will either be *very* beautiful, or absolutely ugly. And we may again easily determine, if we are not willing in such a case to trust our feelings, which of these is indeed the case, by this simple rule, that if the rare occurrence is the result of the complete fulfilment of a natural law, it will be beautiful; if of the violation of a natural law, it will be ugly. For instance, a sapphire is the result of the complete and perfect fulfilment of the laws of aggregation in the earth of alumina, and it is therefore beautiful; more beautiful than clay, or any other of the conditions of that earth. But a square leaf on any tree would be ugly, being a violation of the laws of growth in trees, and we ought to feel it so.

Now then, I proceed to argue in this manner from what we see in the woods and fields around us; that as they are evidently meant for our delight, and as we always feel them to be beautiful, we may assume that the forms into which their leaves are cast, are indeed types of beauty, not of extreme or perfect, but average beauty. And finding that they invariably terminate more or less in pointed arches, and are not square-headed, I assert the pointed arch to be one of the forms most fitted for perpetual contemplation by the human mind; that it is one of those which never weary, however often repeated; and that therefore, being both the strongest in structure, and a beautiful form (while the square head is both weak in structure, and an ugly form), we are unwise ever to build in any other.

You will find, on the other hand, that the language of the Bible is specifically distinguished from all other early literature, by its delight in natural imagery; and that the dealings of God with His people are calculated peculiarly to awaken this sensibility within them. Out of the monotonous valley of Egypt they are instantly taken into the midst of the mightiest mountain scenery in the peninsula of Arabia; and that scenery is associated in their minds with the immediate manifestation and presence of the Divine Power; so that mountains for ever afterwards become invested with a peculiar sacredness in their minds: while their descendants being placed in what was then one of the loveliest districts upon the earth, full of glorious vegetation, bounded on one side by the sea, on the north by 'that goodly mountain' Lebanon, on the south and east by deserts, whose barrenness enhanced by their contrast the sense of the perfection of beauty in their own land, they became, by these means, and by the touch of God's own hand upon their hearts, sensible to the appeal of natural scenery in a way in which no other people were at the time. And their literature is full of expressions, not only testifying a vivid sense of the power of nature over man, but showing that *sympathy with natural things themselves*, as if they had human souls, which is the especial characteristic of true love of the works of God.

Ruskin: *Lectures on Art and Painting*

9

THE NINETEENTH CENTURY: SCIENCE AND MATERIALISM

The nineteenth century was a period of spiritual and moral crisis, concluding with Nietzsche's prophetic warning concerning 'nihilism' (belief in nothing), and his famous cry 'God is dead'. The German philosophical tradition, initiated by Kant, culminated in the early part of the century with Schopenhauer's pessimistic philosophy which described nature as a godless domain of endless and pointless strife, one in which humanity was inexorably imprisoned. This theme was later to find scientific expression in Darwin's theory of evolution by natural selection, which dispensed with the need for God as a designer of the intricate and seemingly purposeful workings of living things. The image of nature 'red in tooth and claw' (the phrase was the poet Tennyson's) was one which reflected something of the prevailing economic reality of Victorian Britain in which the values of progress and self-reliance were pursued often at the price of social and personal distress on a wide scale. It also reflected, in its ruthless reductionism, the growing confidence of science, under the banner of Positivism, in explaining the operations of the natural world in purely materialistic and rational terms. The theories of the German physicist Helmholtz concerning the nature of energy were not just technical advances within the confines of pure science, but had wide philosophical repercussions, encouraging the view that all the complex workings of nature, including living things and even mind itself, could be explained from within the closed circle of matter and energy. It was this development which inspired the biologist Haeckel to maintain, at the end of the century, that science had virtually solved all the riddles of the universe in purely scientific terms. At the same time, a rearguard action was being fought within science itself to preserve a different view of nature. For example biologists such as Driesch argued that living things could not be reduced to matter and energy, but needed to be explained in terms of a vital, purposeful, non-material principle, a theory called 'vitalism'. And the Russian anarchist/geographer Kropotkin directly confronted the Darwinist trend with his view that evolution is driven as much by mutual aid and co-operation as by strife and competition.

In the following passages by the historian F A Lange (1828–1875), the physicist Hermann Helmholtz (1821–1894), and the biologist Ernst Haeckel (1834–1919) we can see unambiguous expressions of the growing confidence of science in the nineteenth century with its increasingly powerful materialistic view of nature which, by reducing all phenomena to matter and energy, was colonizing the natural world on behalf of human knowledge and industry.

Materialism always rests upon the contemplation of nature; but in our own days it cannot content itself with a possible explanation of natural events by means of its theory: it must take its stand upon scientific research, and it gladly accepts this forum, because it is convinced that here it must win its cause. Many of our Materialists go so far as to represent the philosophy to which they attach themselves as a necessary consequence of the scientific spirit – as a natural result of the enormous development and advance which the natural sciences have attained since the speculative method has been abandoned, and the exact and systematic investigation of facts has taken its place ...

We have seen how in antiquity Materialism remained sterile because it adhered doggedly to its great dogma of atoms and their motion, and had little sense for new and bold ideas. The Idealistic school, on the contrary, especially the Platonists and Pythagoreans, gave antiquity the richest fruits of scientific knowledge.

In modern times an incomparably more favourable account of Materialism can be given as regards its participation in inventions and discoveries. Atomism, which once only led to speculations as to the possibility of phenomena, has become since Gassendi the basis of physical investigation into the actual. The mechanical theory of the world has since Newton gradually dominated our whole apprehension of nature. Thus, if we only leave out of view the 'limits of natural knowledge', Materialism is now not only the result, but, strictly speaking, the very presupposition of all scientific study.

Lange: *The History of Materialism*

No matter what it was called – the *archeus*, the *anima inscia*, the vital force, the healing force of nature, or whatever – the power to develop the body according to plan and to accommodate it suitably to external conditions remained the most basic property of this hypothetical controlling principle postulated by vitalistic theory...

It is apparent, however, that this notion runs directly counter to the law of the conservation of force. If a vital force were to suspend for a time the action of gravity on a body, it could be raised without work to any height desired, and if the action of gravity were subsequently restored, it would perform work of any amount desired. Thus work could be obtained without expense out of nothing...

In reality, however, there is no evidence that the living organism can perform the slightest trace of work without a corresponding consumption of energy. If we consider the work done by animals, we find it similar in every respect to that done by a steam engine. Animals, like machines, can move and do work only if they are continuously supplied with fuel (that is to say, food) and air containing oxygen. Both animals and machines give off this material again in a burned state, and both produce simultaneously heat and work...

If, then, the law of the conservation of force holds good for living beings too, it follows that the physical and chemical forces of the material employed in building up the body are in continuous action without interruption ... Physiologists should thus expect an unconditional conformity of the forces of nature to laws.

Helmholtz: *Selected Writings*

The whole of nature is in causal connection with a unitary process of development and that cosmogenesis consists in an unbroken chain of formations through change. That goes just as much for the processes of an organic nature as for the process of organic beings ... Modern science must completely reject any so called 'creation' of the world ... An anthropological 'Creator' exists just as little as any divinely ordered 'moral' world order.

Haeckel: *Theses for the Organization of Monism*

The idea of the conquest of nature and of life itself by science was a common theme throughout the nineteenth century, but it was a theme which had worrisome undertones, intimations of which appear early on in the century in the prophetic novel of Mary Shelley (1797–1851) where the ambition of science to create a human being leads to disastrous consequences. The name 'Prometheus' in the title refers to the Greek mythical figure who stole fire from the gods to give to humankind, but who was condemned to a terrible punishment for his efforts.

From this day natural philosophy [ie science], and particularly chemistry, in the most comprehensive sense of the term, became nearly my sole occupation. I read with ardour those works, so full of genius and discrimination, which modern enquirers have written on these subjects...

One of the phenomena which particularly attracted my attention was the structure of the human frame, and, indeed, any animal endued with life. Whence, I often asked myself, did the principle of life proceed? It was a bold question, and one which has ever been considered as a mystery; yet with how many things are we on the brink of becoming acquainted, if cowardice or carelessness did not restrain our enquiries. I revolved these circumstances in my mind, and determined thenceforth to apply myself more particularly to those branches of natural philosophy which relate to physiology. Unless I had been animated by an almost supernatural enthusiasm, my application to this study would have been irksome, and almost intolerable. To examine the causes of life, we must first have recourse to death. I became acquainted with the science of anatomy: but this was not sufficient; I must also observe the natural decay and corruption of the human body ... I saw how the fine form of man was degraded and wasted; I beheld the corruption of death succeed to the blooming cheek of life; I saw how the worm inherited the wonders of the eye and brain. I paused, examining and analysing all the minutiae of causation, as exemplified in the change from life to death, and death to life, until from the midst of this darkness a sudden light broke in upon me – a light so brilliant and wondrous, yet so simple, that while I became dizzy with the immensity of the prospect which it illustrated, I was surprised, that among so many men of genius who had directed their enquiries towards the same science, I alone should be reserved to discover so astonishing a secret...

No one can conceive the variety of feelings which bore me onwards like a hurricane, in the first enthusisam of my success. Life and death appeared to me ideal bounds, which I should first break through, and pour a torrent of light into our dark world. A new species would bless me as its creator and source; many happy and excellent natures would owe their being to me. No father could claim the gratitude of his child so completely as I should deserve theirs. Pursuing these reflections, I thought, that if I could bestow animation upon lifeless matter, I might in the process of time (although I now found it impossible) renew life where death had apparently devoted the body to corruption.

These thoughts supported my spirits, while I pursued my undertaking with unremitting ardour. My cheek had grown pale with study, and my person had become emaciated with confinement. Sometimes, on the very brink of certainty, I failed; yet still I clung to the hope which the next day or the next hour might realise. One secret which I alone possessed was the hope to which I had dedicated myself; and the moon gazed on my midnight labours, while, with unrelaxed and breathless eagerness, I pursued nature to her hiding places.

Shelley: *Frankenstein; or, The Modern Prometheus*

One of the main challenges to traditional beliefs about the natural world posed by the advance of science concerned the nature of life: could it be explained in the same terms and by means of the same theories and concepts as the rest of the physical universe, or did it represent something fundamentally different? Hans Driesch (1867–1941) was one of a steadily diminishing band of biologists who argued for the latter.

The main question of Vitalism is not whether the processes of life can properly be called purposive: it is rather the question if the purposiveness in those processes is the result of a special *constellation of factors known already* to the sciences of the inorganic, or if it is the result of an *autonomy* peculiar to the processes themselves. For that there is, as a matter of fact, much that is purposive in vital phenomena is merely an immediate deduction from the definition of the concept of purpose itself, and from the application of this definition to living beings.

In the language of everyday life, we designate as purposive such actions as experience shows to contribute directly or indirectly to a definitely desired end – or of which this is at any rate assumed. I judge all purposiveness in actions from my own standpoint: that is to say, I know for myself when my actions deserve the predicate purposive, because I know my own objects. With this I start. The actions of other men I describe as purposive if I understand the object which they have in view: that is to say, if I can imagine that that object could be my own, and consider them in relation to that object.

But I do not limit the application of the word purposive to the actions of other men: I extend it already in everyday life in two directions: and from this extension arises, on the one hand, the application of the word purposive or teleological to biology in general, and, on the other, the fundamental problem of biology itself.

I describe as purposive a great deal of animal movement, not only in certain of the higher animals whose movements are actually called actions, but also that group of movements which, in view of their constancy and coherence, are usually referred to not as actions but as instincts or reflexes. From these to the movements of plants which turn either towards or away from the light is a very short step, and it is only one step further to describe as purposive also those movements of growth which create out of the germ the complete organisms of animals and plants in a typical succession.

In this way, then, we finally get all phenomena in the living being which can be shown to be directed to a single point, thought of in some sense as an end, subordinated to the *purely descriptive* concept of purposiveness. From what we have said it will be seen that a certain arbitrariness is unavoidable in the designation of any event as teleological, for we can only proceed here by analogy. This arbitrariness, however, is not of any great consequence, as it may be stated once and for all that the term is used at this stage merely to give a certain orientation and nothing more.

We have already said that, in order to describe a process as purposive, it must be connected with the idea of an end: it is thereby implied that the concept of teleology is extended to many processes of very different kinds, and also that it is limited to the organic in the first place, at least in so far as so-called natural objects in the narrower sense are concerned. For it is only in relation to organisms that the possibility of an end thus arbitrarily postulated can be thought of, at any rate without further consideration. This is due, among other things, essentially to the fact that relation to an end implies two things: in the first place, the special adaptation of the process in question to an end (or better, its position in a system of objects thus typically adapted), and secondly, its appearance in an indefinite number of individuals or examples – in short, its unlimited plurality. This is a postulate which in nature is fulfilled in organic natural bodies, and at the first glance only in them. We can therefore describe very many biological processes as purposive.

Driesch: *The History and Theory of Vitalism*

The idea of evolution is one of the most important factors in shaping modern attitudes to the natural world and to humanity's place within it. Charles Darwin (1809–1882) did not discover the idea, but his theory of evolution by natural selection offered a serious challenge to traditional views about humankind's supernatural origins, to its supposed natural pre-eminence over the animals, and to beliefs about the divine origins of the order of nature. The idea of the 'struggle for existence' put paid to earlier ideas about 'universal harmony', and the old 'argument from design' proved especially vulnerable to Darwinism. A rather different image of nature is conjured out of evolutionary theory by the Russian geographer/anarchist Peter Kropotkin (1842–1921).

How will the struggle for existence . . . act in regard to variation? Can the principle of selection, which we have seen is so potent in the hands of man, apply under nature? I think we shall see that it can act most efficiently. Let the endless number of slight variations and individual differences occurring in our domestic productions, and, in a lesser degree, in those under nature, be borne in mind; as well as the strength of the hereditary tendency. Under domestication, it may be truly said that the whole organisation becomes in some degree plastic. But the variability, which we almost universally meet with in our domestic productions, is not directly produced by man; he can neither originate varieties, nor prevent their occurrence; he can only preserve and accumulate such as do occur. Unintentionally he exposes organic beings to new and changing conditions of life, and variability ensues; but similar changes of conditions might and do occur under nature.

Let it also be borne in mind how infinitely complex and close-fitting are the mutual relations of all organic beings to each other and to their physical conditions of life; and consequently what infinitely varied diversities of structure might be of use to each being under changing conditions of life. Can it, then, be thought improbable, seeing that variations useful to man have undoubtedly occurred, that other variations useful in some way to each being in the great and complex battle of life should occur in the course of many successive generations? If such do occur, can we doubt (remembering that many more individuals are born than can possibly survive) that individuals having any advantage, however slight, over others, would have the best chance of surviving and of procreating their kind? On the other hand, we may feel sure that any variation in the least degree injurious would be rigidly destroyed. This preservation of favourable individual differences and variation, and the destruction of those which are injurious, I have called Natural Selection, or the Survival of the Fittest...

Several writers have misapprehended or objected to the term Natural Selection. Some have even imagined that natural selection induces variability, whereas it implies only the preservation of such variations as arise and are beneficial to the being under its conditions of life. No one objects to agriculturists speaking of the potent effects of man's selection; and in this case the individual differences given by nature, which man for some object selects, must of necessity first occur. Others have objected that the term selection implies conscious choice in the animals which become modified; and it has even been urged that, as plants have no volition, natural selection is not applicable to them! In the literal sense of the word, no doubt, natural selection is a false term; but who ever objected to chemists speaking of the elective affinities of the various elements? – and yet an acid cannot strictly be said to elect the base with which it in preference combines...

Authors of the highest eminence seem to be fully satisfied with the view that each species has been independently created. To my mind it accords better with what we know of the laws impressed on matter by the Creator, that the production and extinction of the past and present inhabitants of the world should have been due to secondary causes, like those determining the birth and death of the individual. When I view all beings not as special creations, but as the lineal descendants of some few beings which lived long before the first bed of the Cambrian system was deposited, they seem to me to become ennobled . . .

It is interesting to contemplate a tangled bank, clothed with many plants of many kinds, with birds singing on the bushes, with various insects flitting about, and with worms crawling through the damp earth, and to reflect that these elaborately constructed forms, so different from each other, and dependent on each other in so complex a manner, have all been produced by laws acting around us. These laws, taken in the largest sense, being Growth with Reproduction; inheritance which is almost implied by reproduction; variability from the indirect and direct action of the conditions of life, and from use and disuse: a Ratio of Increase so high as to lead to a Struggle for Life, and as a consequence to Natural Selection, entailing Divergence of Character and the Extinction of less-improved forms. Thus, from the war of nature, from famine and death, the most exalted object which we are capable of conceiving, namely, the production of the higher animals, directly follows. There is grandeur in this view of life, with its several powers, having been originally breathed by the Creator into a few forms or into one; and that, whilst this planet has one cycling on according to the fixed law of gravity, from so simple a beginning endless forms most beautiful and most wonderful have been, and are being evolved.

Darwin: *Origin of Species*

The conception of struggle for existence as a factor of evolution, introduced into science by Darwin and Wallace, has permitted us to embrace an immensely wide range of phenomena in one single generalization, which soon became the very basis of our philosophical, biological, and sociological speculations. An immense variety of facts: – adaptations of function and structure of organic beings to their surroundings; physiological and anatomical evolution; intellectual progress, and moral development itself, which we formerly used to explain by so many different causes, were embodied by Darwin in one general conception. We understood them as continued endeavours – as a struggle against adverse circumstances – for such a development of individuals, races, species and societies, as would result in the greatest possible fullness, variety, and intensity of life. It may be that at the outset Darwin himself was not fully aware of the generality of the factor which he first invoked for explaining one series only of facts relative to the accumulation of individual variations in incipient species. But he foresaw that the term which he was introducing into science would lose its philosophical and its only true meaning if it were to be used in its narrow sense only – that of a struggle between separate individuals for the sheer means of existence. And at the very beginning of his memorable work he insisted upon the term being taken in its 'large and metaphorical sense including dependence of one being on another, and including (which is more important) not only the life of the individual, but success in leaving progeny' ...

As soon as we study animals – not in laboratories and museums only, but in the forest and the prairie, in the steppe and the mountains – we at once perceive that though there is an immense amount of warfare and extermination going on amidst various species, and especially amidst various classes of animals, there is, at the same time, as much, or perhaps even more, of mutual support, mutual aid, and mutual defence amidst animals belonging to the same species or, at least, to the same society. Sociability is as much a law of nature as mutual struggle. Of course it would be extremely difficult to estimate, however roughly, the relative numerical importance of both these series of facts. But if we resort to an indirect test, and ask Nature: 'Who are the fittest: those who are continually at war with each other, or those who support one another?' we at once see that those animals which acquire habits of mutual aid are undoubtedly the fittest. They have more chances to survive, and they attain, in their respective classes, the highest development of intelligence and bodily organization. If the numberless facts which can be brought forward to support this view are taken into account, we may safely say that mutual aid is as much a law of animal life as mutual struggle, but that, as a factor of evo-lution, it most probably has a far greater importance, inasmuch as it favours the development of such habits and characters as insure the maintenance and further development of the species, together with the greatest amount of welfare and enjoyment of life for the individual, with the least waste of energy

Happily enough, competition is not the rule either in the animal world or in mankind. It is limited among animals to

154

exceptional periods, and natural selection finds better fields for its activity. Better conditions are created by the *elimination of competition* by means of mutual aid and mutual support. In the great struggle for life – for the greatest possible fullness and intensity of life with the least waste of energy – natural selection continually seeks out the ways precisely for avoiding competition as much as possible. The ants combine in nests and nations; they pile up their stores, they rear their cattle – and thus avoid competition; and natural selection picks out of the ants' family the species which know best how to avoid competition, with its unavoidably deleterious consequences. Most of our birds slowly move southwards as the winter comes, or gather in numberless societies and undertake long journeys – and thus avoid competition. Many rodents fall asleep when the time comes that competition should set in; while other rodents store food for the winter, and gather in large villages for obtaining the necessary protection when at work. The reindeer, when the lichens are dry in the interior of the continent, migrate towards the sea. Buffaloes cross an immense continent in order to find plenty of food. And the beavers, when they grow numerous on a river, divide into two parties, and go, the old ones down the river, and the young ones up the river – and avoid competition. And when animals can neither fall asleep, nor migrate, nor lay in stores, nor themselves grow their food like the ants, they do what the titmouse does, and what Wallace . . . has so charmingly described: they resort to new kinds of food – and thus, again, avoid competition.

'Don't compete! – competition is always injurious to the species, and you have plenty of resources to avoid it!' That is the *tendency* of nature, not always realized in full, but always present. That is the watchword which comes to us from the bush, the forest, the river, the ocean. 'Therefore combine – practise mutual aid! That is the surest means for giving to each and to all the greatest safety, the best guarantee of existence and progress, bodily, intellectual, and moral.' That is what Nature teaches us; and that is what all those animals which have attained the highest position in their respective classes have done. That is also what man – the most primitive man – has been doing; and that is why man has reached the position upon which we stand now, as we shall see in the subsequent chapters devoted to mutual aid in human societies.

Kropotkin: *Mutual Aid: A Factor of Evolution*

The primary interest of Karl Marx (1818–1883) was not the natural world but the world of economics and politics. Nevertheless he believed that philosophies of nature, while seeming to stand beyond everyday human strife, are in fact shaped by more fundamental attitudes and practices at the social level, and that our relationship with nature has to be understood in the context of historical factors. In his early writings he showed especial concern for the way in which modern modes of production had wrenched humankind painfully out of its hitherto close relationship with nature, a concern with strong Romantic overtones.

For labour, *life activity, productive life* itself, appears to man in the first place merely as a *means* of satisfying a need – the need to maintain physical existence. Yet the productive life is the life of the species. It is life-engendering life. The whole character of a species – its species-character – is contained in the character of its life activity; and free, conscious activity is man's species-character. Life itself appears only as a *means to life.*

The animal is immediately one with its life activity. It does not distinguish itself from it. It is *its life activity.* Man makes his life activity itself the object of his will and of his consciousness. He has conscious life activity. It is not a determination with which he directly merges. Conscious life activity distinguishes man immediately from animal life activity. It is just because of this that he is a species-being. Or it is only because he is a species-being that he is a conscious being, i.e., that his own life is an object for him. Only because of that is his activity free activity. Estranged labour reverses this relationship, so that it is just because man is a conscious being that he makes his life activity, his *essential being*, a mere means to his *existence.*

In creating *a world of objects* by his practical activity, in his *work upon* inorganic nature, man proves himself a conscious species-being, ie, as a being that treats the species as its own essential being, or that treats itself as a species-being. Admittedly animals also produce. They build themselves nests, dwellings, like the bees, beavers, ants, etc. But an animal only produces what it immediately needs for itself or its young. It produces one-sidedly, whilst man produces universally. It produces only under the dominion of immediate physical need, whilst man produces even when he is free from physical need and only truly produces in freedom therefrom. An animal produces only itself, whilst man reproduces the whole of nature. An animal's product belongs immediately to its physical body, whilst man freely confronts his product. An animal forms objects only in accordance with the standard and the need of the species to which it belongs, whilst man knows how to produce in accordance with the standard of every species, and knows how to apply everywhere the inherent standard to the object. Man therefore also forms objects in accordance with the laws of beauty.

It is just in his work upon the objective world, therefore, that man really proves himself to be a *species-being*. This production is his active species-life. Through this production, nature appears as *his* work and his reality. The object of labour is, therefore, the *objectification of man's species-life*: for he duplicates himself not only, as in consciousness, intellectually, but also actively, in reality, and therefore he sees himself in a world that he has created. In tearing away from man the object of his production,therefore, estranged labour tears from him his *species-life*, his real objectivity as a member of the species, and transforms his advantage over animals into the disadvantage that his inorganic body, nature, is taken away from him.

Marx: *Economic and Philosophical Manuscripts*

Thus on the one hand production which is founded on capital creates universal industry – ie surplus labour, value-producing labour; on the other hand it creates a system of general exploitation of natural human attributes, a system of general profitability, whose vehicles seem to be just as much science, as all the physical and intellectual characteristics. There is nothing which can escape, by its own elevated nature or self-justifying characteristics, from this cycle of social production and exchange. Thus capital first creates bourgeois society and the universal appropriation of nature and of social relationships themselves by the members of society. Hence the great civilising influence of capital, its production of a stage of society compared with which all earlier stages appear to be merely *local progress* and idolatry of nature. Nature becomes for the first time simply an object for mankind, purely a matter of utility; it ceases to be recognised as a power in its own right; and the theoretical knowledge of its independent laws appears only as a stratagem designed to subdue it to human requirements, whether as the object of consumption or as the means of production. Pursuing this tendency, capital has pushed beyond national boundaries and prejudices, beyond the deification of nature and the inherited, self-sufficient satisfaction of existing needs confined within well-defined bounds, and the reproduction of the traditional way of life.

Marx: *Grundrisse*

The idea of following closely the ways of nature in pursuit of virtue and happiness, which is an ancient principle that has roots in Eastern as well as Western philosophy, was under severe threat in the materialistic and Utilitarian atmosphere of the nineteenth century. While Marx examined it from the point of view of economic and historical forces, the English philosopher John Stuart Mill (1806–1873) approached the question from a more abstract angle, subjecting it to a close philosophical analysis.

Let us then consider whether we can attach any meaning to the supposed practical maxim of following Nature ... in which Nature stands for that which takes place without human intervention. In Nature as thus understood, is the spontaneous course of things which left to themselves, the rule to be followed in endeavouring to adapt things to our use? But it is evident at once that the maxim, taken in this sense, is not merely, as it is in the other sense, superfluous and unmeaning, but palpably absurd and self-contradictory. For while human action cannot help conforming to Nature in the one meaning of the term, the very aim and object of action is to alter and improve Nature in the other meaning. If the natural course of things were perfectly right and satisfactory, to act at all would be a gratuitous meddling, which as it could not make things better, must make them worse. Or if action at all could be justified, it would only be when indirect obedience to instincts, since these might perhaps be accounted part of the spontaneous order of Nature; but to do anything with forethought and purpose, would be a violation of that perfect order. If the artificial is not better than the natural, to what end are all the arts of life? To dig, to plough, to build, to wear clothes, are direct infringements of the injunction to follow nature.

Accordingly, it would be said by everyone, even of those most under the influence of the feelings which prompt the injunction, that to apply it to such cases as those just spoken of, would be to push it too far. Everybody professes to approve and admire many great triumphs of Art over Nature: the junction by bridges of shores which Nature had made separate, the draining of Nature's marshes, the excavation of her wells, the dragging to light of what she has buried at immense depths in the earth; the turning away of her thunderbolts by lightning rods, of her inundations by embankments, of her ocean by breakwaters. But to commend these and similar feats, is to acknowledge that the ways of Nature are to be conquered, not obeyed: that her powers are often towards man in the position of enemies, from whom he must wrest, by force and ingenuity, what little he can for his own use, and deserves to be applauded when that little is rather more than might be expected from his physical weakness in comparison to those gigantic powers. All praise of Civilization, or Art, or Contrivance, is so much dispraise of Nature; an admission of imperfection, which it is man's business and merit, to be always endeavouring to correct or mitigate...

With regard to the hypothesis, that all natural impulses, all propensities sufficiently universal and sufficiently spontaneous to be capable of passing for instincts, must exist for good ends, and ought to be only regulated, not repressed; this is of course true of the majority of them, for the species could not have continued to exist unless most of its inclinations had been directed to things needful or useful for its preservation. But unless the instincts can be reduced to a very small number indeed, it must be allowed that we have also bad instincts which it should be the aim of education not simply to regulate but to extirpate, or rather (what can be done even to an instinct) to starve them by disuse. Those who are inclined to multiply the number of instincts, usually include among them one which they call destructiveness: an instinct to destroy for destruction's sake. I can conceive no good reason for preserving this, no more than another propensity which if not an instinct is very like one, what has been called the instinct of domination; a delight in exercising despotism, in holding other beings in subjection to our will. The man who takes pleasure in the mere exertion of authority, apart from the purpose for which it is to be employed, is the last person in whose hands one would willingly entrust it. Again, there are persons who are cruel by character, or, as the phrase is, naturally cruel; who have a real pleasure in inflicting, or seeing the infliction of pain. This kind of cruelty is not mere hard heartedness, absence of pity or remorse; it is a positive thing; a particular kind of voluptuous excitement. The East, and Southern Europe, have afforded, and probably still afford, abundant examples of this hateful propensity. I suppose it will be granted that this is not one of the natural inclinations which it would be wrong to suppress. The only question would be whether it is not a duty to suppress the man himself along with it.

But even if it were true that every one of the elementary impulses of human nature has its good side, and may by a sufficient amount of artificial training be made more useful than hurtful; how little would this amount to, when it must in any case be admitted that without such training all of them, even those which are necessary to our preservation, would fill the world with misery, making human life an exaggerated likeness of the odious scene of violence and tyranny which is exhibited by the rest of the animal kingdom, except in so far as tamed and disciplined by man. There, indeed, those who flatter themselves with the notion of reading the purposes of the Creator in his works, ought in consistency to have seen grounds for inferences from which they have shrunk. If there are any marks at all of special design in creation, one of the things most evidently designed is that a large proportion of all animals should pass their existence in tormenting and devouring other animals. They have been lavishly fitted out with the instruments necessary for that purpose; their strongest instincts impel them to it, and many of them seem to have been constructed incapable of supporting themselves by any other food. If a tenth part of the pains which have been expended in finding benevolent adaptations in all nature, had been employed in collecting evidence to blacken the character of the Creator, what scope for comment would not have been found in the entire existence of the lower animals, divided, with scarcely an exception, into devourers and devoured, and a prey to a thousand ills from which they are denied the faculties necessary for protecting themselves! If we are not obliged to believe the animal creation to be the work of a demon, it is because we need not suppose it to have been made by a Being of infinite power. But if imitation of the Creator's will as revealed in nature, were applied as a rule of action in this case, the most atrocious enormities of the worst men would be more than justified by the apparent intention of Providence that throughout all animated nature the strong should prey upon the weak...

Conformity to nature, has no connection whatever with right and wrong. The idea can never be fitly introduced into ethical discussions at all, except, occasionally and partially, into the question of degrees of culpability. To illustrate this point, let us consider the phrase by which the greatest intensity of condemnatory feeling is conveyed in connection with the idea of nature – the word unnatural. That a thing is unnatural, in any precise meaning which can be attached to the word, is no argument for its being blamable; since the most criminal actions are to a being like man, not more unnatural than most of the virtues. The acquisition of virtue has in all ages been accounted a work of labour and difficulty, while the *descensus Averni* on the contrary is of proverbial facility: and it assuredly requires in most persons a greater conquest over a greater number of natural inclinations to become eminently virtuous than transcendently vicious. But if an action, or an inclination, has been decided on other grounds to be blamable, it may be a circumstance in aggravation that it is unnatural, that is, repugnant to some strong feeling usually found in human beings; since the bad propensity, whatever it be, has afforded evidence of being both strong and deeply rooted, by having overcome that repugnance. This presumption of course fails if the individual never had the repugnance: and the argument, therefore, is not fit to be urged unless the feeling which is violated by the act, is not only justifiable and reasonable, but is one which it is blamable to be without.

The corresponding plea in extenuation of a culpable act because it was natural, or because it was prompted by a natural feeling, never, I think, ought to be admitted. There is hardly a bad action ever perpetrated which is not perfectly natural, and the motives to which are not perfectly natural feelings. In the eye of reason, therefore, this is no excuse, but it is quite 'natural' that it should be so in the eyes of the multitude; because the meaning of the expression is, that they have a fellow feeling with the offender. When they say that something which they cannot help admitting to be blamable, is nevertheless natural, they mean that they can imagine the possibility of their being themselves tempted to commit it. Most people have a considerable amount of indulgence towards all acts of which they feel a possible source within themselves, reserving their rigour for those which, though perhaps really less bad, they cannot in any way understand how it is possible to commit. If an action convinces them (which it often does on very inadequate grounds) that the person who does it must be a being totally unlike themselves, they are seldom particular in examining the precise degree of blame due to it, or even if blame is properly due to it at all. They measure the degree of guilt by the strength of their antipathy; and hence differences of opinion, and even differences of taste, have been objects of as intense moral abhorrence as the most atrocious crimes.

Mill: *Nature*

The American pragmatist philosopher William James (1842–1910) is also concerned in the following passage to probe some of the philosophical assumptions that underlie our views about nature, specifically the distinction between a 'monist' and a 'pluralistic' outlook – is the universe in the final analysis a single indivisible whole or a multiplicity of phenomena? – an issue which has been at the heart of many of the debates about nature over the centuries.

But what at bottom is meant by calling the universe many or by calling it one?

Pragmatically interpreted, pluralism or the doctrine that it is many means only that the sundry parts of reality *may be externally related*. Everything you can think of, however vast or inclusive, has on the pluralistic view a genuinely 'external' environment of some sort or amount. Things are 'with' one another in many ways, but nothing includes everything, or dominates over everything. The word 'and' trails along after every sentence. Something always escapes. 'Ever not quite' has to be said of the best attempts made anywhere in the universe at attaining all-inclusiveness. The pluralistic world is thus more like a federal republic than like an empire or a kingdom. However much may be collected, however much may report itself as present at any effective centre of consciousness or action, something else is self-governed and absent and unreduced to unity.

Monism, on the other hand, insists that when you come down to reality as such, to the reality of realities, everything is present to *everything* else in one vast instantaneous co-implicated completeness – nothing can in *any* sense, functional or substantial, be really absent from anything else, all things interpenetrate and telescope together in the great total conflux.

For pluralism, all that we are required to admit as the constitution of reality is what we ourselves find empirically realized in every minimum of finite life. Briefly it is this, that nothing real is absolutely simple, that every smallest bit of experience is a *multum in parvo* plurally related, that each relation is one aspect, character, or function, way of its being taken, or way of its taking something else; and that a bit of reality when actively engaged in one of these relations is not *by that very fact* engaged in all the other relations simultaneously. The relations are not *all* what the French call *solidaires* with one another. Without losing its identity a thing can either take up or drop another thing, like the log I spoke of, which by taking up new carriers and dropping old ones can travel anywhere with a light escort.

For monism, on the contrary, everything, whether we realize it or not, drags the whole universe along with itself and drops nothing. The log starts and arrives with all its carriers supporting it. If a thing were once disconnected, it could never be connected again, according to monism. The pragmatic difference between the two systems is thus a definite one. It is just thus, that if a is once out of sight of b or out of touch with it, or, more briefly, 'out' of it at all, then, according to monism, it must always remain so, they can never get together; whereas pluralism admits that on another occasion they may work together, or in some way be connected again. Monism allows for no such things as 'other occasions' in reality – in *real* or absolute reality, that is.

The difference I try to describe amounts, you see, to nothing more than the difference between what I formerly called the each-form and the all-form of reality. Pluralism lets things really exist in the each-form or distributively. Monism thinks that the all-form or collective-unit form is the only form that is rational. The all-form allows of no taking up and dropping of connexions, for in the all the parts are essentially and eternally co-implicated. In the each-form, on the contrary, a thing may be connected by intermediary things, with a thing with which it has no immediate or essential connexion. It is thus at all times in many possible connexions which are not necessarily actualized at the moment. They depend on which actual path of inter-mediation it may functionally strike into: the word 'or' names a genuine reality. Thus, as I speak here, I may look ahead *or* to the right *or* to the left, and in either case the intervening space and air and ether enable me to see the faces of a different portion of this audience. My being here is independent of any one set of these faces...

Here, then, you have the plain alternative, and the full mystery of the difference between pluralism and monism, as clearly as I can set it forth on this occasion. It packs up into a nutshell: – Is the manyness in oneness that indubitably char- acterizes the world we inhabit, a property only of the absolute whole of things, so that you must postulate that one-enormous- whole indivisibly as the *prius* of there being any many at all – in other words, start with the rationalistic block universe, entire, unmitigated, and complete? – or can the finite elements have their own aboriginal forms of manyness in oneness, and where they have no immediate oneness still be continued into one another by intermediary terms – each one of these terms being one with its next neighbors, and yet the total 'oneness' never getting absolutely complete?

James: *A Pluralistic Universe*

In the following passage the German philosopher Friedrich Nietzsche (1844–1900) sets out to demolish a number of the dearly held myths about nature, all of which have been exemplified in the present book: that it is a machine, that it is a living being, that it demonstrates purposefulness, that it bears the marks of beauty and harmony.

Let us beware of thinking the world is a living being. Whither should it spread itself? What should it nourish itself with? How could it grow and multiply? We know indeed more or less what the organic is: and shall we interpret the unspeakably derivative, late, rare, chance phenomena which we perceive only on the surface of the earth into the essential, universal, eternal, as they do who call the universe an organism? I find that disgusting. Let us likewise beware of believing the universe is a machine; it is certainly not constructed so as to perform some operation, we do it far too great honour with the word 'machine'. Let us beware of presupposing that something so orderly as the cyclical motions of our planetary neighbours are the general and universal case; even a glance at the Milky Way gives rise to doubt whether there may not exist far more crude and contradictory motions, likewise stars with eternally straight trajectories and the like. The astral order in which we live is an exception; this order and the apparent permanence which is conditional upon it is in its turn made possible by the exception of exceptions: the formation of the organic. The total nature of the world is, on the other hand, to all eternity chaos, not in the sense that necessity is lacking but in that order, structure, form, beauty, wisdom and whatever other human aesthetic notions we may have are lacking. Judged from the viewpoint of our reason, the unsuccessful cases are far and away the rule, the exceptions are not the secret objective, and the whole contraption repeats its theme, which can never be called a melody, over and over again to eternity – and ultimately even the term 'unsuccessful case' is already a humanization which contains a reproof. But how can we venture to reprove or praise the universe! Let us beware of attributing to it heartlessness and unreason or their opposites: it is neither perfect nor beautiful nor noble, and has no desire to become any of these; it is by no means striving to imitate mankind! It is quite impervious to all our aesthetic and moral judgements! It has likewise no impulse to self-preservation or impulses of any kind; neither does it know any laws. Let us beware of saying there are laws in nature. There are only necessities: there is no one to command, no one to obey, no one to transgress. When you realize that there are no goals or objectives, then you realize, too, that there is no chance: for only in a world of objectives does the word 'chance' have any meaning. Let us beware of saying that death is the opposite of life. The living being is only a species of the dead, and a very rare species.

Nietzsche: *The Gay Science*

10

THE TWENTIETH CENTURY: POSITIVISM AND ITS RIVALS

The trends and conflicts of the nineteenth century continue unresolved into the twentieth, and as we move into the twenty-first century these conflicts have come to assume proportions which seem to threaten life itself. One big difference, though, is that the scientific and technological triumphalism of the earlier period, which was then a characteristic of the advanced Western nations, has come, through European imperialism and commercial expansion, to dominate the whole globe. Positivism is philosophically perhaps most typical of the first half of our century, which is roughly the limit of the scope of this chapter. It is a philosophy which celebrates most powerfully the sense of the domination of nature through the power of the human mind. According to this way of thinking, any attitude to nature other than the strictly scientific is consigned to the subjective realms of emotion and poetry, and vitalism is finally expunged from the scientific agenda. Existentialism, in its concern for the subjective world of human consciousness and freedom, is in some ways the diametric opposite of Positivism, yet it shares with it the idea that values arise from human beings and that nature is entirely neutral, even indifferent to human concerns. These two attitudes coalesce in the writings of Bertrand Russell for whom nature is nothing but a chance collocation of atoms, devoid of meaning, in which man 'snatches a few brief moments of life before Death's inexorable decree', and where science offers nothing but 'a firm foundation of unyielding despair'. The image of nature as a machine still holds sway here, and from a purely instrumental point of view has proved most profitable. But at the same time a subversive sub-culture has sought to keep alive and even to amplify a more traditional and more metaphysical conception of nature. The French philosopher Bergson and the Anglo-American philosopher Whitehead are representative of such an alternative view of nature, one which emphasizes creativity rather than deterministic mechanism, process rather than substance, the whole rather than the parts. This view links together the human and the natural realms, and pictures the world as an ever-interacting flow of energy, in a way which was characterised by the South African philosopher-statesman Jan

Smuts as 'holistic'. This term has become widely used in the second half of the century to represent a new, if traditionally based, view of nature, one which has arisen in part from developments within science itself, and which is vaunted by its supporters to overcome the limiting and dispiriting aspects of Positivistic and mechanistic philosophies of nature. But that is a different story.

Moritz Schlick (1882–1936) was the leader of a group of scientists and philosophers known as the Vienna Circle who, during the 1920s and '30s, set out the principles of logical Positivism according to which the meanings of words are tied to empirical verification. Schlick concluded from this that vitalistic terms such as 'purpose', when applied to the natural world, are strictly speaking meaningless; hence his use of 'scare quotes' for this word.

The concepts most frequently adduced in connection with the explanation of organic life are those of purpose and purposiveness.

The processes of metabolism and regeneration, and the adaptation of the various organs and functions to one another, appear extremely 'purposive'. They all seem to be directed toward a supreme goal, sometimes directly, sometimes in a roundabout fashion. The goal is the preservation and development of the living organisms, both of the individual and of the species. It is this purposiveness of the organisms and their functions which represents itself to many thinkers as the genuine miracle of life that distinguishes it from the lifeless. Hence it is only too understandable that reference to the teleology of organic life constituted throughout the ages the strongest argument in favor of the autonomy of organic life.

A careful analysis of the concepts is indispensable for a clarification of the questions surrounding this issue. First of all, what are we to understand by 'purpose'? No doubt this is a concept derived from human action. What we call purpose is nothing but the anticipated outcome of our actions. In each action that is consciously carried out, the goal of the action is envisaged by consciousness. Hence, the existence of a purpose presupposes the presence of a consciousness capable of representation. Wherever consciousness is absent or wherever a conceptual system is utilized which does not refer to consciousness, it is therefore impossible to speak of 'purposes' in the original sense of this word. In accordance with what we said before, this term should really be banished from biology right from the start. If it is to be retained at all, then this can be done only by assigning a new meaning to the term 'purpose'. Such a procedure should be followed only in case of extreme need, for any such change in the meaning of a word only too easily produces much misunderstanding.

Schlick: *The Philosophy of Organic Life*

In the following passages by the French biologist Jacques Monod (1910–1976) and the English philosopher Bertrand Russell (1872–1970) we can see typical examples of the way in which, under the influence of the prevailing Positivistic outlook, twentieth-century thinkers have sought remorselessly to draw the inevitable conclusions about humanity's place in the natural world from the scientific ideas of the previous century.

We say that [mutations] are accidental, due to chance. And since they constitute the *only* possible source of modifications in the genetic text, itself the *sole* repository of the organism's hereditary structures, it necessarily follows that chance *alone* is the source of every innovation, of all creation in the biosphere. Pure chance, absolutely free but blind, at the very root of the stupendous edifice of evolution: this central concept of modern biology is no longer one among other possible or even conceivable hypotheses. It is today the *sole* conceivable hypothesis, the only one compatible with observed and tested fact. And nothing warrants the supposition (or the hope) that conceptions about this should, or ever could, be revised.

There is no scientific position, in any of the sciences, more destructive of anthropocentrism than this one, and no other more unacceptable to the intensely teleonomic creatures that we are. So for every vitalist or animist ideology this is the concept or rather the spectre to be exorcised at all costs...

Modern societies accepted the treasures and the power offered them by science. But they have not accepted – they have scarcely even heard – its profounder message: the defining of a new and unique source of truth, and the demand for a thorough revision of ethical premises, for a complete break with the animist tradition, the definitive abandonment of the 'old covenant', the necessity of forging a new one. Armed with all the powers, enjoying all the riches they owe to science, our societies are still trying to live by and to teach systems of values already blasted at the root by science itself...

[Man] must at last awake out of his millennary dream and discover his total solitude, his fundamental isolation. He must realize that, like a gypsy, he lives on the boundary of an alien world; a world that is deaf to his music, and as indifferent to his hopes as it is to his suffering or his crimes.

Monod: *Chance and Necessity*

To Dr Faustus in his study Mephistopheles told the history of the Creation, saying:

'The endless praises of the choirs of angels had begun to grow wearisome; for, after all, did He not deserve their praise? Had He not given them endless joy? Would it not be more amusing to obtain undeserved praise, to be worshipped by beings whom He tortured? He smiled inwardly, and resolved that the great drama should be performed.

'For countless ages the hot nebula whirled aimlessly through space. At length it began to take shape, the central mass threw off planets, the planets cooled, boiling seas and burning mountains heaved and tossed, from black masses of cloud hot sheets of rain deluged the barely solid crust. And now the first germ of life grew in the depths of the ocean, and developed rapidly in the fructifying warmth into vast forest trees, huge ferns springing from the damp mold, sea monsters breeding, fighting, devouring, and passing away. And from the monsters, as the play unfolded itself, Man was born, with the power of thought, the knowledge of good and evil, and the cruel thirst for worship. And Man saw that all is passing in this mad, monstrous world, that all is struggling to snatch, at any cost, a few brief moments of life before Death's inexorable decree. And Man said: "There is a hidden purpose, could we but fathom it, and the purpose is good; for we must reverence something, and in the visible world there is nothing worthy of reverence." And Man stood aside from the struggle resolving that God intended harmony to come out of chaos by human efforts. And when he followed the instincts which God had transmitted to him from his ancestry of beasts of prey, he called it Sin, and asked God to forgive him. But he doubted whether he could be justly forgiven, until he invented a divine Plan by which God's wrath was to have been appeased. And seeing the present was bad, he made it yet worse, that thereby the future might be better. And he gave God thanks for the strength that enabled him to forgo even the joys that were possible. And God smiled; and when he saw that Man had become perfect in renunciation and worship, he sent another sun through the sky, which crashed into Man's sun; and all returned again to nebula.

' "Yes," he murmured, "it was a good play; I will have it performed again." '

Such, in outline, but even more purposeless, more void of meaning, is the world which Science presents for our belief. Amid such a world, if anywhere, our ideals henceforward must find a home. That Man is the product of causes which had no prevision of the end they were achieving; that his origin, his growth, his hopes and fears, his loves and his beliefs, are but the outcome of accidental collocations of atoms; that no fire, no heroism, no intensity of thought and feeling, can preserve an individual life beyond the grave; that all the labours of the ages, all the devotion, all the inspiration, all the noonday brightness of human genius, are destined to extinction in the vast death of the solar system, and that the whole temple of Man's achievement must inevitably be buried beneath the debris of a universe in ruins – all these things, if not quite beyond dispute, are yet so nearly certain, that no philosophy which rejects them can hope to stand. Only within the scaffolding of these truths, only on the firm foundation of unyielding despair, can the soul's habitation henceforth be safely built.

How, in such an alien and inhuman world, can so powerless a creature as Man preserve his aspirations untarnished? A strange mystery it is that Nature, omnipotent but blind, in the revolutions of her secular hurryings through the abysses of space, has brought forth at last a child, subject still to her power, but gifted with sight, with knowledge of good and evil, with the capacity of judging all the works of his unthinking Mother. In spite of Death, the mark and seal of parental control, Man is yet free, during his brief years, to examine, to criticise, to know, and in imagination to create. To him alone, in the world with which he is acquainted, this freedom belongs; and in this lies his superiority to the resistless forces that control his outward life.

Russell: 'A Free Man's Worship'

Starting not from science but from human consciousness and the human condition, the French Existentialist philosopher Jean-Paul Sartre (1905–1980) arrived at a conclusion similar to that of Monod and Russell, namely that nature has no value except that which we project on to it. The sense of the world's absurdity obdurately confronts human freedom, and is experienced through mentally stripping the world of its customary veneer of words and concepts.

I was sitting, stooping forward, head bowed, alone in front of this black, knotty mass, entirely beastly, which frightened me. Then I had this vision.

It left me breathless. Never, until these last few days, had I understood the meaning of 'existence'. I was like the others, like the ones walking along the seashore, all dressed in their spring finery. I said, like them, 'The ocean *is* green; that white speck up there *is* a seagull,' but I didn't feel that it existed or that the seagull was an existing seagull; usually existence hides itself. It is there, around us, in us, it is *us*, you can't say two words without mentioning it, but you can never touch it. When I believed I [*sic*] was thinking about it, I must believe that I was thinking nothing, my head was empty, or there was just one word in my head, the word 'to be'. Or else I was thinking ... how can I explain it? I was thinking of *belonging*, I was telling myself that the sea belonged to the class of green objects, or that the green was a part of the quality of the sea. Even when I looked at things, I was miles from dreaming that they existed: they looked like scenery to me. I picked them up in my hands, they served me as tools, I foresaw their resistance. But that all happened on the surface. If anyone had asked me what existence was, I would have answered, in good faith, that it was nothing, simply an empty form which was added to external things without changing anything in their nature. And then all of a sudden, there it was, clear as day: existence had suddenly unveiled itself. It had lost the harmless look of an abstract category; it was the very paste of things, this root was kneaded into existence. Or rather the root, the park gates, the bench, the sparse grass, all that had vanished: the diversity of things, their individuality, were only an appearance, a veneer. This veneer had melted, leaving soft, monstrous masses, all in disorder – naked, in a frightful, obscene nakedness ...

The word absurdity is coming to life under my pen; a little while ago, in the garden, I couldn't find it, but neither was I looking for it: I didn't need it: I thought without words, on things, *with* things. Absurdity was not an idea in my head, or the sound of a voice, only this long serpent dead at my feet, this wooden serpent. Serpent or claw or root or vulture's talon, what difference does it make. And without formulating anything clearly, I understood that I had found the key to Existence, the key to my Nauseas, to my own life. In fact, all that I could grasp beyond that returns to this fundamental absurdity. Absurdity: another word; I struggle against words; down there I touched the thing. But I wanted to fix the absolute character of this absurdity here. A movement, an event in the tiny coloured world of men is only relatively absurd: by relation to the accompanying circumstances. A madman's ravings, for example, are absurd in relation to the situation in which he finds himself, but not in relation to his delirium. But a little while ago I made an experiment with the absolute or the absurd. This root – there was nothing in relation to which it was absurd. Oh, how can I put it in words? Absurd: in relation to the stones, the tufts of yellow grass, the dry mud, the tree, the sky, the green benches. Absurd, irreducible; nothing – not even a profound, secret upheaval of nature – could explain it. Evidently I did not know everything, I had not seen the seeds sprout, or the tree grow. But faced with this great wrinkled paw, neither ignorance nor knowledge was important: the world of explanations and reasons is not the world of existence. A circle is not absurd, it is clearly explained by the rotation of a straight segment around one of its extremities. But neither does a circle exist. This root, on the other hand, existed in such a way that I could not explain it. Knotty, inert, nameless, it fascinated me, filled my eyes, brought me back unceasingly to its own existence. In vain to repeat: 'This is a root' – it didn't work any more. I saw clearly that you could not pass from its function as a root, as a breathing pump, to *that*, to this hard and compact skin of a sea lion, to this oily, callous, headstrong look. The function explained nothing: it allowed you to understand generally that it was a root, but not *that one* at all. This root, with its colour, shape, its congealed movement, was . . . below all explanation.

Sartre: *Nausea*

Simone de Beauvoir (1908–1986) was close to Sartre both personally and philosophically, nevertheless in her seminal work on woman she offers an image of an adolescent girl's intimate relationship with nature – one of liberation and fulfilment – which is quite different from Sartre's alienating picture, and points to a theme in later feminist writings which argues that the West's exploitative attitude to nature is gender-related.

[How] splendid a refuge the adolescent girl finds in the fields and woods. At home, mother, law, customs, routine hold sway, and she would fain escape these aspects of her past; she would in her turn become a sovereign subject. But, as a member of society, she enters upon adult life only in becoming a woman; she pays for her liberation by an abdication. Whereas among plants and animals she is a human being; she is freed at once from her family and from the males – a subject, a free being. She finds in the secret places of the forest a reflection of the solitude of her soul and in the wide horizons of the plains a tangible image of her transcendence; she is herself this limitless territory, this summit flung up towards heaven; she can follow these roads that lead towards the unknown future, she will follow them; seated on the hilltop, she is mistress of the world's riches, spread out at her feet, offered for the taking. In the rush of water, the shimmer of light, she feels a presentiment of the joys, the tears, the ecstasies she has not yet known; the ripples on the pool, the dappled sunlight, give vague promise of the adventurings of her own heart.

Scents and colours speak a mysterious language, but one word sounds out triumphantly clear; the word *life*. Existence is not merely an abstract destiny set down in city records; it is the rich fleshly future. To have a body no longer seems a blemish to be ashamed of; in the desires that under the maternal eye the girl repudiates, she can recognise the sap that rises in the trees; she is no longer accursed, she lays claim proudly to her kinship with the leaves and flowers; she crumples a corolla, and she knows that one day a living prey will fill her empty hands. The flesh is no longer a defilement: it means joy and beauty. At one with earth and sky, the young girl is that vague breath which animates and kindles the universe, and she is each sprig of heather; an organism rooted in the soil and in infinite consciousness, she is at once spirit and life; her being is imperious and triumphant like that of the earth itself.

de Beauvoir: *The Second Sex*

─────────────

The French philosopher Henri Bergson (1859–1941), who achieved considerable acclaim in the early years of this century before Logical Positivism and Existentialism caught on, put forward an evolutionary philosophy which, with its idea that the universe is essentially creative, and therefore more like an organism than a machine, provided a counterblast to the reductionist materialism of the nineteenth century.

The neo-Darwinians are probably right, we believe, when they teach that the essential causes of variation are the differences inherent in the germ borne by the individual, and not the experiences or behaviour of the individual in the course of his career. Where we fail to follow these biologists, is in regarding the differences inherent in the germ as purely accidental and individual. We cannot help believing that these differences are the development of an impulsion which passes from germ to germ across the individuals, that they are therefore not pure accidents, and that they might well appear at the same time, in the same form, in all the representatives of the same species, or at least in a certain number of them. Already, in fact, the theory of *mutations* is modifying Darwinism profoundly on this point. It asserts that at a given moment, after a long period, the entire species is beset with a tendency to change. The *tendency to change*, therefore, is not accidental. True, the change itself would be accidental, since the mutation works, according to De Vries, in different directions in the different representatives of the species. But, first we must see if the theory is confirmed by many other vegetable species (De Vries has verified it only by the *Oenothera Lamarckiana*), and then there is the possibility, as we shall explain further on, that the part played by chance is much greater in the variation of plants than in that of animals, because, in the vegetable world, function does not depend so strictly on form. Be that as it may, the neo-Darwinians are inclined to admit that the periods of mutation are determinate. The direction of the mutation may therefore be so as well, at least in animals, and to the extent we shall have to indicate.

We thus arrive at a hypothesis like Eimer's, according to which the variations of different characters continue from generation to generation in definite directions. This hypothesis seems plausible to us, within the limits in which Eimer himself retains it. Of course, the evolution of the organic world cannot be predetermined as a whole. We claim, on the contrary, that the spontaneity of life is manifested by a continual creation of new forms succeeding others. But this indetermination cannot be complete; it must leave a certain part to determination. An organ like the eye, for example, must have been formed by just a continual changing in a definite direction. Indeed, we do not see how otherwise to explain the likeness of structure of the eye in species that have not the same history. Where we differ from Eimer is in his claim that combinations of physical and chemical causes are enough to secure the result. We have tried to prove, on the contrary, by the example of the eye, that if there is 'orthogenesis' here, a psychological cause intervenes.

Certain neo-Lamarckians do indeed resort to a cause of a psychological nature. There, to our thinking, is one of the most solid positions of neo-Lamarckism. But if this cause is nothing but the conscious effort of the individual, it cannot operate in more than a restricted number of cases – at most in the animal world, and not at all in the vegetable kingdom. Even in animals, it will act only on points which are under the direct or indirect control of the will. And even where it does act, it is not clear how it could compass a change so profound as an increase of complexity: at most this would be conceivable if the acquired characters were regularly transmitted so as to be added together; but this transmission seems to be the exception rather than the rule. A hereditary change in a definite direction, which continues to accumulate and add to itself so as to build up a more and more complex machine, must certainly be related to some sort of effort, far more independent of circumstances, an effort common to most representatives of the same species, inherent in the germs they bear rather than in their substance alone, an effort thereby assured of being passed on to their descendants.

So we come back, by a somewhat roundabout way, to the idea we started from, that of an *original impetus* of life, passing from one generation of germs to the following generation of germs through the developed organisms which bridge the interval between the generations. This impetus, sustained right along the lines of evolution among which it gets divided, is the fundamental cause of variations, at least of those that are regularly passed on, that accumulate and create new species. In general, when species have begun to diverge from a common stock, they accentuate their divergence as they progress in their evolution. Yet, in certain definite points, they may evolve identically; in fact, they must do so if the hypothesis of a common impetus be accepted. This is just what we shall have to show now in a more precise way, by the same example we have chosen, the formation of the eye in molluscs and vertebrates. The idea of an 'original impetus', moreover, will thus be made clearer.

Bergson: *Creative Evolution*

Bergson's influence can be found in the thinking of Alfred North Whitehead (1861–1947) whose 'process philosophy' was also aimed at elaborating an organicist model of nature, and in replacing the concept of 'substance' with that of 'event'. This idea was developed by the American philosopher/theologian Charles Hartshorne (1897–) into Process Theology according to which God is not outside the world but a participant in the process of cosmic evolution.

The doctrine which I am maintaining is that the whole concept of materialism only applies to very abstract entities, the products of logical discernment. The concrete enduring entities are organisms, so that the plan of the *whole* influences the very characters of the various subordinate organisms which enter into it. In the case of an animal, the mental states enter into the plan of the total organism and thus modify the plans of the successive subordinate organisms until the ultimate smallest organisms, such as electrons, are reached. Thus an electron within a living body is different from an electron outside it, by reason of the plan of the body. The electron blindly runs either within or without the body; but it runs within the body in accordance with its character within the body; that is to say, in accordance with the general plan of the body, and this plan includes the mental state. But the principle of modification is perfectly general throughout nature, and represents no property peculiar to living bodies. In subsequent lectures it will be explained that this doctrine involves the abandonment of the traditional scientific materialism, and the substitution of an alternative doctrine of organism.

I shall not discuss Mill's determinism, as it lies outside the scheme of these lectures. The foregoing discussion has been directed to secure that either determinism or free will shall be of some relevance, unhampered by the difficulties introduced by materialistic mechanism, or by the compromise of vitalism. I would term the doctrine of these lectures, the theory of *organic mechanism*. In this theory, the molecules may blindly run in accordance with the general laws, but the molecules differ in their intrinsic characters according to the general organic plans of the situations in which they find themselves...

I have also sketched an alternative philosophy of science in which *organism* takes the place of *matter*. For this purpose, the mind involved in the materialist theory dissolves into a function of organism. The psychological field then exhibits what an event is in itself. Our bodily event is an unusually complex type of organism and consequently includes cognition. Further, space and time, in their most concrete signification, become the locus of events. An organism is the realisation of a definite shape of value. The emergence of some actual value depends on limitation which excludes neutralising cross-lights. Thus an event is a matter of fact which by reason of its limitation is a value for itself; but by reason of its very nature it also requires the whole universe in order to be itself.

Whitehead: *Science and the Modern World*

God orders the universe, according to panentheism [God in everything], by taking into his own life all the currents of feeling in existence. He is the most irresistible of influences precisely because he is himself the most open to influence. In the depths of their hearts all creatures (even those able to 'rebel' against him) defer to God because they sense him as the one who alone is adequately moved by what moves them. He alone not only knows but feels (the only adequate knowledge, where feeling is concerned) how they feel, and he finds his own joy in sharing their lives, lived according to their own free decisions, not fully anticipated by any detailed plan of his own. Yet the extent to which they can be permitted to work out their own plan depends on the extent to which they can echo or imitate on their own level the divine sensitiveness to the needs and precious freedom of all. In this vision of a deity who is not a supreme autocrat, but a universal agent of 'persuasion', whose 'power is the worship he inspires' (Whitehead), that is, flows from the intrinsic appeal of his infinitely sensitive and tolerant relativity, by which all things are kept moving in orderly toge-therness, we may find help in facing our task of today, the task of contributing to the democratic self-ordering of a world whose members not even the supreme orderer reduces to mere subjects with the sole function of obedience.

Hartshorne: *The Divine Relativity*

In about the same period and under the same influence, the South African Jan Smuts (1870–1950) was also expounding an organicist philosophy, in the course of which he coined the word 'holism', a term which has played a central role in much subsequent discussion on environmental and ecological questions.

Both matter and life consist of unit structures whose ordered grouping produces natural wholes which we call bodies or organisms. This character of 'wholeness' meets us everywhere and points to something fundamental in the universe. Holism ... is the term here coined for this fundamental factor operative towards the creation of the universe. Its character is both general and specific or concrete, and it satisfies our double requirement for a natural evolutionary starting-point.

Wholes are not mere artificial constructions of thought; they point to something real in the universe, and Holism is a real operative factor, a *vera causa*. There is behind Evolution no mere vague creative impulse or *Élan vital*, but something quite definite and specific in its operation, and thus productive of the real concrete character of cosmic Evolution. The idea of wholes and wholeness should therefore not be confined to the bio-logical domain; it covers both inorganic substances and the highest manifestations of the human spirit. Taking a plant or animal as a type of a whole, we notice the fundamental holistic characters as a unity of parts which is so close and intense as to be more than the sum of its parts; which not only gives a particular conformation or structure to the parts, but so relates and determines them in their synthesis that their functions are altered; the synthesis affects and determines the parts, so that they function towards the 'whole'; and the whole and the parts therefore reciprocally influence and determine each other, and appear more or less to merge their individual characters: the whole is in the parts and the parts are in the whole, and this synthesis of whole and parts is reflected in the holistic character of the functions of the parts as well as of the whole.

There is a progressive grading of this holistic synthesis in Nature, so that we pass from (*a*) mere physical mixtures, where the structure is almost negligible, and the parts largely preserve their separate characters and activities or functions, to (*b*) chemical compounds, where the structure is more synthetic and the activities and functions of the parts are strongly influenced by the new structure and can only with difficulty be traced to the individual parts; and, again, to (*c*) organisms, where a still more intense synthesis of elements has been effected, which impresses the parts or organs far more intimately with a unified character, and a system of central control, regulation and co-ordination of all the parts and organs arises; and from organism, again, on to (*d*) Minds or psychical organs, where the Central Control acquires consciousness and a freedom and creative power of the most far-reaching character; and finally to (*e*) Personality, which is the most evolved whole among the structures of the universe, and becomes a new orientative, originative centre of reality. All through this progressive series the character of wholeness deepens; Holism is not only creative but self-creative, and its final structures are far more holistic than its initial structures. Natural wholes are always composed of parts; in fact the whole is not something additional to the parts, but is just the parts in their synthesis, which may be physico-chemical or organic or psychical or personal. As Holism is a process of creative synthesis, the resulting wholes are not static but dynamic, evolutionary, creative. Hence Evolution has an ever-deepening inward spiritual holistic character; and the wholes of Evolution and the evolutionary process itself can only be understood in reference to this fundamental character of wholeness. This is a universe of whole-making. The explanation of Nature can therefore not be purely mechanical; and the mechanistic concept of Nature has its place and justification only in the wider setting of Holism. In its organic application, in particular, the 'whole' will be found a much more useful term in science than 'life', and will render the prevailing mechanistic interpretation largely unnecessary.

A natural whole has its 'field', and the concept of fields will be found most important in this connection also. Just as a 'thing' is really a synthesised 'event' in the system of Relativity, so an organism is really a unified, synthesised section of history, which includes not only its present but much of its past and even its future. An organism can only be explained by reference to its past and its future as well as its present; the central structure is not sufficient and literally has not enough in it to go round in the way of explanation; the conception of the field therefore becomes necessary and will be found fruitful in biology and psychology no less than in physics.

Smuts: *Holism and Evolution*

While seeking to maintain the principle of our moral responsibility for nature, Karl Barth (1886–1968), one of the leading Protestant theologians of the twentieth century, also reaffirmed the radical ontological distinction between humans and animals, and along with that the 'otherness' of God in relation to his creation.

Our starting-point must be that in this matter too, as a living being in co-existence with non-human life, man has to think and act responsibly. The responsibility is not the same as he has to his own life and that of his fellow-men. Only analogically can we bring it under the concept of respect for life. It can only follow the primary responsibility at a distance. If we try to bring animal and vegetable life too close to human, or even class them together, we can hardly avoid the danger of regarding and treating human life, even when we really want to help, from the aspect of the animal and vegetable, and therefore in a way which is not really apposite. But why should we not be faced here by a responsibility which, if not primary, is a serious secondary responsibility?

The special responsibility in this case rests primarily on this, that the world of animals and plants forms the indispensable living background to the living-space divinely allotted to man and placed under his control. As they live, so can he. He is not set up as lord over the earth, but as lord on the earth which is already furnished with these creatures. Animals and plants do not belong to him; they and the whole earth can belong only to God. But he takes precedence of them. They are provided for his use. They are his 'means of life'. The meaning of the basis of this distinction consists in the fact that he is the animal creature to whom God reveals, entrusts and binds Himself within the rest of creation, with whom He makes common cause in the course of a particular history which is neither that of an animal nor of a plant, and in whose life-activity He expects a conscious and deliberate recognition of His honour, mercy and power. Hence the higher necessity of his life, and his right to that lordship and control. He can exercise it only in the responsibility thus conferred upon him.

But this lordship, and the responsibility which it confers, is in the first instance a differentiated one in respect of the animals and plants. Let us take first the case of plants. We can say unequivocally of these that man may and should exercise his creaturely and relative sovereignty by using them for food. There comes in here what we have stated to be the right of satisfying the animal needs and impulses of man. Man's vegetable nourishment, or the preceding harvest, is not the destruction of vegetation but a sensible use of its superfluity. The only possible limits lie in the nature of man as a rational being and beyond that is his vocation in relation to God and his fellow-men . . .

The question of this human lordship and its corresponding responsibility becomes more difficult when it is a matter of the relation between man and beast. Here, too, lordship can have the primary meaning of requisitioning, disciplining, taming, harnessing, exploiting and making profitable use of the surplus forces of nature in the animal world. For what is human lordship over the beast if it cannot take this form of 'domesticating' animals? . . .

Responsibility within limits of lordship as understood in this way will consist in what is proposed for our consideration in Prov. 12: 'A righteous man regardeth the life of his beast: but the tender mercies of the wicked are cruel.' Even within these limits there is still quite enough human stupidity, severity, caprice and irrationality at work and needing to be curbed. Respect for the fellow-creature of man, created with him on the sixth day and so closely related to him, means gratitude to God for the gift of so useful and devoted a comrade, and this gratitude will be translated into a careful, considerate, friendly and above all understanding treatment of it, in which sympathetic account is taken of its needs and the limits of its possibilities.

Barth: *Church Dogmatics*

While Karl Barth was wary of the idea of 'reverence for life', as veering dangerously towards theological liberalism, even paganism, his fellow Protestant theologian Albert Schweitzer (1875–1965), partly under the influence of Gandhi and Hindu thought, placed this notion at the heart of his ethical thinking.

The great fault of all ethics hitherto has been that they believed themselves to have to deal only with the relations of man to man. In reality, however, the question is what is his attitude to the world and all life that comes within his reach. A man is ethical only when life, as such, is sacred to him, that of plants and animals as that of his fellow-men, and when he devotes himself helpfully to all life that is in need of help. Only the universal ethic of the feeling of responsibility in an ever-widening sphere for all that lives – only that ethic can be founded in thought. The ethic of the relation of man to man is not something apart by itself: it is only a particular relation which results from the universal one.

The ethic of Reverence for Life, therefore, comprehends within itself everything that can be described as love, devotion, and sympathy whether in suffering, joy, or effort.

The world, however, offers us the horrible drama of Will-to-Live divided against itself. One existence holds its own at the cost of another: one destroys another. Only in the thinking man has the Will-to-Live become conscious of the other will-to-live, and desirous of solidarity with it. This solidarity, however, he cannot completely bring about, because man is subject to the puzzling and horrible law of being obliged to live at the cost of other life, and to incur again and again the guilt of destroying and injuring life. But as an ethical being he strives to escape whenever possible from this necessity, and as one who has become enlightened and merciful to put a stop to this disunion (*Selbstentzweiung*) of the Will-to-Live so far as the influence of his own existence reaches. He thirsts to be permitted to preserve his humanity, and to be able to bring to other existences release from their sufferings.

The Reverence for Life, therefore, which has arisen in the thinking Will-to-Live, contains world- and life-affirmation and the ethical fused together. Its aim is to create values, and to realize progress of different kinds which shall serve the material, spiritual, and ethical development of men and mankind. While the unthinking modern world- and life-affirmation stumbles about with its ideals won by discovery and invention, the thinking world- and life-affirmation sets up the spiritual and ethical perfecting of mankind as the highest ideal, and an ideal from which alone all other ideals of progress get their real value.

Schweitzer: *My Life and Thought*

The French scientist-theologian Pierre Teihard de Chardin (1881–1955) attempted to blend evolution theory and Christian theology in a single synthesis, a 'cosmogenesis' in which nature and consciousness are seen as evolving towards a final spiritual unity called the 'Omega Point'.

The astronomers have lately been making us familiar with the idea of a universe which for the last few thousand million years has been expanding in galaxies from a sort of primordial atom. This perspective of a world in a state of explosion is still debated, but no physicist would think of rejecting it as being tainted with philosophy or finalism. The reader should keep this example before him when he comes to weigh up the scope, the limitations and the perfect scientific legitimacy of the views I have here put forward. Reduced to its ultimate essence, the substance of these long pages can be summed up in this simple affirmation: that if the universe, regarded sidereally, is in process of spatial expansion (from the infinitesimal to the immense), in the same way and still more clearly it presents itself to us, physico-chemically, as in process of organic *involution* upon itself (from the extremely simple to the extremely complex) – and, moreover, this particular involution 'of complexity' is experimentally bound up with a correlative increase in interiorisation, that is to say in the psyche or consciousness.

In the narrow domain of our planet (still the only one within the scope of biology) the structural relationship noted here between complexity and consciousness is experimentally incontestable and has always been known. What gives the standpoint taken in this book its originality is the affirmation, at the outset, that the particular property possessed by terrestrial substances – of becoming more vitalised as they become increasingly complex – is only the local manifestation and expression of a trend as universal as (and no doubt even more significant than) those already identified by science: those trends which cause the cosmic layers not only to expand explosively as a wave but also to condense into corpuscles under the action of electro-magnetic and gravitational forces, or perhaps to become de-materialised in radiation: trends which are probably strictly inter-connected, as we shall one day realise.

If that be so, it will be seen that consciousness (defined experimentally as the specific effect of organised complexity) transcends by far the ridiculously narrow limits within which our eyes can directly perceive it.

On the one hand we are logically forced to assume the existence in rudimentary form (in a microscopic, ie an infinitely diffuse, state) of some sort of psyche in every corpuscle, even in those (the mega-molecules and below) whose complexity is of such a low or modest order as to render it (the psyche) imperceptible – just as the physicist assumes and can calculate those changes of mass (utterly imperceptible to direct observation) occasioned by slow movement.

On the other hand, there precisely in the world where various physical conditions (temperature, gravity, etc) prevent complexity reaching a degree involving a perceptible radiation of consciousness, we are led to assume that the involution, temporarily halted, will resume its advance as soon as conditions are favourable.

Regarded along its axis of complexity, the universe is, both on the whole and at each of its points, in a continual tension of organic doubling-back upon itself, and thus of interiorisation. Which amounts to saying that, for science, life is always under pressure everywhere; and that where it has succeeded in breaking through in an appreciable degree, nothing will be able to stop it carrying to the uttermost limit the process from which it has sprung.

It is in my opinion necessary to take one's stand in this actively convergent cosmic setting if one wants to depict the phenomenon of man in its proper relief and explain it fully and coherently.

Teilhard de Chardin: *The Phenomenon of Man*

SOURCES AND ACKNOWLEDGEMENTS

I Nature as a Living Being: Non-European Traditions

'The Creation Hymn', in O'Flaherty, Wendy (ed and trans) (1981) *The Rig Veda: An Anthology*, Penguin Books, Harmondsworth, pp25–6. Copyright © Wendy Doniger O'Flaherty. Reproduced by permission of Penguin Books Ltd.

The Atharva Veda, in Zaehner, R C, (ed and trans) (1966) *Hindu Scriptures*, J M Dent & Sons, New York. Reproduced by permission of David Campbell Publishing.

The Mundaka Upanishad and *The Chandogya Upanishad*, in Mascaro, Juan, (ed and trans) (1965) *The Upanishads*, Penguin Books, Harmondsworth, pp77–8. Copyright © Juan Mascaro, 1965. Reproduced by permission of Penguin Books Ltd.

Mahayana Buddhist Sutra, in du Barry, W T (ed) (1972) *The Buddhist Tradition in India, China and Japan*, Vintage Books, New York. Copyright © 1972 Random House Inc. Reproduced by permission of the publisher.

Mahayana Buddhist Sutra, in Conze, Edward (ed and trans) (1959) *Buddhist Scriptures*, Penguin Books, Harmondsworth.

Lao-Tzu *Tao Te Ching*, Verses 1, 2, 4, 5, 17, 56, 76, 128, Penguin Books, Harmondsworth, 1963, pp57, 58, 62, 82, 93. Copyright © D C Lau, 1963. Reproduced by permission of Penguin Books Ltd.

Chuang-Tzu, quoted in Chan, Wing-Tsit, (1963) *A Source Book of Chinese Philosophy*, Princeton University Press, Princeton. Reproduced by permission of the publishers.

Kuo-Hsiang, quoted in Yu-Lan, Fung, (1952) *A History of Chinese Philosophy*, Vol. 1, trans Der Bodde, Princeton University Press, Princeton. Reproduced by permission of the publisher.

Hsun-Tzu, quoted in *A Source Book of Chinese Philosophy*, *op cit*. Reproduced by permission of the publisher.

Kuan-Tzu, quoted in *A History of Chinese Philosophy*, *op cit*. Reproduced by permission of the publisher.

Chuang-Tzu, quoted in *A Source Book of Chinese Philosophy*, *op cit*. Reproduced by permission of the publisher.

Luther Standing Bear (1933) *Land of the Spotted Eagle*, University of Nebraska Press, Nebraska, reprinted from *Land of the Spotted Eagle*, by Luther Standing Bear. Reproduced by permission of the University of Nebraska Press. Copyright © 1933, by Luther Standing Bear, renewal copyright 1960 by May Jones.

2 From Myth to Philosophy: The Classical World

Aristotle *Metaphysics*, 1:5, in Ross, W D (ed) (1908) *The Works of Aristotle*, The Clarendon Press, Oxford, Vol 8. Reproduced by permission of Oxford University Press.

Heraclitus *Fragments 20–3* and *41–4* in Burnet, John (1930) *Early Greek Philosophy*, Adam and Charles Black, London. Reproduced by permission of the publisher.

Plato *Timaeus*, Sections 1, 4, 5, in Lee, Desmond (trans) (1965) Penguin Books, Harmondsworth, pp.42–5. Copyright © H D P Lee, 1965, 1971, 1977. Reproduced by permission of Penguin Books Ltd.

Aristotle *Physics*, 2:3, in *The Works of Aristotle*, *op cit*, Vol 2, 1930. Reproduced by permission of Oxford University Press.

—*Physics*, 2:8, in *The Works of Aristotle*, *op cit*, Vol 2, 1930. Reproduced by permission of Oxford University Press.

—*Historia Animalium* (Study of Animals) 8:1, in *The Works of Aristotle*, *op cit*, Vol 4, 1916. Reproduced by permission of Oxford University Press.

—*De Caelo* (On the Heavens), 290b12, in *The Works of Aristotle*, *op cit*, Vol 2, 1930. Reproduced by permission of Oxford University Press.

Cicero *On the Nature of the Gods*, 2:5, in Loeb, (ed) (1933) Heinemann, London.

Lucretius *On the Nature of the Universe*, in Latham, R E (trans) (1951) Penguin Books, Harmondsworth, pp31–3, 39–41, 107. Copyright © R E Latham, 1951. Reproduced by permission of Penguin Books Ltd.

Sophocles *Antigone*, in E F Watling (trans) (1974) *The Theban Plays*, Penguin Books, Harmondsworth, p135. Copyright © E F Watling, 1947, 1974. Reproduced by permission of Penguin Books Ltd.

Epicetus *Discourses*, Ch 16, Everyman, London, 1910. Reproduced by permission of David Campbell Publishing.

Aristotle *The Politics*, 1:8, in *The Works of Aristotle*, *op cit*, Vol 10, 1921. Reproduced by permission of Oxford University Press.

3 Nature in the Hands of God: The Judaeo–Christian–Islamic Traditions

The Book of Genesis, from Bks 1, 2, 3, 9, in Knox, R (trans) (1955) The Holy

Bible, Burns & Oates Ltd, London, Reproduced by permission of the publisher, Burns & Oates Ltd.

Psalms 8 and 148, in The Holy Bible, *op cit*. Reproduced by permission of the publisher.

St Augustine *Enchiridion*, in Dods, Marcus (trans) (1871–7) *Works of St Augustine* Vol 9, T & T Clark Ltd, Edinburgh. Reproduced by permission of the publisher.

— *Confessions*, 13:30–1, in Pine-Coffin, R S (trans) (1961) Penguin Books, Harmondsworth, pp343–4. Copyright © R S Pine-Coffin, 1961. Reproduced by permission of Penguin Books Ltd.

Plotinus *The Enneads*, 8:1 and 9, in O'Brien Elmer, S J (ed and trans) (1975) *The Essential Plotinus*, Hacket Publishing Company Inc, Indianapolis. By permission of the publisher, all rights reserved.

Maimonides *The Guide of the Perplexed*, 2:1, in Pines Schlomo (trans) (1963) University of Chicago Press, Chicago. Reproduced by permission of the publisher.

Abelard *Epitome Theologiae Christianae* (The Essence of Christian Theology), in Migne, *Patr. Lat*, Vol 178, 1726–7, quoted in Lovejoy, A O (1984), *The Great Chain of Being*, Harvard University Press, Cambridge, Mass.

Aquinas, St Thomas, *Summa Theologiae*, Vol 1, Qus 2 and 22, in Clark, M T (ed and trans) (1972) *An Aquinas Reader*, Doubleday & Co Inc, New York.

—*Summa Contra Gentiles*, 3:2:112, in the English Dominican Fathers (trans) (1928) Burns & Oates, London. Reprinted by permission of the publishers, Burns & Oates Ltd.

Assisi, St Francis of 'Song of Brother Sun and of All Creatures', in Price, L Shirly, (1959) *St Francis of Assisi*, A R Mowbray, London. Reprinted by permission of Cassell plc.

Dante *The Banquet*, in Hillard, Katharine (trans) (1889) Routledge, London.

The Koran, 14:1, in Dawood, N J (trans) (1956) Penguin Books, Harmondsworth, pp304–5. Copyright © N J Dawood, 1956, 1959, 1966, 1968, 1974, 1990. Reproduced by permission of Penguin Books Ltd.

4 Magic, Mysticism, and Harmony in the Renaissance

Petrarch 'The Ascent of Mont Ventoux' from a letter to Francesco de'Robert, in Cassirer, E, Kristeller, P and Herman Randall, J (eds and trans) (1948) *The Renaissance Philosophy of Man*, Chicago University Press, Chicago. Copyright © 1948 by the University of Chicago, by permission of the publisher.

The Malleus Maleficarum of Heinrich Kraemer and Johannes Sprenger (*The Witches' Hammer*), 1:1 in Summers, Montague (ed and trans) (1971) Dover Publications Inc, New York.

Hermetica: The Greek Corpus Hermeticum 5:3–11, in Copenhaver, Brian P (trans) (1992) Cambridge University Press, Cambridge. Reproduced by permission of the publisher.

Kepler, Johann (1599) Letter to Herwart von Hohenberg, in Ross, J B and McLaughlin, M M (eds and trans) (1977) *The Portable Renaissance Reader*, Penguin Books, Harmondsworth. Copyright 1953, renewed © 1981 by Viking Penguin Inc. Reproduced by Permission of Viking Penguin, a division of Penguin Books USA Inc.

— 'Dedication' of the *Mysterium Cosmographicum*, in Goodman, D C (ed) 1973 *Science and Religious Belief 1600–1900*, John Wright & Sons in association with The Open University Press, by permission of Butterworth–Heinemann.

Ficino, Marsilio, *Letters*, 2:1, in *The Renaissance Philosophy of Man*, *op cit*, copyright 1948 by the University of Chicago. Reproduced by permission of the publisher.

Castiglione, Baldasar, *The Book of the Courtier*, in Bull, George (trans) (1967) Penguin Books, Harmondsworth, p332. Copyright © George Bull, 1967. Reproduced by permission of Penguin Books Ltd.

Shakespeare, William *The Merchant of Venice*, 5:1, in Harbage, Alfred (ed) (1969) *The Complete Works of Shakespeare*, Penguin Books, Harmondsworth.

Agrippa, Cornelius *On the Occult Philosophy*, quoted in Hersey, G L (1976) *Pythagorean Palaces*, Cornell University Press, Ithaca. Reproduced by permission of G L Hersey.

da Vinci, Leonardo in Richter, I A (ed and trans) (1952) *The Notebooks of Leonardo da Vinci*, Oxford University Press, Oxford. Reproduced by permission of Oxford University Press.

della Mirandola, Pico *Oration on the Dignity of Man*, in *The Renaissance Philosophy of Man*, *op cit*. Reproduced by permission of the publisher.

Marlowe, Christopher *The Tragical History of the Life and Death of Doctor Faustus*, 1:1, in Jump, J D (ed) (1962) Manchester University Press, Manchester. Reproduced by permission of the publisher.

Montaigne, Michel de 'On Cruelty', in Creech, M A (ed and trans) (1987) *The Essays of Michel de Montaigne*, Allen Lane, The Penguin Press, Harmondsworth. Reproduced by permission of Penguin Books Ltd.

Pascal, Blaise *The Pensées*, 184, in Cohen, J M (trans) Penguin Books (1961), Harmondsworth.

Shakespeare, William *Troilus and Cressida*, 1:3, in Craig, W J (ed) (1954) *The Complete Works of William Shakespeare*, Oxford University Press, Oxford. Reproduced by permission of Oxford University Press.

Donne, John 'An Anatomie of the World', Lines 191–246, in Smith, E J (ed) (1971) *John Donne: The Complete English Poetry*, Penguin Books, Harmondsworth.

189

Cusa, Nicholas of *On Learned Ignorance*, in *The Portable Renaissance Reader*, *op cit*. Copyright 1953, renewed © 1981 by Viking Penguin, a division of Penguin Books USA. Inc.

5 'The Magnificent Clockwork': Nature as Machine

Copernicus, Nicholas *On the Revolutions of the Heavenly Bodies*, in Duncan, A M (ed and trans) (1976) David & Charles, Newton Abbot; 2nd edition (1993) Easton Press, Norwalk, Connecticut. Reproduced by permission of Dr A M Duncan.

Osiander, Andreas in *On the Revolutions of the Heavenly Bodies*, *op cit*. Reproduced by permission of Dr A M Duncan.

Bacon, Francis *The Great Instauration*, in Anderson, Fulton H (ed) (1960) *Francis Bacon: The New Organon and Related Writings*, Bobbs-Merrill Co, Indianapolis; reprinted with the permission of Macmillan Publishing Company from Bacon, Francis in Anderson, Fulton H (ed) *The New Organon and Related Writings*, © by Macmillan Publishing Company.

—*The New Organon*, Aphorisms 2:52, 1:81, 1:84, 1:97, 1:98, 1:129, in *Francis Bacon: The New Organon and Related Writings*, *op cit*, reprinted with the permission of Macmillan Publishing Company from Bacon, Francis in Anderson, Fulton H (ed) *The New Organon and Related Writings*, © by Macmillan Publishing Company.

Galilei, Galileo *Early Notebooks*, 6th Question: 'Are the Heavens Animated', in Wallace, William W (trans) (1977) *Galileo's Early Notebooks*, University of Notre Dame Press, Notre Dame. Reproductory permission of the publisher.

—*The Assayer*, in Drake, Stillman (trans) (1957) *Discoveries and Opinions of Galileo*, Doubleday Anchor Books Inc, New York. © 1957 by Stillman Drake. Used by permission of Doubleday, a division of Bantam Doubleday Dell Publishing Group Inc.

—*The Starry Messenger*, in *Discoveries and Opinions of Galileo*, *op cit*. © 1957 by Stillman Drake. Used by permission of Doubleday, a division of Bantam Doubleday Dell Publishing Group Inc.

Descartes, René *Principles of Philosophy*, XLVIII, in Anscombe, E and Geach, P T (eds and trans) (1970) *Descartes: Philosophical Writings*, Thomas Nelson & Sons Ltd, London. Reproduced by permission of the publisher.

—*Meditations on First Philosophy*, VI, in *Descartes: Philosophical Writings*, op cit. Reproduced by permission of the publisher.

—*Principles of Philosophy*, XLVI, in *Descartes: Philosophical Writings*, *op cit*. Reproduced by permission of the publisher.

—*Principles of Philosophy*, CCIII, in *Descartes: Philosophical Writings*, *op cit*. Reproduced by permission of the publisher.

— Letter to Henry More in Kenny, Anthony (trans) (1970) *Descartes: Philosophical Letters*, Basil Blackwell, Oxford. Reproduced by permission of the publisher.

—*Principles of Philosophy*, III, in *Descartes: Philosophical Writings*, *op cit*. Reproduced by permission of the publisher.

Boyle, Robert *The Excellency of the Mechanical Hypothesis*, in Stewart, M A (ed) (1979) *Selected Philosophical Papers of Robert Boyle*, Manchester University Press, Manchester. Reproduced by permission of the publisher.

Newton, Isaac *Principia Mathematica* in Cajori, F (ed) in Motte, Andrew (ed and trans) (1960) in *Isaac Newton: Mathematical Principles of Natural Philosophy and his System of the World*, University of California Press, Berkeley. Copyright © 1934 renewed 1962 Regents of the University of California, reprinted with permission.

—in Cohen, I B (ed (1952) *Newton's Opticks*, Dover Publications, New York. Reproduced by permission of the publisher.

6 The Order of Nature in the Age of Enlightenment

Pope, Alexander *An Essay on Man*, Epistle I, Bobbs-Merrill Co, Indianapolis, 1965. Reprinted with the permission of Macmillan Publishing Company from Brady, Frank (ed) *An Essay on Man* by Alexander Pope, Copyright © 1965 by Macmillan Publishing Company.

Leibniz, G W *Principles of Nature and of Grace, Founded on Reason*, Sections 3–4 and 10–13, in Parkinson, G H R (1973) *Leibniz: Philosophical Writings*, J M Dent & Sons, London. Reproduced by permission of David Campbell Publishing.

Ray, John *The Wisdom of God as Manifested in the Works of the Creation*, in *Science and Belief: Copernicus to Darwin*, Open University Course ASMST 283, Block IV, Unit 1, The Open University Press, Milton Keynes, 1974.

Derham, William *Physico-Theology*, in Goodman, D C (ed) (1973) *Science and Religious Belief 1600–1900*, John Wright & Sons in Association with The Open University Press, UK. Reproduced by permission of Butterworth-Heinemann.

Wilkins, John *Of the Principles and Duties of Natural Religion*, in *Science and Belief: Copernicus to Darwin*, *op cit*.

Paley, William *Natural Theology* in Young, Francis, (ed) (1892) Ward, Lock & Co, London.

Shaftesbury, Earl of *The Moralists*, Sections 64–7 and 97–9, in Green, Stanley (ed) (1964) *Characteristics*, Vol 2, Bobbs Merrill, New York, reprinted with the permission of Macmillan Publishing Company from Green, Stanley (ed) *Characteristics of Men, Manners, Opinions, Times* by Anthony, Earl of Shaftesbury, copyright © 1964 by Macmillan Publishing Company.

Joseph Addison, 'The Harmony of the World', *The Spectator*, No 40, 2 July, 1712.

d'Holbach, Baron *The System of Nature*, in *Science and Religious Belief 1600–1900, op cit*. Reproduced by permission of Butterworth-Heinemann.

Kant, Immanuel *Critique of Judgement*, in Bernard, J H (trans) (1914) Macmillan, London. Reproduced by permission of Macmillan Ltd.

—*Natural History and Theory of the Heavens*, in Hastie, W (ed and trans) (1900) *Kant's Cosmology*, James Maclehose & Sons, Glasgow.

Spinoza, Benedict de *Ethics*, in Boyle, Andrew (trans) (1959) J M Dent & Sons, London. Reproduced by permission of David Campbell Publishing.

7 The Romanticization of Nature

Rousseau, Jean-Jacques *A Discourse on the Origin of Inequality*, in Cole, G D H (trans) (1973) *The Social Contract & Discourses*, J M Dent & Sons, London. Reproduced by permission of David Campbell Publishing.

—*Émile*, in Foxley, Barbara, (trans) (1974) Dent & Sons, London. Reproduced by permission of David Campbell Publishing.

—*Reveries of a Solitary Stroller* 'Fifth Promenade', Routledge, London, 1927.

Wollstonecraft, Mary 'On Poetry and Our Relish for the Beauties of Nature', in Todd, Janet (1989) *A Wollstonecraft Anthology*, Polity Press, Cambridge. Reproduced by permission of the publisher.

Goethe, Johann von *The Sufferings of Young Werther*, in Morgan, Bayard Quincy (trans) (1976) John Calder (Publishers) London, copyright this translation John Calder (Publishers) Ltd 1976, reprinted by Permission of The Calder Educational Trust, London.

—*Aphorisms on Nature*, in Huxley, T H (1869) 'Nature: Aphorisms by Goethe' in *Nature*, 1869.

Fichte, Johann Gottlieb *The Vocation of Man*, in Smith, William (trans) (1889) *The Popular Works of Johann Gottlieb Fichte*, Vol 1, Trubner & Co, London.

Schelling, Friedrich von *Ideas for the Philosophy of Nature*, in Harris, E and Heath, P (trans) (1988) Cambridge University Press, Cambridge. Reproduced by permission of the publisher.

Coleridge, S T *Philosophical Lectures* in Coburn, Kathleen (ed) (1949) The Pilot Press, London.

Blake, William 'Notebook Drafts', in Stevenson, W H (ed) (1971) *The Poems of William Blake*, Longmans, London.

Keats, John 'Lamia' in Barnard, John (ed) (1973) *Keats: Complete Poems*, Penguin Books, Harmondsworth.

Wordsworth, William 'Lines Written a Few Miles Above Tintern Abbey', in Hutchinson, T (ed) (1936) *Wordsworth: Poetical Works*, Oxford University Press, Oxford. Reproduced by permission of Oxford University Press.

Humboldt, Alexander von *Cosmos: A Sketch of a Physical Description of the Universe*, in Otte, E C (trans) (1901) George Bell & Sons, London.

8 The Nineteenth Century: Romantic Twilight

Schopenhauer, Arthur *The World as Will and Representation*, in Payne E F J (ed and trans) (1966) Dover Publications, New York. Reproduced by permission of the publisher.

—*On the Basis of Morality*, in Payne, E F (trans) (1965) Bobbs-Merrill Co, New York, reprinted with the permission of Macmillan Publishing Company from Payne, E F J (ed) *On the Basis of Morality* by Arthur Schopenhauer, copyright © 1965 by Macmillan Publishing Company.

Bentham, Jeremy *An Introduction to the Principles of Morals and Legislation*, in Burns, J H and Hart, H L A (eds) (1970) The Athlone Press, London. Copyright © The University of London 1970, by permission of The Athlone Press Ltd.

Emerson, Ralph Waldo 'The Oversoul', in Paul, Sherman (ed) (1978) *Emerson's Essays on Nature*, J M Dent & Sons, London. Reproduced by permission of David Campbell Publishing.

Thoreau, Henry David *Walden and Civil Disobedience*, Penguin Books, Harmondsworth, 1983.

Whitman, Walt *Specimen Days*, July 22nd, 1878, 'Hours for the Soul', in Kaplan, J (ed) (1982) *Walt Whitman: Complete Poetry & Collected Prose*, Viking Press, New York.

Dickinson, Emily 'Nature, the gentlest mother', in Liscott, R N (1959) *Selected Poems and Letters of Emily Dickinson*, Doubleday Anchor Books, New York. Reproduced by permission of the Executrix of the Estate of Robert N Linscott.

Muir, John 'A Voyage to Alaska', in Wolfe, Linnie Marsh (ed) (1966) *John of the Mountains: The Unpublished Journals of John Muir*, University of Wisconsin Press, Madison.

—(1898) 'The Wild Parks and Forest Reservations of the West', in *Atlantic Monthly* LXXXI.

Jefferies, Richard *The Story of My Heart*, in Hooker, S J (ed) (1947) Constable, London, 1947. Reproduced by permission of the publisher.

Ruskin, John (1905) *Lectures on Art and Painting*, George Allen & Unwin, London.

9 The Nineteenth Century: Science and Materialism

Lange, Friedrich *The History of Materialism*, in Thomas, EC (trans) (1974) Arno Press, New York, by permission of Ayer Company Publishers, Salem, New Hampshire.

Helmholtz, Hermann in Kahl, R (ed) (1971) *Selected Writings of Hermann von Helmholtz*, Wesleyan University Press, Middletown.

Haeckel, Ernst *Theses for the Organization of Monism*, in Nagy, M (trans) in *Philosophical Issues in the Psychology of C.G. Jung*, State University of New York Press, Albany, 1991.

Shelley, Mary *Frankenstein; or, The Modern Prometheus*, in Smith, J M (ed) (1992) St Martin's Press, Boston.

Driesch, Hans (1914) *The History and Theory of Vitalism*, Macmillan, London, by permission of Macmillan Ltd.

Darwin, Charles *The Origin of Species by Natural Selection*, J M Dent & Sons, London, undated. Reproduced by permission of David Campbell Publishing.

Kropotkin, Peter (1902) *Mutual Aid: A Factor of Evolution*, William Heinemann, London.

Marx, Karl *Economic and Philosophical Manuscripts*, in Marx, K and Engels, F *Collected Works* Vol 13, Lawrence & Wishart, 1975. Reproduced by permission of the publisher.

Marx, Karl, *Grundrisse*, Macmillan, London, 1971, by permission of Macmillan Ltd.

Mill, John Stuart *Nature, the Utility of Religion, and Theism*, in Cohen, M (ed) (1961) *The Philosophy of John-Stuart Mill*, Random House, New York.

James, William (1907) *A Pluralistic Universe*, Longmans Green, London.

Nietzsche, Friedrich *The Gay Science*, in Hollingdale, R J (ed and trans) (1977) *A Nietzsche Reader*, Penguin Books, Harmondsworth, pp200–1. Copyright © R J Hollingdale, 1977. Reproduced by permission of Penguin Books Ltd.

10. The Twentieth Century: Positivism and its Rivals

Schlick, Moritz *The Philosophy of Organic Life*, in Feigl, H and Brodbeck, M (eds) (1953) *Readings in the Philosophy of Science*, Appleton–Century–Crofts, New York.

Monod, Jacques (1974) *Chance and Necessity*, William Collins, London. Reproduced by permission of HarperCollins Publishers Ltd, and Alfred Knopf Inc, © 1971.

Russell, Bertrand (1963) 'A Free Man's Worship', in *Mysticism and Logic*, Unwin Hyman, London. Reproduced by permission of the publisher.

Sartre, Jean-Paul *Nausea*, in Alexander, Lloyd (trans) (1964) New Directions Publishing Corp, New York. Copyright © 1964 New Directions Publishing Corp, reprinted by permission of the publisher.

de Beauvoir, Simone *The Second Sex*, in Parshley, H M (ed and trans) (1972) Penguin Books, Harmondsworth. Reproduced by permission of Jonathan Cape.

Bergson, Henri *Creative Evolution* in Mitchell, A (trans) (1911) Macmillan, London. Reproduced by permission of Macmillan Ltd.

Whitehead, Alfred North (1945) *Science and the Modern World*, Cambridge University Press, Cambridge. Reproduced by permission of the publisher.

Hartshorne, Charles (1948) *The Divine Relativity*, Yale University Press, New Haven, copyright © 1982 Yale University. Reproduced by permission of the publisher.

Smuts, Jan *Holism and Evolution* (1973) Greenwood, Westport.

Barth, Karl (1961) *Church Dogmatics*, Vol. 4, T & T Clark Ltd, Edinburgh. Reproduced by permission of the publisher.

Schweitzer, Albert *My Life and Thought*, in Campion, C T (trans) (1933) George Allen & Unwin, London. Reproduced by permission of Rhena Schweitzer Muller.

Teilhard de Chardin *The Phenomenon of Man* (1959) Collins, London. Reproduced by permission of the publisher.

FURTHER READING

Barbour, I (1966) *Issues in Science and Religion*, SCM Press, London. Examines lucidly some of the major points of conflict between science and religion associated with, for example, Galileo and Darwin.

Batchelor, M and Brown, K. (eds) (1992) *Buddhism and Ecology*, Cassell, London. A set of readings indicating the relevance and the impact of Buddhism with regard to modern environmental thinking.

Baumer, F (1977) *Modern European Thought: Continuity and Change in Ideas, 1600–1950*, Macmillan, New York. A wide-ranging study of the development of modern Western thought.

Berman, M (1981) *The Reenchantment of the World*, Cornell University Press, Ithaca. A study of the development of, and challenges to, the mechanistic world-view that has dominated Western thought since the scientific revolution.

Bookchin, M (1990) *The Philosophy of Social Ecology: Essays in Dialectical Naturalism*, Black Rose Books, New York. Develops an ecological philosophy from a socio-political point of view, but critical of many aspects of recent environmentalist thinking.

Bowler, P (1992) *The Fontana History of the Environmental Sciences*, Fontana, London. A comprehensive survey of the origins and development of environmental science and ecology.

Campbell, J (1974) *The Masks of God*, Souvenir Press, London. A multi-volume work which offers a comprehensive survey of the world's myths and primitive religions.

Capra, F (1982) *The Turning Point*, Wildwood House, London. Draws on ancient and modern sources to show how a revolution in our outlook on the natural world is occurring at the present time, as our model of the world moves from a mechanistic to an organic one.

Cavendish, R (1987) *A History of Magic*, Arkana, London. Traces the course of magical theory and practice that runs beneath the surface of the history of Western civilization.

Collingwood, R (1960) *The Idea of Nature*, Oxford University Press, London. A brief but wide-ranging account of the great cosmologies and world-views of the Western tradition, from Thales to the twentieth century.

Cooper, J (1990) *Taoism*, Mandala, London. A survey of Taoist philosophy, examining its central concepts, and its attitude towards the natural world and our place within it.

Devall, B and Sessions, G (1985) *Deep Ecology*, Gibbs Smith, Salt Lake City. Explores the philosophical, psychological, and sociological roots of today's environmental movement and its challenge to traditional human-centred assumptions.

Elliot, R and Gare, A (eds) (1983) *Environmental Philosophy: A Collection of Readings*, The Open University Press, Milton Keynes. Represents some of the efforts of contemporary philosophers to respond to the environmental crisis.

Goldsmith, E (1992) *The Way: An Ecological World View*, Rider, London. Puts forward fundamental principles of an ecological world-view.

Gore, A (1992) *Earth in Balance: Forging a New Common Purpose*, Earthscan, London. Study by a leading US politician of the crises facing the global environment, and an outline of measures to deal with them.

Huxley, A (ed) (1958) *The Perennial Philosophy*, Fontana, London. A selection of writings, mostly of a mystical or metaphysical nature, from many different cultures and traditions, that seeks to identify a universal philosophy.

Lovejoy, A (1974) *The Great Chain of Being*, Harvard University Press, Cambridge, Mass. A study of the development of a conception of the universe which has underpinned attitudes to nature from Plato to the eighteenth century.

Marshall, P (1992) *Nature's Web: An Exploration of Ecological Thinking*, Simon & Schuster, London. Traces in detail the development of ecological thinking from its origins in ancient religions and philosophies, East and West, to the present.

Merchant, C (1982) *The Death of Nature: Women, Ecology and the Scientific Revolution*, Wildwood House, London. Examines attitudes to nature in the Scientific Revolution, especially the idea of the world as a machine, in the light of women's issues and ecology.

Nash, R (1989) *The Rights of Nature: A History of Environmental Ethics*, University of Wisconsin Press, Madison. Charts in detail the history of modern philosophical, religious and ethical beliefs regarding nature.

Passmore, J (1974) *Man's Responsibility for Nature: Ecological Problems and Western Traditions*, Duckworth, London. An examination, from the point of view of philosophy and of the history of ideas, of environmental and ecological issues.

Pepper, D (1984) *The Roots of Modern Environmentalism*, Routledge, London. Provides wide-ranging historical and philosophical background to modern environmental thinking.

Ponting C (1991) *A Green History of the World*, Sinclair Stevenson, London. An account of the environmental impact, and ecological consequences, of human activity throughout history.

Sheldrake, R (1990) *The Rebirth of Nature: The Greening of Science and God*, Rider, London. Traces the mythological and historical roots of animistic and mechanistic views of nature, arguing that we are on the threshold of a new understanding.

Singer, P (1976) *Animal Liberation: Towards an End to Man's Inhumanity to Animals*, Jonathan Cape, London. A philosophical analysis of the moral issues concerning our treatment of animals.

Skolimowski, H (1992) *Living Philosophy: Eco-Philosophy as a Tree of Life*, Arkana, London. The author develops a comprehensive eco-philosophy which is built on the concept of evolution and the spiritual development of humanity.

Thomas, K (1984) *Man and the Natural World: Changing Attitudes in England 1500–1800*, Penguin Books, Harmondsworth. A detailed historical account of changing attitudes towards the natural world in the early modern period.

Tillyard, E (1963) *The Elizabethan World-Picture*, Penguin, Harmondsworth. A sketch of the dominant attitude towards nature and the cosmos at the time of the Renaissance, making use of English literature of the Elizabethan period.

Toulmin, S and Goodfield, J (1963) *The Fabric of the Heavens*, Penguin, Harmondsworth. Traces the stages of development of cosmological thinking from the ancient Greek to the Scientific Revolution.

Whitehead, A (1925) *Science and the Modern World*, Cambridge University Press, Cambridge. Many times reprinted, this classic work offers a view of the history of scientific and cosmological thinking from an organicist viewpoint.

Worster, D (1985) *Nature's Economy: A History of Ecological Ideas*, Cambridge University Press, Cambridge. Discusses a variety of thinkers and ideas, from the eighteenth century onwards, that have shaped our modern conception of nature and of our place in it.